POWER 팡팡

토플 영단어

Magic English
Power **팡팡 토플영단어**
ⓒ 조영재 2003

초판 1쇄 발행일 | 2003년 12월 5일

지은이 | 조영재
펴낸이 | 이정원

펴낸곳 | 도서출판 들녘미디어
등록일자 | 1995년 5월 17일
등록번호 | 10-1162
주소 | 서울시 마포구 합정동 366-2 삼주빌딩 3층
전화 | (마케팅) 02-323-7849, (편집) 02-323-7366
팩시밀리 | 02-338-9640
홈페이지 | www.ddd21.co.kr

ISBN 89-86632-97-7 (13740)

MAGIC ENGLISH

POWER팡팡

조영재 지음

토플 영단어

들녘미디어

필자는 1995년부터 미국 뉴욕에서 학원을 열어 토플과 SAT(미국 수능시험)를 가르쳤고, 1999년부터는 한국에서 중·고등학생, 대학생 그리고 일반인들에게 토플을 가르쳐왔다. 그동안의 경험에 비추어볼 때, 한국 학생들의 영어 학습의 특성은 어휘 부분을 무척 열심히 한다는 것이다. 그래서 상당히 많은 양의 단어를 외우는 데 시간을 투자하지만, 정작 토플이나 SAT 시험을 치를 때 본인이 외운 단어가 나오더라도 정답을 제대로 찾지 못할 뿐만 아니라 문장을 제대로 해석하지도 못한다. 이는 단어를 외우기는 했어도 그 의미를 모르고 있기 때문에 생긴 결과다. 하나하나의 단어에 대해 얼마나 깊이 있게 이해하는지를 중요하게 여기는 미국인들의 시각에서 출제되는 시험(토플 혹은 SAT)을 준비하는 이들은 그에 따라 대비를 해야 골치 아픈 단어와 독해를 쉽게 해결할 수 있다.

미국에서 출판되는 단어책의 문제점

미국인들은 얼마나 많은 양의 단어를 알고 있는가가 아니라 하나하나의 단어에 대해 얼마나 깊이 있게 이해하는지를 더 중요하게 여긴다. 미국 단어책을 보면 단어가 1,000개도 채 되지 않지만 유의어나 예문을 아주 풍부하게 곁들인다. 즉, 단어를 외우는 것이 아니라 문장에서 단어가 얼마나 다양하게 사용되는지에 중점을 둔다. 하지만 예문에 사용되고 있는 단어들의 뜻을 모를 경우 예문을 제대로 이해하지 못하는 문제가 발생한다.

한국에서 출판되는 단어책의 문제점

요즘 한국에서도 과거처럼 무작정 많은 단어를 싣는 것이 아니라 단어의 뜻과 유의어를 위주로 하는 책들이 많이 나오고 있다. 그런데 아쉽게도 여기에도 문제점이 있다. 단어가 문맥에 따라 다양하게 해석되면 그에 따른 유의어나 반의어도 각각 달라지기 때문에 제대로 구분해서 제시해주어야 하는데, 그런 점을 충분히 반영하지 못해 도리어 학생들에게 혼동을 주는 것이다. 그리고 공부하는 이들도 단어가 실제 문장에서 어떻게 사용되는지 이해하기보다는 유의어든 반의어든 무작정 외우려고 덤벼든다. 취미로 어휘 공부하는 이들이야 어떤 식으로 공부해도 상관없지만, 짧은 시간에 고득점을 원하는 수험생들에겐 지극히 비효율적인 방법이다. 특히 토플 독해에서는 지문에 나오는 단어가 거의 정해져 있으며, 어휘 문제에서 답으로 제시되는 유의어 또한 정해져 있어 수능용 단어를 제아무리 많이 외우고 있다 해도 쓸모가 없다. 따라서 무작정 단어를 외우는 것보다는 시험에 자주 나오는 단어 위주로, 그중에서도 답으로 자주 사용되는 유의어를 집중적으로 공부하는 것이 효율적이다.

이 책의 특징

그동안 한국 학생들을 가르쳐온 필자의 경험을 토대로, 토플을 막 시작하려는 이들이 독해에서 알아야 할 기본적인 단어들을 모아 상황에 맞는 적절한 해석을 소개하고 그 유의어들을 중점적으로 공부할 수 있도록 했다. 특히 이 책은 토플에 이미 출제된 단어들만 선별해서 다루었다. 한국에서 시행되는 시험과는 달리 토플, 그중에서도 어휘 문제는 일정 단어들이 반복해서 출제되지만, 똑같은 단어가 출제되더라도 매번 다른 의미로 전환되는 것이 보통이다. 그러므로 '이 단어는 이런 뜻'이라는 식의 단편적인 암기는 효과가 없다. 하나의 단어에서 파생되는 다양한 의미를 이해하고 있어야 한다. 또한 이 책은 기존 미국 단어책이 가진 문제점을 보완하여 예문에 나오는 단어들의 뜻과 상황에 따른 뜻 변화도 함께 정리해 놓았다. 따라서 예문까지 열심히 공부한다면 아득하기만 한 어휘 공부에서 확실한 자신감을 가지게 될 것이다.

이 책은 이렇게 활용하라

　대부분의 수험생들은 책을 구입하면 1주일 혹은 열흘 이내에 마스터하려는 의욕에 가득 차 덤벼들지만 막상 4, 5일이 지나면 흐지부지되다가 결국은 책의 반도 공부하지 못하는 경우가 많다.

1 | 25과로 구성되어 있는 이 책을 월요일부터 금요일까지 매일 한 과씩 공부하고, 주말에는 그 주에 외웠던 단어들을 복습하도록 하자. 이렇게 차근차근 해나가면 5주면 마스터할 수 있다. 이것은 CBT 200점(PBT 530점)을 받는 중급 정도의 어휘실력이 있는 수험생들을 기준으로 했으며, 어휘력이 약한 학생들은 좀더 여유를 가지고 2, 3달 정도의 시간을 투자해야 한다. 물론 기본 단어들을 열심히 공부해야 되지만 예문에서도 잘 모르는 단어가 있다면 역시 충분한 시간을 두고 공부하도록 하자.

2 | 예문에 덧붙인 해석은 전체 문장을 쉽게 이해하기 위한 참고용으로 활용하자. 어휘 위주의 책이라 각 단어의 의미를 부각시켜 해석하다보니 의역보다는 직역이라 문장 전체의 흐름이 자연스럽지 못할 수도 있기 때문이다.

3 | 한 과가 끝날 때마다 실려 있는 Review Test로 반복 학습의 효과를 높이자. Review Test에서는 이미 공부한 문장들이 나온다. 앞에 나온 문장을 다시 싣는 것은 직접 문장을 해석하면서 배운 단어를 제대로 해석할 수 있는지 확인하려는 의도에서다. 그리고 Review Test에서 답으로 제시된 단어들 또한 중요한 단어이니 열심히 공부하기 바란다. 해답 설명란에서 단어의 과거형이나 복수형은 원형이나 단수형으로 풀이했다.

4 | 맨 뒷부분에 실린 '기출 단어 리스트'를 효과적으로 활용하자. 단기간에 토플시험을 치러야 할 수험생들을 위해 두 번 이상 어휘 시험에 나왔던 단어를 책의 맨 뒷부분에 '기출 단어 리스트'로 묶어놓았다.

이 책의 강점

＊기출 단어 375개를 재구성하여 → 높은 적중률과 학습 효과 배가

＊단순한 유의어/반의어가 아니라 → 뜻에 따라 구분된 유의어/반의어 제시

＊토플시험에 자주 나오는 단어로 구성된 → 단기 점검 '기출단어 목록'

차례

■ 들어가는 글 004

First Week

Lesson 01_ 011

Lesson 02_ 023

Lesson 03_ 035

Lesson 04_ 047

Lesson 05_ 059

Second Week

Lesson 06_ 071

Lesson 07_ 083

Lesson 08_ 095

Lesson 09_ 107

Lesson 10_ 119

Third Week

Lesson 11_ 131

Lesson 12_ 143

Lesson 13_ 155

Lesson 14_ 167

Lesson 15_ 179

Fourth Week

Lesson 16_ 191

Lesson 17_ 203

Lesson 18_ 215

Lesson 19_ 227

Lesson 20_ 239

Fifth Week

Lesson 21_ 251

Lesson 22_ 263

Lesson 23_ 275

Lesson 24_ 287

Lesson 25_ 299

■ Index 311

■ 기출단어 목록 336

L e s s o n 01

ruin

migrate

simultaneous(ly)

vessel

vacant

resource(s)

gradual(ly)

boost

persist

aim

minute

inappropriate(ly)

load

admire

brevity

ruin

v. **1_파괴하다** destroy

2_손해를 내다 damage, harm, spoil

n. **1_파손** destruction, downfall

2_잔재 remains, relic

During the Civil War, steam-boating on the lower Mississippi River was **ruined**. 남북전쟁 동안, 미시시피 강 하류의 증기선이 파괴되었다.

steam n. 증기, 기운 v. 증기를 내다, 증발하다

There's only the mountain in the direction, and higher up an old **ruin**, an abandoned castle. 이 방향에는 오직 산과 높게 솟은 낡은 잔재인 버려진 성만 있다.

direction n. 방향, 지시

abandoned adj. 버림받은, 유기된=forsaken

migrate

v. **1_이동하다** journey, travel

2_이주하다 emigrate, immigrate

When birds **migrate**, they sometimes fly in formation. 새들이 이동을 할 때는 때때로 대형을 갖춰 날아간다.

formation n. 형상, 육성, 구조

migration

n. 1_이동

2_이주

The persecution of Jews led to the **migration** of Soviet Jews to Israel. 유대인의 박해 때문에 소련계 유대인이 이스라엘로 이주하게 되었다.

persecution n. 박해

lead to ~을 이르게 하다

migratory

adj. 1_이동성의

2_이주하는

simultaneous(ly)

adj.(adv.)

동시에 발생하는 concurrent

The **simultaneous** release of the album and the movie created a lot of buzz. 앨범과 영화의 동시 발매는 세상을 떠들썩하게 했다.

release　n. 개봉, 발매, 석방　v. 자유롭게 하다, 놓아주다

buzz　n. 웅성거리는 소리, 소문=rumor　v. 윙윙 소리를 내다

Glass-fiber cables can carry hundreds of telephone conversation **simultaneously**. 유리 섬유 케이블로 인해 수백 통의 전화 통화가 동시에 가능하게 되었다.

carry　v. ~을 전달하다, ~을 나르다, 진행하다, 받치다=support

conversation　n. 대화

vessel

n. **1_용기** container

2_그릇 vase

3_배 boat, ship

This drinking **vessel** was made from copper. 이 음료 용기는 구리로 만들어졌다.

copper　n. 구리

On January 29, 1778, Captain James Cook took his two **vessels** into a small harbor on the island of Kauai. 1778년 1월 29일, 임스 쿡 선장은 그의 배 두 척을 카우아이 섬의 작은 항구로 가져갔다.

harbor　n. 항구　v. 숨기다, (생각, 계획 등을) 마음속에 품다

vacant

adj. **비어 있는** empty, unoccupied, void

Many city dwellers are turning **vacant** lots into thriving
gardens. 많은 도시 거주자들이 공터를 훌륭한 공원으로 바꾸고 있다.

dweller n. 거주자

turn into (~의 질, 형상 따위를) 바꿔놓다=change

lot n. 부지, 제비뽑기, 몫, 운명

thrive v. 번성하다=prosper, 무럭무럭 자라다

garden n. 공원, 정원

vacancy

n. 빈 상태 emptiness, vacuum

resource(s)

n.(pl) **1_자원, 물자** asset, wealth
2_수완 skill, ability, ingenuity

Some schools don't have enough **resources** to educate
their students properly. 어떤 학교들은 학생들을 올바르게
교육시킬 만한 충분한 물자를 갖고 있지 않다.

educate v. 교육시키다

properly adv. 올바르게, 알맞게=fittingly, 정당하게=rightly

Even while making political statement, Ben Shahn was in
full command of his technical **resources**. 벤 샨은 정치적
연설을 행하고 있을 때조차도, 그의 기술적 수완을 충분히
발휘했다.

statement n. 성명, 진술=testimony

command n. 운용력, 명령 v. ~을 명하다

gradual(ly) adj(adv.)

1_점차적인 slow

≠rapid, speedy

2_단계적인 deliberate

One may expect her recovery from surgery to be **gradual** rather than speedy. 그녀는 수술 후 빠른 회복보다는 점진적으로 회복될 것이다.

recovery n. 회복, 되찾은 것   **surgery** n. 수술

During the years before the American Civil War, differences between the North and the South **gradually** came to focus on the question of slavery. 미국의 남북전쟁이 발발하기 전 몇 년 동안, 남북 사이의 차이점이 점점 노예문제로 집중되어졌다.

focus v. 집중하다, 초점을 모으다 n. 초점, 핵심

question n. 문제점=issue, 질문 v. 질문하다, ~에 대해 의심을 품다

boost

v. **1_상승하다** elevate, improve, raise

2_올리다 elevate, lift, raise

n. **1_도움** aid, help

2_지지, 후원 endorsement

Grocery prices were **boosted** again last month. 식료품 가격이 지난달에 다시 올랐다.

The candidate received a **boost** on Monday when *The New York Times* endorsed him in an editorial. 그 후보는 〈뉴욕타임스〉가 월요일 사설에서 그를 지지하자 큰 힘을 얻었다.

candidate n. 후보

endorse v. 지지하다, (어음, 서류 등에) 배서하다

editorial n. 사설 adj. 편집장의, 사설의

persist

v. **1_주장하다** insist

2_고수하다 persevere, continue, endure

You should call your doctor if the symptom **persists**.
증상이 지속되면 의사에게 전화해야 한다.
symptom n. 증상

persistent(ly)

adj.(adv.) 1_끈덕진 insistent

2_지속적인 continuous

Brooks Adams failed to find the universal law of commerce
that he **persistently** sought. 브룩스 애덤스는 그가 끊임없이
추구했던 상업의 일반적인 법칙을 찾아내지 못했다.
universal adj. 일반적인, 전체의, 우주의
law n. 법, 규칙
commerce n. 상업, 무역=trade

aim

n. **1_목표** purpose, intention

2_목적 goal, end

v. **1_겨냥하다** point, direct

2_갈망하다 aspire to, try for

The governor's **aim** is to increase state income. 그 주지사의
목표는 주의 소득을 늘리는 것이다.
governor n. 주지사, 지배자
state n. 주, 국가, 상태 v. 말하다
income n. 소득, 수입

The peace talks **aimed** at ending the conflict between North
and South Korea. 평화 회담은 남북한의 갈등을 종식시킬 목적이었다.
peace n. 평화, 평온 **talk** n. 협상, 수업, 연설 v. 말하다

minute

adj. **작은** small, tiny, miniscule, infinitesimal

≠huge, vast, enormous, massive, colossal

Living things consist of **minute** structures called cells.
생물은 세포라고 불리는 작은 구조들로 이루어져 있다.

inappropriate(ly)

adj.(adv.)

1_적절하지 않은 unsuitable, improper

2_잘못된 wrong, unbecoming

The audience felt that the speaker's remark was
inappropriate for such a grave issue. 청중들은 그 연사의
소견이 그렇게 중대한 문제에 적절하지 않다고 느꼈다.

audience n. 청중, 관객, 관중, 독자

speaker n. 연설가, 강연가

The New River in North Carolina is **inappropriately**
named because it is five hundred million years old.
노스캐롤라이나에 있는 뉴 강은 이름이 부적절하게 붙여졌다. 왜냐하면
그 강은 5억 년이나 되었기 때문이다.

name v. ~에 이름을 지어주다, (가격, 날짜 등을) 지정하다 n. 이름

load

n. **1_짐** cargo

2_부담 burden

3_과제 assignment

v. **1_(짐 등을) 싣다**

2_권총에 총알을 장전하다

The professor decided to take some of the **load** off the students when they began to complain. 학생들이 불평하기 시작했을 때 교수는 그들의 부담을 좀 덜어주기로 결심했다.
complain v. 불평을 말하다, 고소하다

The police officer got shot when he was trying to **load** his gun. 그 경찰은 총알을 장전하고 있을 때 총에 맞았다.

admire

v. **존중하다, 존경하다** esteem, respect, idolize

I **admire** his work for its richness and profoundness. 나는 풍부함과 심오함 때문에 그의 작품을 존경한다.
richness n. 풍부함
profoundness n. 심오함

admiration

n. 감탄 respect

The crowd was filled with **admiration** for the player's will to win. 그 선수의 승리에 대한 의지에 관중들은 감탄하고 있었다.
crowd n. 관중, 대중 v. (장소가) 붐비다, 만원이다

brevity

n. **1_(시간, 기간의) 짧음** short

2_간결함 briefness, conciseness

Epigrams are sayings characterized by wit and **brevity**.

풍자시는 재치와 간결함의 특색을 갖춘 말이다.

epigram n. (짧은) 풍자시

saying n. 명언, 발언, 말하기

characterize v. ~의 특색을 나타내다, (~이라고) 간주하다

wit n. 재치, 이성

Lesson 01 Review Test

01 During the Civil War, steam-boating on the lower Mississippi River was **ruined**.

    ⓐ delayed   ⓑ taxed

    ⓒ destroyed   ⓓ rerouted

02 Even while making political statement, Ben Shahn was in full command of his technical **resources**.

    ⓐ abilities   ⓑ senses

    ⓒ facts   ⓓ accents

03 During the years before the American Civil War, differences between the North and the South **gradually** came to focus on the question of slavery.

    ⓐ angrily   ⓑ guiltily

    ⓒ actively   ⓓ slowly

04 When birds **migrate**, they sometimes fly in formation.

    ⓐ grow from feathers   ⓑ move from one place to another

    ⓒ feel death is near   ⓓ search for food and water

05 Brooks Adams failed to find the universal law of commerce that he **persistently** sought.

    ⓐ halfheartedly   ⓑ hurriedly

    ⓒ continuously   ⓓ slyly

06 Living things consist of **minute** structures called cells.

    ⓐ numerous   ⓑ variable

    ⓒ diverse   ⓓ tiny

07 The New River in North Carolina is **inappropriately** named because it is five hundred million years old.

    ⓐ quaintly   ⓑ unsuitably

    ⓒ indiscreetly   ⓓ peculiarly

08 The professor decided to take some of the **load** off the students when they began to complain.

    ⓐ group   ⓑ burden

    ⓒ return   ⓓ issue

09 I **admire** his work for its richness and profoundness.

    ⓐ recognize   ⓑ exploit

    ⓒ tolerate   ⓓ esteem

10 Glass-fiber cables can carry hundreds of telephone conversation **simultaneously**.

    ⓐ with safety   ⓑ without direction

    ⓒ in little space   ⓓ at the same time

11 Many city dwellers are turning **vacant** lots into thriving gardens.

    ⓐ costly   ⓑ empty

    ⓒ small   ⓓ shady

12 Epigrams are sayings characterized by wit and **brevity**.

    ⓐ rhythm   ⓑ conciseness

    ⓒ brilliance   ⓓ scorn

13 On January 29, 1778, Captain James Cook took his two **vessels** into a small harbor on the island of Kauai.

    ⓐ assistants   ⓑ cargoes

    ⓒ ships   ⓓ guns

14 Grocery prices were **boosted** again last month.

    ⓐ attacked   ⓑ stabilized

    ⓒ fixed   ⓓ raised

15 The governor's **aim** is to increase state income.

    ⓐ promise   ⓑ duty

    ⓒ proposal   ⓓ goal

01	c	ⓐ delay=v. 지연되다 ⓑ tax=v. 세금을 부과하다 ⓓ reroute=v. 코스를 변경하다
02	a	ⓑ sense=n. 감각 ⓒ fact=n. 사실 ⓓ accent=n. 악센트
03	d	ⓐ angrily=adv. 성나서 ⓑ guiltily=adv. 죄를 범한 듯이 ⓒ actively=adj. 활동적으로
04	b	ⓐ grow from feathers=깃털에서부터 자라다 ⓒ feel death is near=죽음이 가깝다고 느끼다 ⓓ search for food and water=먹이와 물을 찾다
05	c	ⓐ halfheartedly=adv. 마음이 내키지 않게 ⓑ hurriedly=adv. 급히 ⓓ slyly=adv. 교활하게
06	d	ⓐ numerous=adj. 매우 많은 ⓑ variable=adj. 일정하지 않은 ⓒ diverse=adj. 다양한
07	b	ⓐ quaintly=adv. 별나고 아름답게 ⓒ indiscreetly=adv. 무분별하게 ⓓ peculiarly=adj. 독특하게
08	b	ⓐ group=n. 그룹 ⓒ return=n. 귀환 ⓓ issue=n. 논점
09	d	ⓐ recognize=v. 인식하다 ⓑ exploit=v. 이용하다 ⓒ tolerate=v. 허용하다
10	d	ⓐ with safety=안전하게 ⓑ without direction=방향이 없이 ⓒ in little space=작은 공간에서
11	b	ⓐ costly=adj. 값이 비싼 ⓒ small=adj. 작은 ⓓ shady=adj. 그늘이 많은
12	b	ⓐ rhythm=n. 리듬 ⓒ brilliance=n. 탁월 ⓓ scorn=n. 경멸
13	c	ⓐ assistant=n. 조수 ⓑ cargo=n. 짐 ⓓ gun=n. 총
14	d	ⓐ attack=v. 공격하다 ⓑ stabilize=v. ~을 안정시키다 ⓒ fix=v. 고치다
15	d	ⓐ promise=n. 약속 ⓑ duty=n. 책임 ⓒ proposal=n. 제안

L e s s o n 02

rescue

last

found

eradicate

abundant(ly)

leading

widespread

analogy

spur

marvel

bond

monumental

moist

diverse

trigger

rescue

v. **1_구하다, 구조하다** save
2_회복하다 recover

n. **구출, 구조**

When Washington, D. C. was burned in 1814, Dolley Madison **rescued** many official papers from the White House. 1814년 워싱턴이 불에 탔을 때, 돌리 매디슨은 백악관의 많은 공문서들을 구해냈다.

official adj. 직무상의 n. (정부의) 관리, 공무원(civil servant)

The economic crisis called for the federal government to come to the **rescue**. 경제위기가 회복되기 위해서는 연방정부의 도움이 필요했다.

crisis n. 위기, 국면 **call for** ~을 요구하다
federal adj. 연방의 **government** n. 정부

last

adj. **마지막** final, ultimate
≠first, initial

v. **1_계속하다** continue
2_견디어내다 endure, persevere

He believes that this is his **last** bid to be elected president. 그는 이것이 대통령으로 선출되기 위한 그의 마지막 시도라고 생각한다.

bid n. 시도, 입찰(의 기회), 노력 v. ~을 얻으려 하다
elect v. (~의 직책에) 선출되다, ~을 선택하다

The Depression in the United States **lasted** until the beginning of the Second World War. 미국의 불황은 제2차 세계대전 초까지 계속됐다.

depression n. 공황, 불황, 저하, 우울

found

v. **1_설립하다** establish, set up, erect

2_시작하다 originate, launch

3_기초를 두다 base

The Women's Army Corps was **founded** in 1942. 여군 부대는 1942년에 창설되었다.

Is the article a complete fabrication or is it **founded** on reality? 이 기사는 완벽한 날조인가 아니면 사실에 기초를 둔 것인가?

article n. 기사, 논문, 한 품목, 물품

founder

n. 설립자

Founding Fathers

n. 미국 건국의 인물들

eradicate

v. **1_뿌리째 뽑다** uproot, wipe out

2_근절하다, 박멸하다 destroy, exterminate

The intention of Social Security was to **eradicate** poverty in America. 미국 사회보장제도의 취지는 가난을 뿌리뽑는 것이었다.

social adj. 사회복지의, 사회의

security n. 보호수단, 안전, 보증금

intention n. 의도, 목적, 목표

poverty n. 가난, 빈곤, 부족

The Salk vaccine is a major factor in the fight to **eradicate** polio. 솔크 백신은 소아마비를 근절하기 위한 분투에 있어서 중요한 요소다.

major adj. 중요한, 대표적인   **factor** n. 요소, 요인

abundant(ly)

adj.(adv.)

풍부한 ample, plentiful, rich

≠scarce, lacking, sparse

Blue-green algae grow **abundantly** in salt marshes.

청녹조류는 염습지에서 풍부하게 자란다.

abundance

n. 많음, 풍부함 profusion, wealth, affluence ≠ scarcity, shortage, paucity

Lack of human contacts led to the variety and **abundance** of wildlife in the Demilitarized Zone(DMZ). DMZ에는 사람과의 접촉이 없어서 야생 생물이 풍부하고 다양하다.

lack n. 결여, 결핍, 부족한 것 v. 결핍되다

variety n. 다양(성), 갖가지 다른 것, 종류

wildlife n. 야생 생물

leading

adj. **대표적인, 선두의** foremost, first, principal, front, chief, primary

Insect pests are among the **leading** causes of crop failure.

충해는 흉작의 대표적인 원인 중의 하나다.

So far, he is the **leading** candidate in the election. 지금까지, 그는 선거에서 가장 앞선 후보다.

widespread

adj. **널리 퍼진** pervasive, extensive, disseminated, far-reaching

≠ limited, confined

As both a religion and a social force, Puritanism has had a **widespread** influence in the United States. 종교와 사회적 세력으로서, 청교도주의는 미국 전체에 영향을 끼치고 있다.

religion n. 종교

force n. 세력, 영향력, 효력, 폭력

influence n. 영향, 작용

analogy

n. **유사, 비슷함** similarity, resemblance, parallel

≠ disparity

The fear of smallpox, which terrorized the eighteenth century, has no **analogy**. 18세기를 위협했던 천연두처럼 요즘은 그러한 공포를 야기하는 병은 없다.

fear n. 두려움, 근심, 염려 v. 두려워하다

terrorize v. ~을 무서워하게 하다, 위협하다

analogous

adj. 닮은 comparable, akin, corresponding

spur

v. **자극하다, 장려하다** urge, encourage, stimulate

≠ hinder, prevent, discourage, thwart

n. **동기** incentive, motive

The National Industrial Recovery Act was designed to **spur** industry. 국가산업 회복결의서는 산업을 장려하기 위해 만들어졌다.

act n. 법령, 행위, 시늉 v. 행동하다, 집무하다

The instructor thought that harsh criticisms would act as a **spur** to increase his students' effort. 그 선생님은 신랄한 비판이 학생들의 노력을 증대시키는 자극제 역할을 하리라고 생각했다.

harsh adj. 신랄한, 엄한, 거친

marvel

n. **놀라운 일, 경이** astonishment, sensation, spectacle, wonder

v. **감탄하다, 놀라다** wonder, gape

When the Erie Canal was built in the 1820's, it was the engineering **marvel** of its time. 1820년대 이리 운하가 건설되었을 때, 그것은 당시 기술공학의 경이였다.

build v. 짓다, 건축하다, ~을 늘리다

We **marveled** at the sight of the Empire State Building. 우리는 엠파이어 스테이트 빌딩의 광경에 감탄했다.

sight n. 광경, 경치, 시각, 일견 v. ~을 발견하다

bond

n. **연맹, 맺음, 결속** union, link, attachment

v. **접착하다** bind, tie, weld

≠separate, sever, detach

Communication is one of the most important **bonds** that hold cultural systems together. 커뮤니케이션은 문화적 체계를 유지하는 가장 중요한 결속력의 하나다.

bondage

n. 속박, 감금 slavery, captivity, servitude ≠ freedom, liberty

Most people in the third world countries live their entire lives in **bondage** to hunger and poverty. 제3세계 국가 사람들 대부분은 전 생애를 기아와 가난의 노예로 살아간다.

monumental

adj. **1_대단히 큰** huge, enormous, massive, vast

2_대단한 significant, enduring, outstanding

≠insignificant, trivial, negligible

In 1974 Henry Aaron broke Babe Ruth's **monumental** lifetime record of 714 home runs. 1974년에, 헨리 아론은 베이브 루스의 714번 홈런이라는 대단한 생애기록을 깼다.

break v. (기록을) 깨뜨리다, 부수다, ~을 끝내다, 고장나다 n. 틈, 운, 기회

lifetime adj. 일생(동안)의, 평생의

moist

adj. **축축한, 습기 있는** damp, wet, humid, muggy,

≠dry, parched, arid

Food must be **moist** in order to have a taste. 음식은 맛을
지니기 위해서 축축해야 한다.

in order to ~하기 위하여

taste n. 맛, 시식 v. 맛보다, 경험하다

moisture

n. 1_수분 dampness, wetness

2_습기 humidity

diverse

adj. **다양한, 다른** various, dissimilar

≠identical, corresponding

diversified

adj. 변화가 많은, 다채로운 varied,
assorted

The economy of Dallas, Texas, is strong and **diversified**.
텍사스 주 댈러스의 경제는 강력하고 변화가 많다.

diversify

v. 다채롭게 하다 vary, branch
out, mix

diversity

n. 다양성 difference,
distinctiveness, variety

One of the unique aspects of American society is its
diversity. 미국 사회의 독특한 면 중의 하나는 다양성이다.

trigger

v. **유발하다** set off, cause, generate, spark, touch off

≠inhibit, prevent, stop

n. **방아쇠**

The flower bud of a water lily opens at sunset since its opening is **triggered** by the decreased light. 수련 봉오리는 해질녘에 피어난다. 왜냐하면 그것의 개화는 감소된 빛에 의해 유발되기 때문이다.

bud   n. 봉오리 v. 싹트다

sunset   n. 일몰 ≠ sunrise, 말기, 만년

decrease   v. 서서히 줄다 ≠ increase

Lesson 02 Review Test

01 When Washington, D.C. was burned in 1814, Dolley Madison **rescued** many official papers from the White House.

ⓐ stole   ⓑ filed

ⓒ hid   ⓓ saved

02 The Depression in the United States **lasted** until the beginning of the Second World War.

ⓐ was avoided   ⓑ continued

ⓒ had been restrained   ⓓ deteriorated

03 The Women's Army Corps was **founded** in 1942.

ⓐ supported   ⓑ established

ⓒ discovered   ⓓ emphasized

04 The Salk vaccine is a major factor in the fight to **eradicate** polio.

ⓐ completely destroy   ⓑ carefully disguised

ⓒ sustain   ⓓ contain

05 Blue-green algae grow **abundantly** in salt marshes.

ⓐ primarily   ⓑ slowly

ⓒ on plants   ⓓ in great numbers

06 Insect pests are among the **leading** causes of crop failure.

ⓐ expected   ⓑ chief

ⓒ natural   ⓓ least

07 As both a religion and a social force, Puritanism has had **a widespread** influence in the United States.

    ⓐ a disturbing   ⓑ a complex

    ⓒ an annoying   ⓓ a far-reaching

08 The fear of smallpox, which terrorized the eighteenth century, has no **analogy**.

    ⓐ occurrence   ⓑ remnants

    ⓒ witnesses   ⓓ parallel

09 The National Industrial Recovery Act was designed to **spur** industry.

    ⓐ tax   ⓑ stimulate

    ⓒ censure   ⓓ rebuke

10 When the Erie Canal was built in the 1820's, it was the engineering **marvel** of its time.

    ⓐ wonder   ⓑ dispute

    ⓒ frustration   ⓓ model

11 Communication is one of the most important **bonds** that hold cultural systems together.

    ⓐ obligations   ⓑ links

    ⓒ duties   ⓓ needs

12 In 1974 Henry Aaron broke Babe Ruth's **monumental** lifetime record of 714 home runs.

    ⓐ archaic   ⓑ degrading

    ⓒ outstanding   ⓓ entire

13 Food must be **moist** in order to have a taste.

ⓐ appetizing ⓑ nutritious

ⓒ damp ⓓ chewed

14 The economy of Dallas, Texas, is strong and **diversified**.

ⓐ inflated ⓑ stable

ⓒ varied ⓓ well-regulated

15 The flower bud of a water lily opens at sunset since its opening is **triggered** by the decreased light.

ⓐ alleviated ⓑ endured

ⓒ set off ⓓ covered up

01	**d**	ⓐ steal=v. ~을 훔치다 ⓑ file=v. 정리하여 보관하다 ⓒ hide=v. 숨기다
02	**b**	ⓐ avoid=v. 피하다 ⓒ restrain=v. 제지(방해)하다 ⓓ deteriorate=v. 나빠지게 하다
03	**b**	ⓐ support=v. 지지하다 ⓒ discover=v. 발견하다 ⓓ emphasize=v. 강조하다
04	**a**	ⓑ carefully disguised=조심스럽게 변장한 ⓒ sustain=v. 떠받치다 ⓓ contain=v. 포함하다
05	**d**	ⓐ primarily=adv. 첫째로 ⓑ slowly=adv. 천천히 ⓒ on plants= 식물(초목) 위에
06	**b**	ⓐ expect=v. 기대하다 ⓒ natural=adj. 자연의 ⓓ least=adj. 가장 적은(작은)
07	**d**	ⓐ disturbing=adj. 불안하게 하는 ⓑ complex=adj. 복잡한 ⓒ annoying=adj. 성가신
08	**d**	ⓐ occurrence=n. 발생 ⓑ remnant=n. 나머지 ⓒ witness=n. 목격자
09	**b**	ⓐ tax=n. 세금 ⓒ censure=n. 비난 ⓓ rebuke=n. 비난
10	**a**	ⓑ dispute=n. 논쟁 ⓒ frustration=n. 좌절 ⓓ model=n. 모델
11	**b**	ⓐ obligation=n. 의무 ⓒ duty=n. 의무 ⓓ need=n. 필요
12	**c**	ⓐ archaic=adj. 고풍의 ⓑ degrading=adj. 품위를 떨어뜨리는 ⓓ entire=adj. 전체의
13	**c**	ⓐ appetizing=adj. 식욕을 돋우는 ⓑ nutritious=adj. 영양이 되는 ⓓ chew=v. 씹다
14	**c**	ⓐ inflated=adj. 팽창한 ⓑ stable=adj. 안정된 ⓓ well-regulated=adj. 잘 정돈된
15	**c**	ⓐ alleviate=v. 완화하다 ⓑ endure=v. 참다 ⓓ cover up=싸서 감추다

shift

symptom

initiate

modification

devote

important

trace

emit

unique

outmoded

succumb

exhaustive(ly)

distinguish

threat(en)

pure

shift

v. **이동하다, 바꾸다** move, change

n. **1_변천** deviation, reversal

2_교대(시간)

Because he is a night person, John prefers to work during the evening **shift**. 존은 야행성이기 때문에, 저녁조 근무 시간대에 일하는 것을 더 좋아한다.

shifting

adj. 이동하는, 바뀌는 moving, changing

The **shifting** layers of the earth's center continue to make earthquakes inevitable. 지구 중심의 이동층들은 끊임없이 지진이 일어나도록 만든다.

symptom

n. **1_징조** sign, omen

2_증상 condition, sign

The **symptoms** of influenza are fever, headache, and muscular pain. 유행성 감기의 증상은 발열, 두통 그리고 근육통이다.

fever n. 발열, 열병, 열광 v. ~을 흥분시키다

headache n. 두통, 난처한 사람, 골칫거리

muscular adj. 근육의, 강건한, 강렬한

pain n. 고통, 괴로움, 고뇌=anguish, 고생 v. 아픔을 주다, 괴롭히다

initiate

v. **시작하다, 창설하다** begin, originate, commence

n. **초보자** beginner, novice, neophyte

The term "New Deal" applies to the program of reform and recovery **initiated** by President Franklin D. Roosevelt. "뉴딜"이란 용어는 프랭클린 D. 루스벨트 대통령에 의해 시작된 경기회복과 재건 프로그램에 적용된 말이다.

term   n. (학술) 용어, 말투, (약정) 기간, 관계   v. ~이라고 부르다=name

apply   v. 적용하다, 활용하다, 바르다, ~에 전념하다

reform   n. 개선, 개혁   v. ~을 보다 좋게 하다, 개심시키다

recovery   n. 회복, 복귀, ~을 되찾기, 회복에 소요되는 시간

modification

n. **수정, 변경** alteration, refinement, change

Although many **modifications** have been made in it, the game known in the United States as football can be traced directly to the English game of rugby. 많은 수정이 이루어지고 있지만, 미국에서 풋볼로 알려진 그 경기는 영국의 럭비경기에서 바로 그 유래를 찾을 수 있다.

although   conj. 비록 ~일지라도, ~이기는 하나, ~이지만=though

trace to   ~까지 거슬러 올라가다, ~에 유래하다

directly   adv. 바로, 똑바로, 정확히, 직접으로

modify

v. 1_ 수정하다 alter

2_ 완화하다, 조절하다

moderate, adjust

devote

v. **(노력, 돈, 시간 따위를) 바치다** dedicate, concentrate,
reserve, occupy oneself

Much of the space in the National Gallery of Art is **devoted**
to paintings presented to the museum by Andrew Mellon.
국립 미술관의 많은 공간이 앤드류 멜론이 박물관에 기증한 그림들로
채워져 있다.

space n. 공간, 우주, 장소, (기차, 비행기 등의) 자리 v. 간격을 두고 배치하다

present v. 증정하다, 제시하다 adj. 출석해 있는 ≠ absent, 마음속에 있는 n. 현재

devoted

adj. 충실한, 헌신적인 faithful,
ardent, devout
≠ distant, detached

devotion

n. 헌신, 전심, 강한 애착
commitment, affection

important

adj. **중요한** significant, essential, vital, integral, fundamental,
critical, major
≠ unimportant, insignificant, minor, weak, trivial,
petty

A dog's most **important** sense is that of smell. 개의 가장
중요한 감각은 후각이다.

sense n. 오감의 하나, 감각, 기분=feeling, 의식, 제정신 v. ~을 느끼다

smell n. 후각, 냄새
v. ~의 냄새가 나다, ~의 냄새를 맡다=sniff, 탐지하다=detect

trace

n. **1_ 발자취, 흔적** track, trail

v. **1_ 추적하다** chase, pursue

2_ 조사하다 investigate

The bank robber disappeared without a **trace**. 은행 강도는 흔적도 없이 사라졌다.

Nineteenth-century scholars tried to **trace** the origins of modern languages to ancient Hebrew. 19세기 학자들은 고대 히브리어에서 현대 언어의 기원을 찾으려고 노력했다.

scholar n. 학자

origin n. 기원, 출처=source, 발생, 원인, 혈통=ancestry

modern adj. 근대의≠ancient, 현대의, 현대적인 n. 현대인

emit

v. **1_ 방출하다** discharge, secrete

　　　　≠ absorb, suck up

2_ 발산하다 give out

　　　　≠ take in

Cathode **emits** electrons in a controlled environment. 음극은 제어된 환경에서 전자를 방출한다.

control v. 제어하다, 지배하다 n. 지배, 관리, 억제, 제어, 지배력

environment n. 환경, 자연환경, 주위

unique

adj. **독특한** only, exceptional, extraordinary, peerless, unparalleled, remarkable

≠ numerous, common, ordinary, familiar

In his novels, Upton Sinclair showed his **unique** genius for recreating social history. 그의 소설에서, 업톤 싱클레어는 사회 역사를 재현하는 데 있어 독특한 천재성을 보여주었다.

genius n. 비범한 재능, 천재

recreate v. 재현(재생)하다, ~을 개조하다, 기분 전환을 하다

outmoded

adj. **유행에 뒤떨어진, 구식의** outdated, obsolete, unfashionable

≠ up-to-date, current, fashionable

One out of five bridges in the United States is **outmoded**. 미국에 있는 교량 다섯 개 중 한 개는 구식이다.

bridge n. 다리, 연락, 함교 v. 다리를 놓다, ~에게 중개 역할을 하다

succumb v. **1_굴복하다** submit, yield, surrender

2_압도되다 ≠ hold out, persist, persevere, endure

In Nathaniel Hawthorn's "The Scarlet Letter", Reverend Dimmesdale **succumbed** to Hester's charms. 너새니엘 호손의 『주홍 글씨』에서 딤즈데일 목사는 헤스터의 매력에 굴복했다.

reverend n. 목사=minister, 성직자=clergyman

charm n. 애교, 부적 v. 황홀하게 하다

exhaustive(ly) adj. **철저한** thorough, complete, comprehensive
(adv.) ≠ partial, incomplete, superficial

The researcher's sources for his findings were **exhaustive**. 자신의 결론에 대한 그 조사원의 자료는 철저했다.

source n. 자료, 원인=origin, 출처

finding n. 결론, 발견물, 찾아냄, 결정

Although the work needs to be done more **exhaustively**, efforts have been made to collect the songs and ballads of the American Revolution. 연구가 더 철저하게 이루어져야 하지만, 독립전쟁의 노래와 발라드를 모으기 위한 노력이 이루어지고 있다.

distinguish

v. **구별하다** differentiate, mark, single out

There is something about Mary that **distinguishes** her from her peers. 메리에게는 친구들과 구별되는 뭔가가 있다.

peer n. 친구, 동료 v. 자세히 보다

distinguished

adj. 유명한 eminent, notable, noted, acclaimed, illustrious, renowned, famed, famous, celebrated

≠ mediocre, ordinary

Deems Taylor was **distinguished** both as a music critic and as a composer. 딤스 테일러는 음악 평론가 겸 작곡가로서 유명했다.

---

threat(en)

n.(v) **1_협박, 위협** intimidation, terror, menace
≠ reassurance, encouragement

2_징조 sign, omen

From the look of the sky, there is a **threat** of rain. 하늘을 보니, 비가 올 것 같다.

threatened

adj. 멸종 위기에 있는 endangered

threatening(ly)

adj.(adv.) 협박하는, 위협하는 menacing

When bothered by other animals or humans, some species of horned lizards will posture **threateningly** and squirt blood from their eyes. 어떤 뿔도마뱀 종은 동물이나 사람에게 위협을 당하면, 위협하는 자세를 취하며 눈에서 피를 뿜어낸다.

species n. 종, 종류=kind

pure

adj. **1_순수한** innocent

2_청결한 unspoiled, clean

≠ corrupt

3_섞이지 않은 unadulterated

≠ mixed, adulterated

Chemically **pure** iron has relatively few commercial uses.

화학적으로 순수한 철은 비교적 상업적인 용도가 거의 없다.

iron n. 철, 강함, 다리미

Lesson 03 Review Test

01 Cathode **emits** electrons in a controlled environment.
- ⓐ chases
- ⓑ discharges
- ⓒ blocks
- ⓓ gives

02 Chemically **pure** iron has relatively few commercial uses.
- ⓐ mixed
- ⓑ corrupt
- ⓒ unadulterated
- ⓓ threatened

03 The **shifting** layers of the earth's center continue to make earthquakes inevitable.
- ⓐ moving
- ⓑ constant
- ⓒ lowering
- ⓓ burning

04 Nineteenth-century scholars tried to **trace** the origins of modern languages to ancient Hebrew.
- ⓐ dedicate
- ⓑ alter
- ⓒ connect
- ⓓ begin

05 When bothered by other animals or humans, some species of horned lizards will posture **threateningly** and squirt blood from their eyes.
- ⓐ significantly
- ⓑ completely
- ⓒ menacingly
- ⓓ encouragingly

06 The **symptoms** of influenza are fever, headache, and muscular pain.
- ⓐ signs
- ⓑ dangers
- ⓒ warnings
- ⓓ affections

07 A dog's most **important** sense is that of smell.

ⓐ endangered　　　　　　　　ⓑ trivial

ⓒ noted　　　　　　　　　　　ⓓ significant

08 Deems Taylor was **distinguished** both as a music critic and as a composer.

ⓐ acclaimed　　　　　　　　　ⓑ proclaimed

ⓒ denounced　　　　　　　　　ⓓ criticized

09 The term "New Deal" applies to the program of reform and recovery **initiated** by President Franklin D. Roosevelt.

ⓐ concluded　　　　　　　　　ⓑ altered

ⓒ originated　　　　　　　　　ⓓ moderated

10 Much of the space in the National Gallery of Art is **devoted to** paintings presented to the museum by Andrew Mellon.

ⓐ reserved for　　　　　　　　ⓑ detached to

ⓒ unconcerned with　　　　　　ⓓ terrorized by

11 In his novels, Upton Sinclair showed his **unique** genius for recreating social history.

ⓐ peerless　　　　　　　　　　ⓑ numerous

ⓒ huge　　　　　　　　　　　　ⓓ partial

12 In Nathaniel Hawthorn's "The Scarlet Letter", Reverend Dimmesdale **succumbed to** Hester's charms.

ⓐ yielded to　　　　　　　　　ⓑ held out against

ⓒ intimidated by　　　　　　　ⓓ wished for

13 One out of five bridges in the United States is **outmoded**.

    ⓐ outdated   ⓑ renovated

    ⓒ remodeled   ⓓ ignored

14 Although the work needs to be done more **exhaustively**, efforts have been made to collect the songs and ballads of the American Revolution.

    ⓐ faithfully   ⓑ vitally

    ⓒ exceptionally   ⓓ thoroughly

15 Although many **modifications** have been made in it, the game known in the United States as football can be traced directly to the English game of rugby.

    ⓐ dedications   ⓑ criticisms

    ⓒ changes   ⓓ tracks

01	b	ⓐ chase=v. 뒤쫓다 ⓒ block=v. 막다(봉쇄하다) ⓓ give=v. 주다
02	c	ⓐ mixed=adj. 혼합된 ⓑ corrupt=adj. 타락한 ⓓ threatened=adj. 멸종위기에 있는
03	a	ⓑ constant=adj. 불변의, 부단한 ⓒ lowering=adj. 저하시키는 ⓓ burning=adj. 불타는
04	c	ⓐ dedicate=v. 바치다 ⓑ alter=v. 변경하다 ⓓ begin=v. 시작하다
05	c	ⓐ significantly=adv. 의미심장하게 ⓑ completely=adv. 완전히 ⓓ encouragingly=adv. 격려하여
06	a	ⓑ danger=n. 위험 ⓒ warning=n. 경고 ⓓ affection=n. 애정
07	d	ⓐ endangered=adj. 절멸 직전의 ⓑ trivial=adj. 하찮은 ⓒ noted=adj. 유명한
08	a	ⓑ proclaim=v. 선언하다 ⓒ denounce=v. 비난하다 ⓓ criticize=v. 비평(비판)하다
09	c	ⓐ conclude=v. 끝내다 ⓑ alter=v. 변경하다 ⓓ moderate=v. 절제하다
10	a	ⓑ detached=adj. 파견된 ⓒ unconcerned=adj. 관심을 가지지 않은 ⓓ terrorize=v. 위협해서 ~시키다
11	a	ⓑ numerous=adj. 다수의 ⓒ huge=adj. 거대한 ⓓ partial=adj. 부분적인
12	a	ⓑ hold out against=버티다 ⓒ intimidate=v. 협박하다 ⓓ wish=v. 바라다
13	a	ⓑ renovate=v. ~을 새롭게 하다 ⓒ remodel=v. 개작(개조, 개축)하다 ⓓ ignore=v. 무시하다
14	d	ⓐ faithfully=adv. 충실히 ⓑ vitally=adv. 치명적으로 ⓒ exceptionally=adv. 예외적으로
15	c	ⓐ dedication=n. 봉헌, 헌신 ⓑ criticism=n. 비평 ⓓ track=n. 지나간 자취

L e s s o n 04

First Week

provide

forever

mankind

agrarian

locate

laud

lodge

sanction

sovereign

conglomerate

idol

flaw

fruitless(ly)

gifted

imminent

provide

v. **제공하다** supply, furnish, yield

Solar cells have been developed primarily to **provide** electric power for spacecrafts. 태양 전지는 우주선에 전력을 공급하기 위해 우선적으로 개발되었다.

solar adj. 태양의, 태양에서 생기는

cell n. 전지, 세포, 작은 방

provided (that)

conj. ~이라는 조건으로

on condition (that)

The professor will give the student a passing grade for the course, **provided that** he gets an A on the final. 만약 학기말 시험에서 A를 받으면, 그 교수님은 학생에게 과목을 통과하는 점수를 줄 것이다.

forever

adv. **영원히** eternally, indefinitely, infinitely

≠ temporarily, ephemerally

Even the best-built machine will not run **forever** without proper maintenance. 최고로 만들어진 기계라도 적절하게 유지되지 않으면 영원히 작동되지 않을 것이다.

run v. 작동하다, 운영하다, ~을 출판하다 n. 뛰기, 운행

proper adj. 적합한, 고상한=decent, 정규의

maintenance n. 유지, 지속, 보수, 주장

mankind

n. **인류, 인간** humanity, human, human race, people

Soils are renewable resources that support all **mankind**.
흙이란 모든 인류를 지탱시켜주는 재생 가능한 자원이다.

soil n. 흙

renewable adj. 재생 가능한

support v. 유지하다

agrarian

adj. **토지의, 농업의** agricultural

One cause of the Civil War was economic and political
rivalry between the **agrarian** South and the industrial
North. 농업 위주의 남부와 산업 위주인 북부의 경제적 · 정치적 경쟁이
남북전쟁 원인 중의 하나다.

cause n. 원인, 근거, 동기 v. 원인이 되다

economic adj. 경제(상)의

rivalry n. 경쟁, 대립 관계

industrial adj. 산업의, 고도로 발달한 산업을 가진 n. 공업 제품

locate

v. **1_정착하다** settle ≠ leave

   2_찾아내다 find, discover, detect

The committee still hasn't made the decision where to **locate** the new community center. 위원회는 새로운 지역 회관을 어디로 할지 아직까지 결정하지 못했다.

community n. 지역 공동체, (공동의 이익, 직업 등을 가진 사람들의) 사회

located

adj. 위치한 situated, placed, based

location

n. 장소 position, site, spot

The spleen is a small organ **located** beneath the left side of the rib cage. 지라는 흉곽 왼쪽 밑에 위치한 작은 기관이다.

cage n. 골조, 뼈대, 우리, 가두어두는 곳

---

laud

v. **칭찬하다** praise, acclaim, celebrate

Not until his play "Beyond the Horizon" was produced was Eugene O'Neill **lauded** as the foremost creative American playwright. 그의 연극 "지평선을 넘어서"가 제작되기 전까지 유진 오닐은 미국의 대표적인 창의적 극작가로 칭찬받지 못했다.

beyond prep. ~의 저편에

horizon n. 지평선, 한계, 범위

produce v. 제작되다, ~을 낳다, 맺다=bear, 산출하다, 제출하다 n. 농산물

foremost adj. 가장 중요한, 맨 먼저의

creative adj. 창조적인

laudable

adj. 칭찬할 만한, 훌륭한

   admirable, exemplary

lodge

n. **숙박 시설** hut, cabin

v. **1_묵게 하다** accommodate

2_박히다 deposit

We need to book a room at the Sky **Lodge**. 스카이 여관에 우리는 방을 예약해야 한다.

book v. 예약하다

If a foreign object becomes **lodged** in the eye, medical help is necessary. 만약 이물질이 눈에 들어가면, 의학적인 도움이 필요하다.

foreign adj. 이질적인, 외국의, 대외적인

object n. 물체, 목적 v. ~에 반대하다

sanction

v. **1_허가하다** allow, approve

2_제재하다 penalize

n. **1_인가** approval

2_제재 penalty

The UN **sanctioned** Iraq for its failure to comply with the treaty. 협정을 이행하지 않은 것 때문에 UN은 이라크에 제재를 가하였다.

comply v. ~(희망, 요구 등에) 따르다=obey, 응하다 **treaty** n. 협정, 교섭

Among all societies legal marriage is usually accompanied by some kind of ceremony that expresses group **sanction** of the union. 모든 사회에서, 합법적인 결혼에는 일반적으로 그 공동체의 허락을 표현하는 의식이 따른다.

legal adj. 합법적인 **accompany** v. 따라서 일어나다, 동행하다, 반주를 하다

sovereign

n. **지배자** ruler, monarch, king

adj. **자주적인** independent, autonomous, self-governing
≠ powerless, subservient, dependent

The future course of the nation will depend on the action of the **sovereign**. 그 나라의 미래에 대한 방향은 지배자의 행동으로 좌우된다.

course n. 방향, 길, (시간, 사태의) 경과, 과목

depend on 좌우되다, 의존하다

Only **sovereign** states are able to make treaties. 독립적인 국가만이 조약을 맺을 수가 있다.

conglomerate

n. **1_집합(체)** assortment
2_복합 기업(체)

The population of Seattle is a **conglomerate** of people from different ethnic and cultural backgrounds. 시애틀의 인구는 다른 민족적 · 문화적 배경을 가진 사람들의 집합체이다.

population n. 인구

ethnic adj. (소수)민족의 n. 소수민족

cultural adj. 문화적인, 교양의

idol

n. 우상 icon, hero

idolatry

n. 우상 숭배

idolize

v. 우상화하다 venerate, revere

The "Ten Commandments" prohibit any form of **idolatry**.
"십계명"은 어떤 형태의 우상 숭배도 금지하고 있다.

commandment n. 명령=order, instruction

prohibit v. 금지하다=bar, prohibit

Few composers have been so **idolized** during their lifetime
as was Edward MacDowell. 소수의 작곡가들만이 에드워드
맥도웰처럼 살아 생전에 우상화되고 있다.

composer n. 작곡가

flaw

n. 흠 defect, blemish, fault

≠ perfection

Small **flaws** in an object show that it is handmade. 물건에
있는 작은 흠이 이 물건이 수공으로 만들어졌다는 것을 보여준다.

object n. 물체, 목적=goal, purpose, aim

show v. 보여주다, 지적하다=reflect, indicate

fruitless(ly) adj.(adv) **무익한** useless, vain, futile

≠ fruitful, successful, productive, effective

It was a **fruitless** attempt to make peace with the enemy.
적과 평화를 이룬다는 것은 무익한 시도였다.

attempt n. 시도 v. 시도하다

Grounded whales often struggle **fruitlessly** to reenter deep
water. 해저 고래들은 종종 다시 심해로 들어가기 위해 쓸데없는
노력을 한다.

struggle v. 버둥거리다, 노력하다 n. 노력, 고투

deep adj. 깊은, 심오한

gifted   adj. **(천부적인) 재능이 있는** talented, able, skilled

Charles Wilson Peale is generally considered the most **gifted**
of the Philadelphia colonial artists. 찰스 윌슨 필은 일반적으로
필라델피아 식민지 예술가 중에 제일 재능이 뛰어난 예술가로 여겨진다.

generally adv. 일반적으로, 대개, 대체로

consider v. 고려하다＝regard

colonial adj. 식민지의, 미국이 독립하기 전의 시대의

imminent

adj. **절박한, 급박한, 긴급한** immediate, impending,
about to take place

A darkened sky in the daytime is usually an indication that
a storm is **imminent**. 낮에 어두워진 하늘은 대개 태풍이
임박하다는 징조다.

darken v. ~을 어둡게 하다

daytime n. 낮

usually adv. 대개, 평소에는, 보통은

indication n. 징조=sign, 암시, 증거

Lesson 04 Review Test

01 One cause of the Civil War was economic and political rivalry between the **agrarian** South and the industrial North.

ⓐ prosperous   ⓑ old-fashioned

ⓒ agricultural   ⓓ poorly organized

02 Only **sovereign** states are able to make treaties.

ⓐ constitutional   ⓑ powerful

ⓒ legitimate   ⓓ independent

03 Soils are renewable resources that support all **mankind**.

ⓐ gentlemen   ⓑ humans

ⓒ structures   ⓓ culture

04 Grounded whales often struggle **fruitlessly** to reenter deep water.

ⓐ violently   ⓑ desperately

ⓒ in vain   ⓓ at length

05 The spleen is a small organ **located** beneath the left side of the rib cage.

ⓐ caught   ⓑ found

ⓒ ingrown   ⓓ implanted

06 Even the best-built machine will not run **forever** without proper maintenance.

ⓐ eternally   ⓑ smoothly

ⓒ dependably   ⓓ accurately

07 Not until his play "Beyond the Horizon" was produced was Eugene O'Neill **lauded** as the foremost creative American playwright.

    ⓐ compensated   ⓑ secretly named

    ⓒ given preference   ⓓ praised

08 The population of Seattle is **a conglomerate** of people from different ethnic and cultural backgrounds.

    ⓐ a company   ⓑ a fluctuation

    ⓒ an assortment   ⓓ a matching

09 If a foreign object becomes **lodged in** the eye, medical help is necessary.

    ⓐ deposited in   ⓑ invisible to

    ⓒ blurry to   ⓓ isolated in

10 A darkened sky in the daytime is usually an indication that a storm is **imminent**.

    ⓐ about to take place   ⓑ close by

    ⓒ expected to be severe   ⓓ possibly coming

11 Solar cells have been developed primarily to **provide** electric power for spacecrafts.

    ⓐ ensure   ⓑ store

    ⓒ supply   ⓓ secure

12 Few composers have been so **idolized** during their lifetime as was Edward MacDowell.

    ⓐ dissatisfied   ⓑ reviewed

    ⓒ misguided   ⓓ worshipped

13 Small **flaws** in an object show that it is handmade.

    ⓐ requirements   ⓑ details

    ⓒ defects   ⓓ trademarks

14 Charles Wilson Peale is generally considered the most **gifted** of the Philadelphia colonial artists.

    ⓐ talented   ⓑ presented

    ⓒ eccentric   ⓓ sophisticated

15 Among all societies legal marriage is usually accompanied by some kind of ceremony that expresses group **sanction** of the union.

    ⓐ opinion   ⓑ coercion

    ⓒ approval   ⓓ insistence

01	c	ⓐ prosperous=adj. 번영하는 ⓑ old-fashioned=adj. 구식의
		ⓓ poorly organized=조직이 허술한
02	d	ⓐ constitutional=adj. 구성상의, 헌법상의 ⓑ powerful=adj. 강력한 ⓒ legitimate=adj. 합법적인
03	b	ⓐ gentleman=n. 신사 ⓒ structure=n. 구조 ⓓ culture=n. 문화
04	c	ⓐ violently=adv. 맹렬하게 ⓑ desperately=adv. 절망적으로, 필사적으로 ⓓ at length=마침내
05	b	ⓐ catch=v. 잡다 ⓒ ingrown=adj. 안쪽으로 성장한 ⓓ implanted=adj. 끼워진
06	a	ⓑ smoothly=adv. 매끄럽게 ⓒ dependably=adv. 믿음직하게 ⓓ accurately=adv. 정확히
07	d	ⓐ compensate=v. 보상하다 ⓑ secretly named=은밀히 지명된
		ⓒ given preference=우선권이 주어진
08	c	ⓐ company=n. 회사 ⓑ fluctuation=n. 파동 ⓓ matching=adj. 조화되는
09	a	ⓑ invisible=adj. 눈에 안 보이는 ⓒ blurry=adj. 흐릿한 ⓓ isolated=adj. 고립된
10	a	ⓑ close=adj. 가까운 ⓒ expected to be severe=맹렬하리라 예상되는
		ⓓ possibly coming=아마 곧 다가올
11	c	ⓐ ensure=v. 안전하게 하다 ⓑ store=v. 저장, 비축하다 ⓓ secure=v. 안전하게 하다
12	d	ⓐ dissatisfied=adj. 불만스러운 ⓑ review=v. 정밀하게 살피다 ⓒ misguided=adj. 오도된, 잘못 안
13	c	ⓐ requirement=n. 요구(필요) ⓑ detail=n. 세부 ⓓ trademark=n. 상표
14	a	ⓑ present=v. 주다 ⓒ eccentric=adj. 별난 ⓓ sophisticated=adj. 세련된
15	c	ⓐ opinion=n. 의견 ⓑ coercion=n. 강압 ⓓ insistence=n. 주장

house

strike

capture

evidence

fix

relative(ly)

peruse

defeat

coherent

thaw

utter(ly)

outrage

alternative

haphazard

underscore

house

v. **저장하다** store, place

J.P. Morgan **housed** his art and book collections in separate buildings. 모간은 그의 예술품과 서적 수집물을 격리된 건물에 저장했다.

art n. 예술, 기술, 요령

collection n. 수집(물), 기부금

separate adj. 격리된, 독립된 v. 가르다, 나누다=divide

strike

v. **1_치다** hit, attack, raid

2_공격하다 attack, raid

3_파업하다 stop working

n. **1_때리기** blow

2_파업 work stoppage, walkout

The key to a successful surprised attack is to **strike** the enemy off guard. 성공적인 기습 공격의 비결은 적이 방심할 때 공격하는 것이다.

key n. 비결, 요지 adj. 핵심적인=crucial

surprised attack 기습공격 **off guard** 방심하여

America's first successful **strike** took place in Philadelphia in 1786. 미국 최초의 성공적인 파업은 1786년에 필라델피아에서 일어났다.

take place 일어나다=happen, occur

capture

v. **1_포착하다** catch

   2_체포하다 arrest

The artist **captured** the girl's personality in his photograph.
그 사진작가는 자신의 사진에 여자아이의 성격을 포착해냈다.

personality n. 성격, 인품, 인물

photograph n. 사진

After months of a massive manhunt, the police were able
to **capture** three escaped prisoners. 몇 달 동안의 대규모 수배
후에, 경찰은 3명의 탈옥한 죄수들을 체포했다.

massive adj. 대규모, 거대한=vast, huge, enormous

escape v. 탈출하다, 피하다, ~에서 새어나오다

evidence

n. **증거** proof

v. **1_~을 명시하다** reveal

   2_입증하다 prove, confirm

The McCaslin family **evidences** the guilt of slaveholding
more than Faulkner's other characters do. 맥카슬린 가족은
포크너 책 속의 다른 인물들보다 노예소유에 대한 죄책감을 더 많이
보였다.

guilt n. 죄책감

slave n. 노예

holding n. 소유 재산

character n. 등장인물, 성격=personality

fix
v. **1_고치다** repair, mend, work on
2_~에 고정시키다
3_지정하다 designate
4_식사를 준비하다 make

There are numerous manuals available with instructions on how to **fix** a bicycle. 자전거를 고치는 방법을 알려주는 많은 설명서가 있다.

numerous adj. 여러, 많은
manual n. 설명서, 안내서 adj. 수공의, 수동식의
available adj. 수중에 넣을 수 있는, 이용할 수 있는, 도움이 되는

---

relative(ly)
adj.(adv.) **1_상대적인**
2_관계가 있는 relevant, pertinent
3_비교적 comparative

Your answer is not **relative** to my question. 당신의 대답은 내 질문과 관계가 없다.

Relatively young as an educational institution, the junior college had its beginnings in the United States during the 1890's. 교육기관으로는 시작된 지 얼마 안 되는 2년제 대학은 미국에서는 1890년대에 시작되었다.

young adj. 시작된 지 얼마 안 되는, 젊은 n. 젊은이들
institution n. 기관, 관례=custom
junior adj. 낮은, 연하의≠senior

peruse

v. **1_정독하다** examine, study

2_읽다 read

After **perusing** the menu for some time, Sam ordered his meal. 한참 동안 메뉴를 본 다음에, 샘은 식사를 주문했다.

menu n. 메뉴, 식사

some time 오랫동안, 머지않아

order v. 주문하다, 지시하다 n. 순서, 주문, 명령

meal n. 식사

defeat

v. **패배시키다** conquer, crush

n. **패배** loss, downfall

≠ victory, triumph, success

Once its supply lines were broken, it took little time for the army to be **defeated**. 일단 공급선이 끊어지자, 그 군대가 패배하기까지는 불과 얼마의 시간이 걸리지 않았다.

once conj. 일단 adv. 한번 adj. 이전의

supply n. 공급, 재고(량) v. 공급하다

line n. 전선, 선, 줄

He was devastated by his last **defeat**. 그는 자신의 마지막 패배로 충격을 받았다.

devastate v. 충격을 주다, 황폐시키다

coherent

adj. **논리적인** logical, rational

≠ illogical, irrational

We found the professor's talk on nuclear reactors quite **coherent**. 우리는 교수님의 원자로에 대한 수업이 매우 논리적이라고 느꼈다.

find v. 느끼다, 깨닫다, 발견하다=discover

nuclear reactor 원자로

quite adv. 매우=very, 상당히=rather, 전적으로=completely

thaw

v. **1_녹이다** defrost

≠ freeze

2_긴장이 완화되다

n. **1_해동**

2_적대심의 감소

You have to **thaw** the meat before it can be cooked. 고기를 요리하기 전에 먼저 고기를 녹여야 된다.

meat n. 고기, 중심부분, 요점

cook v. 요리하다, (변명 등을) 꾸며대다 n. 요리사

After the summit two countries began to **thaw**. 정상회담 후에 두 나라의 긴장이 완화되기 시작했다.

summit n. 정상회담, 꼭대기=peak

utter(ly)

v. **말하다** say, express

adj.(adv.) 1__ **극적인**

2__ **완전한** complete, total

It's very hard to **utter** "sorry" especially to your love ones.
특히 사랑하는 사람들에게 "미안하다"고 말하는 것이 아주 힘들다.

especially adv. 특히, 두드러지게=markedly

Many doctors and nurses were **utterly** convinced of the
medicine's strength. 많은 의사와 간호사들이 약의 효능에 대해
완전히 확신했다.

convince v. 확신하다, 납득시키다

medicine n. 약=drug

strength n. 효력, 농도, 힘, 강점

outrage

n. **분노** fury, rage, anger

v. **격분하다** anger

He believed drinking heavily was the only way to express
his **outrage**. 그는 술을 많이 마시는 것만이 그의 분노를 표현하는
방법이라고 여겼다.

heavily adv. 많이, 무겁게, 격심하게=severely

express v. 표현하다 n. (기차, 버스의) 급행

I was surprised and **outraged** to see that she had gone ahead
with her plans without consulting us first. 나는 그녀가 먼저
우리와 상의를 하지 않고 그녀의 계획을 진행시켰다는 것에 놀랐고 또한
격분했다.

go ahead 진행하다   **plan** n. 계획

consult v. 상의하다, 상담하다, 조언하다

alternative

n. **1_둘 중의 하나**

2_대안 choice, option, substitute

adj. **(정통적인 것을) 대신하는**

Several **alternatives** to the governor's proposal were
suggested. 주지사의 제안에 대한 여러 대안들이 제시되었다.

proposal n. 제안, 계획=plan, 청혼

suggest v. 제안하다, 암시하다=infer, imply

We need to find several sources of **alternative** energy
before all the current resources are used up. 우리는 현재의
모든 자원이 고갈되기 전에 여러 대체 에너지원들을 찾아야 한다.

source n. 근원, 원인=origin, 출처, 자료

current adj. 현재의, 최신의 n. 흐름, 조류, 해류, 기류, 전류

resources n. 자원, 재산 **use up** ~을 다 써버리다

haphazard

adj. **계획성이 없는** random, accidental

≠ panned, controlled, deliberate

adv. **우연히**

At first glance, a forest appears to be a **haphazard** collection
of trees, shrubs, vines, and flowers. 처음 언뜻 보면, 숲은 나무와
관목, 덩굴과 꽃으로 이루어진 계획성 없는 수집물처럼 보인다.

glance n. 흘끗 보기 v. 언뜻 보다

appear v. 보이다, 나타나다

shrub n. 관목=bush

vine n. 덩굴

underscore

v. **1_ ~에 밑줄을 긋다**

2_ 강조하다 emphasize, stress, underline

≠ underplay, belittle

n. **영화의 백그라운드 뮤직**

Last week's fire **underscores** the necessity of observing safety rules. 지난주의 화재는 안전 규칙을 준수해야 하는 필요성을 강조한다.

fire n. 화재, 불, 정열, 열의

necessity n. 필요성, 필수품

observe v. 지키다=follow, obey; 보다, 관찰하다

safety n. 안전

rule n. 규칙, 풍습, 지배 v. 지배하다, 통치하다

Lesson 05 Review Test

01 Many doctors and nurses were **utterly** convinced of the medicine's strength.
 ⓐ hardly   ⓑ finally
 ⓒ completely   ⓓ rapidly

02 After **perusing** the menu for some time, Sam ordered his meal.
 ⓐ studying   ⓑ hiding
 ⓒ ignoring   ⓓ fingering

03 Several **alternatives to** the governor's proposal were suggested.
 ⓐ solutions to   ⓑ drawbacks to
 ⓒ substitutes for   ⓓ ramifications of

04 The artist **captured** the girl's personality in his photograph.
 ⓐ distorted   ⓑ caught
 ⓒ masked   ⓓ flattered

05 Last week's fire **underscores** the necessity of observing safety rules.
 ⓐ decreases   ⓑ emphasizes
 ⓒ indicates   ⓓ removes

06 **Relatively** young as an educational institution, the junior college had its beginnings in the United States during the 1890's.
 ⓐ Extremely   ⓑ Relevantly
 ⓒ Comparatively   ⓓ Really

07 Once its supply lines were broken, it took little time for the army to be **defeated**.

ⓐ scattered   ⓑ starved

ⓒ wounded   ⓓ conquered

08 The McCaslin family **evidences** the guilt of slaveholding more than Faulkner's other characters do.

ⓐ reveals   ⓑ impairs

ⓒ outdoes   ⓓ prefers

09 I was surprised and **outraged** to see that she had gone ahead with her plans without consulting us first.

ⓐ excited   ⓑ unhappy

ⓒ angered   ⓓ relieved

10 We found the professor's talk on nuclear reactors quite **coherent**.

ⓐ confusing   ⓑ logical

ⓒ irritating   ⓓ long-winded

11 You have to **thaw** the meat before it can be cooked.

ⓐ tenderize   ⓑ defrost

ⓒ season   ⓓ braise

12 J.P. Morgan **housed** his art and book collections in separate buildings.

ⓐ catalogued   ⓑ placed

ⓒ found   ⓓ purchased

13 At first glance, a forest appears to be a **haphazard** collection of trees, shrubs, vines, and flowers.

ⓐ random   ⓑ total

ⓒ graded   ⓓ natural

14 America's first successful **strike** took place in Philadelphia in 1786.

    ⓐ peace march   ⓑ prison riot

    ⓒ work stoppage   ⓓ land reform

15 There are numerous manuals available with instructions on how to **fix** a bicycle.

    ⓐ control   ⓑ ride

    ⓒ repair   ⓓ steer

01	c	ⓐ hardly=adv. 거의 ~않다 ⓑ finally=adv. 마침내 ⓓ rapidly=adv. 빨리
02	a	ⓑ hide=v. 숨기다 ⓒ ignore=v. 무시하다 ⓓ finger=v. 손가락을 대다, 지적하다
03	c	ⓐ solution=n. 해결(책) ⓑ drawback=n. 약점 ⓓ ramification=n. 가지, 지류
04	b	ⓐ distort=v. 뒤틀다 ⓒ mask=v. 감추다 ⓓ flatter=v. 아첨하다
05	b	ⓐ decrease=v. 줄다 ⓒ indicate=v. 나타내다 ⓓ remove=v. 없애다
06	c	ⓐ Extremely=adv. 극히 ⓑ Relevantly=adv. 관련있게, 적절히 ⓓ Really=adv. 정말로
07	d	ⓐ scatter=v. 흩뿌리다 ⓑ starved=adj. 굶주린 ⓒ wounded=adj. 부상한
08	a	ⓑ impair=v. 해치다, 손상시키다 ⓒ outdo=v. ~보다 낫다 ⓓ prefer=v. ~을 더 좋아하다
09	c	ⓐ excited=adj. 흥분한 ⓑ unhappy=adj. 불행한 ⓓ relieve=v. 안도케 하다
10	b	ⓐ confusing=adj. 혼란시키는 ⓒ irritating=adj. 짜증나는 ⓓ long-winded=adj. 지루한
11	b	ⓐ tenderize=v. 연하게 하다 ⓒ season=v. 맛을 내다 ⓓ braise=v. (고기를) 베이컨, 야채와 함께 기름으로 살짝 튀긴 후 오래 끓이다
12	b	ⓐ catalogue=v. 목록을 작성하다 ⓒ find=v. 발견하다 ⓓ purchase=v. 구입하다
13	a	ⓑ total=adj. 전체의 ⓒ grade=v. 등급을 매기다 ⓓ natural=adj. 자연의
14	c	ⓐ peace march=평화 행진 ⓑ prison riot=교도소 폭동 ⓓ land reform= 토지개혁
15	c	ⓐ control=v. 조절하다 ⓑ ride=v. 타다 ⓓ steer=v. 조정하다, ~의 키를 잡다

L e s s o n 06

mirror

wood(s)

convert

peak

seek

consistency

infect

lease

beneath

tend

grant

equivocal(ly)

provocation

bear[1]

proscribe

mirror

n. 거울

v. 1_비추다 reflect

2_반영하다 reflect, echo, represent

The art and literature **mirror** the philosophies and ideas of the changing era. 예술과 문학은 변해가는 시대의 철학과 생각을 반영한다.

literature   n. 문학

philosophy   n. 철학

era   n. 시대, 시기

wood(s)

n. 1_나무

2_목재 timber, lumber, log

3_숲 forest

We need to gather more **wood** for the winter season. 겨울철을 대비해서 더 많은 나무를 모아야 한다.

gather   v. ~을 모으다, ~을 알다, 결론을 내리다, 수확하다

season   n. 철, 계절, 활동기   v. 맛을 들이다, 익다, 단련되다

Woods are important in the conservation of water and wildlife. 숲은 물과 야생 생물의 보호면에서 중요하다.

conservation   n. 보호, 보존, 보호 관리 지구

convert

v. **1_전환하다** change, transform, alter

2_개조하다 modify

The function of ears in hearing is to **convert** the sound waves to nerve impulses. 청각에서의 귀의 역할은 음파를 신경 자극으로 전환시키는 것이다.

function n. 기능, 역할, 행사 v. 작용하다, 기능을 다하다=serve

sound wave 음파   **nerve** n. 신경, 용기, 뻔뻔스러움

impulse n. 자극, 충동

converted

adj. 전향한, 개종한, 개조한

convertible

adj. 바꿀 수 있는 adoptable

n. 지붕이 없는 차

peak

n. **1_끝** edge

2_산꼭대기 mountaintop

adj. **절정에 달하는** climax

v. **최고도까지 올리다** culminate, consummate

During the **peak** hours, you need to pay more for your train fare. 출퇴근 시간에는 기차요금을 더 많이 지불해야 한다.

fare n. 승차 요금, 음식 v. (일이) 되어 나가다

None of the highest **peaks** in Alaska is of volcanic origin. 알래스카의 제일 높은 산꼭대기 그 어느 것도 화산으로 생긴 것이 아니다.

volcanic adj. 화산성의, 화산의, 폭발성의, 격렬한

seek

v. **1_찾다** search for, look for

2_추구하다 strive for

3_요구하다 request

Columbus discovered America while **seeking** a trade route to India. 콜럼버스는 인디아로 가는 무역 항로를 찾던 중에 미대륙을 발견했다.

trade n. 무역, 거래, 교환=exchange, 직업 v. ~을 매매하다, ~을 교환하다

route n. 항로, 길, 수단, 방법 v. 물건을 보내다, 노선을 계획하다

You need to **seek** permission from your supervisor before taking a sick leave. 병가를 떠나기 전에 상사에게 허락을 받아야 한다.

permission n. 허가, 허용 **supervisor** n. 상사, 관리자, 지도 주임

sick leave 병가

consistency

n. **1_일관성** uniformity

≠contradiction

2_조화 harmony

≠ disagreement

consistent

adj. 일치하는 agreeing, suitable

The result was **consistent** with the doctor's diagnosis. 결과는 의사의 진단과 일치했다.

result n. 결과, 효과=effect v. 일어나다, ~으로 끝내다

diagnosis n. 진단, 진찰, 판단, 분석

consistently

adv. 시종 일관되게, 모순 없이

   regularly

Some birds **consistently** return to the same nesting area each spring. 어떤 새들은 봄마다 일관되게 똑같은 서식처로 돌아온다.

nest v. 둥지를 틀다 n. 보금자리, 둥지, (같은 보금자리에 사는 동물의) 떼, 은신처

infect

v. 1_~에 감염시키다

2_~을 물들게 하다 corrupt

3_~을 오염시키다 contaminate, pollute

You have to clean your wound carefully otherwise it would be **infected**. 상처 부위를 아주 조심스럽게 닦아내야 한다. 그렇지 않으면 감염될 것이다.

wound n. 상처, 부상, 고통, 모욕 v. ~에 상처를 입히다, ~을 손상하다

otherwise adv. 그렇지 않으면, 다르게, 다른 점에서는

infection
n. 전염, 감염

infectious
adj. 전염성인 contagious, transmittable

Infectious diseases may be spread by viruses and bacteria. 전염성 병들은 바이러스나 박테리아에 의해 퍼질 수 있다.

spread v. ~을 퍼뜨리다, ~을 펼치다, ~을 늘리다, 분포하다

lease

n. 1_임대 계약서 contract, agreement

2_계약 기간

v. 임대하다 rent

You need to read the **lease** carefully before you sign it. 서명하기 전에 임대 계약서를 주의 깊게 읽어야 한다.

carefully adv. 주의 깊게, 신중히, 꼼꼼히, 정성 들여

Rockefeller Center has **leased** part of its land from Columbia University. 록펠러 센터는 컬럼비아 대학교에 땅의 일부를 임대했다.

part n. 일부, 부분, 한 조각, 기관=organ, 부품, 역할, 배역=role

v. 쪼개다 sever, 떼어놓다 seperate

beneath

prep. **1_~의 아래에** below ≠ above

2_~보다 낮게

3_~보다 이하로

The yellow-necked caterpillar defends itself by squirting an acid secreted **beneath** its thorax. 노란목 쐐기벌레는 흉부 아래에서 분비되는 산을 뿜어내어 스스로를 보호한다.

defend   v. 방어하다, ~을 옹호하다, 항변하다

squirt   v. 분출시키다, 뿜어나오다   n. 분출

secrete   v. ~을 분비하다, ~을 숨기다=conceal

He is so arrogant that he believes almost everyone in the class is **beneath** him. 그는 너무 거만하기 때문에 반에 있는 모든 사람들이 자기 밑에 있다고 생각한다.

arrogant   adj. 거만한, 터무니없는

tend

v. **1_어떤 방향으로 기울다** incline, lean

2_~을 돌보다 look after, attend, care for

≠ neglect, ignore

The Aleutian goose mates for life, but only the female **tends** the eggs. 알류산 열도 거위는 평생 동안 짝을 짓지만 암컷들만 알을 돌본다.

mate   v. 짝짓다, 결혼하다   n. 짝, 배우자, 동료

tendency

n. 1_경향 inclination, propensity

   2_버릇 habit

He has a **tendency** to be late to social occasions. 그는 사교적인 행사에 늦는 경향이 있다.

occasion   n. 행사, 경우, 기회=opportunity

grant

v. **1_ 주다** give
≠ withhold

2_ 수여하다 award

3_ 승인하다 allow, permit
≠ deny, refuse, reject

n. **1_ 허가** permission

2_ 장학금 scholarship, fellowship

The colonists obtained a charter that **granted** them the right to settle in the New World. 미국 초기 개척자들은 신세계에 정착할 권리를 부여해주는 설립 인가서를 구했다.

colonist n. 미국 초기 개척자=pioneer, 식민지 주민, 해외 이주자

settle v. 정착하다, ~을 확정하다, ~을 정하다=decide, 계산하다

equivocal(ly)
adj.(adv.)

1_ 애매(모호)한 ambiguous, vague, uncertain, hazy
≠ definite, clear, certain, unequivocal

2_ 뜻이 모호한 oblique
≠ explicit

Parents who speak **equivocally** may cause their children to become confused. 애매하게 말을 하는 부모들은 아이들에게 혼란을 줄 수 있다.

confuse v. ~을 혼란시키다, ~을 불명확하게 하다, ~을 구별하지 못하다

provocation

n. **1_자극** instigation, incitement

2_도전 challenge

Wild pigs are fierce and courageous fighters and may charge with little or no **provocation**. 야생 돼지들은 사납고 용감한 싸움꾼이며 아무런 자극을 받지 않아도 돌격하기도 한다.

fierce adj. 사나운, 난폭한, 격심한 adv. 지독히

courageous adj. 용감한=brave

charge v. ~에 돌격하다, ~의 요금을 청구하다, 외상으로 사다 n. 경비, 책임

bear¹

v. **1_책임을 지다** take responsibility for

2_부담하다 assume, pay for

The cost of elections in the United States is **borne** by both the government and the private sector. 미국에서 선거비용은 정부와 사기관 둘 다 부담을 한다.

cost n. 비용, 값, 손실 v. 금액이 들다, 잃게 하다

election n. 선거, 투표

private adj. 공적이 아닌, 사적인, 개인에 속하는, 비밀의=secret n. 병졸

sector n. 영역, 활동 분야, 구역

proscribe

v. **1_금지하다** ban, bar, prohibit, forbid

≠ sanction, advocate, approve

2_추방하다 banish, exile

Some conductors **proscribe** sound amplification at their concerts. 어떤 지휘자들은 그들의 연주회에서 음의 확대를 금지한다.

conductor   n. 지휘자, 버스 · 전차 안내원, (열, 전기, 음 등의) 도체

amplification   n. 확대, 증보

concert   n. 연주회, 콘서트   adj. 음악회용의   v. ~을 협정하다, ~을 계획하다

Lesson 06 Review Test

01 Some birds **consistently** return to the same nesting area each spring.

ⓐ occasionally   ⓑ purposely

ⓒ regularly   ⓓ surprisingly

02 The cost of elections in the United States **is borne by** both the government and the private sector.

ⓐ known   ⓑ fought

ⓒ exposed   ⓓ assumed

03 Rockefeller Center has **leased** part of its land from Columbia University.

ⓐ inherited   ⓑ bought

ⓒ acquired   ⓓ rented

04 The colonists obtained a charter that **granted** them the right to settle in the New World.

ⓐ guaranteed   ⓑ taught

ⓒ sent   ⓓ gave

05 The Aleutian goose mates for life, but only the female **tends** the eggs.

ⓐ lays   ⓑ cares for

ⓒ looks at   ⓓ turns

06 Parents who speak **equivocally** may cause their children to become confused.

ⓐ ambiguously   ⓑ angrily

ⓒ abnormally   ⓓ aggressively

07 Wild pigs are fierce and courageous fighters and may charge with little or no **provocation**.

ⓐ protection   ⓑ incitement

ⓒ assistance   ⓓ warning

08 Some conductors **proscribe** sound amplification at their concerts.

ⓐ permit   ⓑ propose

ⓒ demand   ⓓ ban

09 The art and literature **mirror** the philosophies and ideas of the changing era.

ⓐ reflect   ⓑ distort

ⓒ restrict   ⓓ deny

10 **Woods** are important in the conservation of water and wildlife.

ⓐ swamps   ⓑ canyons

ⓒ creeks   ⓓ forests

11 The function of ears in hearing is to **convert** the sound waves to nerve impulses.

ⓐ represent   ⓑ change

ⓒ prove   ⓓ manufacture

12 None of the highest **peaks** in Alaska is of volcanic origin.

ⓐ ridges   ⓑ stones

ⓒ glaciers   ⓓ mountaintops

13 The yellow-necked caterpillar defends itself by squirting an acid secreted **beneath** its thorax.

ⓐ below   ⓑ through

ⓒ out of   ⓓ near

14 **Infectious** diseases may be spread by viruses and bacteria.

    ⓐ Childhood   ⓑ Deadly

    ⓒ Contagious   ⓓ Genetic

15 Columbus discovered America while **seeking** a trade route to India.

    ⓐ mapping   ⓑ hoping for

    ⓒ searching for   ⓓ finding

01	c	ⓐ occasionally=adv. 때때로 ⓑ purposely=adv. 고의로 ⓓ surprisingly=adv. 놀랍게도
02	d	ⓐ know=v. 알다 ⓑ fight=v. 싸우다 ⓒ expose=v. 드러내다
03	d	ⓐ inherit=v. 물려받다 ⓑ buy=v. 사다 ⓒ acquire=v. 얻다
04	d	ⓐ guarantee=v. 보증하다 ⓑ teach=v. 가르치다 ⓒ send=v. 보내다
05	b	ⓐ lay=v. 놓다, 두다 ⓒ look at=~을 보다 ⓓ turn=v. 돌리다
06	a	ⓑ angrily=adv. 노하여 ⓒ abnormally=adv. 비정상적으로 ⓓ aggressively=adv. 공격적으로
07	b	ⓐ protection=n. 보호 ⓒ assistance=n. 원조 ⓓ warning=n. 경고
08	d	ⓐ permit=v. 허락하다 ⓑ propose=v. 제의하다 ⓒ demand=v. 요구하다
09	a	ⓑ distort=v. 비틀다, 왜곡하다 ⓒ restrict=v. 제한하다 ⓓ deny=v. 부인하다
10	d	ⓐ swamp=n. 늪 ⓑ canyon=n. 깊은 협곡 ⓒ creek=n. 작은 내
11	b	ⓐ represent=v. 나타내다, 대표하다 ⓒ prove=v. 증명하다 ⓓ manufacture=v. 제조(제작)하다
12	d	ⓐ ridge=n. 산등성이 ⓑ stone=n. 돌 ⓒ glacier=n. 빙하
13	a	ⓑ through=prep. ~을 통하여 ⓒ out of=~로부터 ⓓ near=prep. ~의 가까이에
14	c	ⓐ Childhood=n. 어린 시절 ⓑ Deadly=adj. 치명적인 ⓓ Genetic=adj. 기원의, 유전의
15	c	ⓐ map=v. ~의 지도를 만들다 ⓑ hope for= ~을 바라다 ⓓ find=v. ~을 발견하다

Lesson 07

aviation

call for

unlike

source

inside

emerge

accrete

wildlife

jurisdiction

theme

inborn

breed

subsequent(ly)

vulnerable

major

aviation

n. 1_비행

2_항공기 산업

3_항공기 airplane, aircraft

aviator

n. 비행사 pilot, flier, airman, astronaut

Amelia Earhart, an American **aviator**, was the first woman to make a solo flight across the Atlantic Ocean. 미국 비행사 아멜리아 에어하트는 대서양을 단독으로 비행 횡단한 최초의 여성이었다.

flight n. 비행, 비행 거리, 도주, 탈출, 도피 v. 떼지어 날다

across prep. 횡단하여, ~을 건너서, ~의 맞은편에

call for

phr- v. 1_불러내다

2_요구하다, 필요하다 require, demand

3_~을 받아 마땅하다 deserve, be worthy of

Positions as teaching assistants **call for** good writing and speaking skills. 보조 교사라는 자리는 훌륭한 쓰기와 말하기 기술이 필요하다.

position n. 자리, 장소, 곳=place, 위치=site, 직위, 심적 태도=attitude

v. ~을 두다

assistant n. 보조원, 어시스턴트, 도움이 되는 것 adj. 도움이 되는, 보좌의

skill n. 기술, 수완, 솜씨

unlike

adj. **다른** different, unrelated, diverse, diversified, in contrast to
≠ like, similar, identical

prep. **~과 닮지 않은**

Unlike gases, liquids are difficult to compress because there is practically no free space between molecules. 기체와는 달리, 액체는 사실상 분자 사이에 여유 공간이 없기 때문에 압축하기가 어렵다.

gas   n. 기체, 가스, 휘발유   v. ~에 가스를 공급하다, 가스를 방출하다

liquid   n. 액체, 유동체=fluid   adj. 액체의, 투명한, 불안정한

compress   v. 압축하다, ~을 꽉 누르다, 요약하다

molecule   n. 분자, 미립자

source

n. **1_근원** origin, seed, root
2_정보원 informant
3_출처
4_자료 material

The **source** of the Mississippi River is located more than two thousand miles from its mouth. 미시시피 강의 근원은 강의 입구로부터 2천 마일 이상 떨어진 곳에 위치해 있다.

mouth   n. 입구, 입   v. 투덜투덜 말하다, 입에 넣다

It is the primary responsibility of journalist to protect the identity of his/her **source**. 저널리스트들은 자신들에게 정보를 제공한 사람들의 신원을 보호하는 것이 가장 기본적인 의무이다.

primary   adj. 기본적인=basic, 근원의=origin, 주요한=chief   n. 제1의 것, 예비 선거

responsibility   n. 의무=duty, 책임, 신뢰성=reliability

protect   v. ~을 보호하다=shield, ~을 지키다

inside

n. **내부** interior
≠exterior

adj. **내면의** internal
≠external

prep. **1_ ~안에**
2_ 지나기 전에

adv. **옥내에** ≠outside

Structurally, the **inside** of early Christian churches was simple. 구조적으로, 초기 기독교 교회의 내면은 간결했다.

structural(ly) adj.(adv.) 구조(상)의, 구조물의, 구조의, 정치(경제) 조직의

early adj. 초기의, 오랜 옛날의, 조금 이른, 머지않은 adv. 일찍이

simple adj. 간결한=plain, 단순한, 수수한, 검소한, 단일의, 하찮은=insignificant

emerge

v. **1_ 나오다** arise, appear, come forth ≠withdraw
2_ 알려지다 come into prominence
3_ 피하다 escape

The train **emerged** from the dust of clouds. 기차가 먼지 더미 속에서 나왔다.

The Abstract Expressionist movement **emerged** in New York City in the 1940's. 추상적 표현파 운동은 1940년대 뉴욕 시에서 알려지기 시작했다.

movement n. 운동, 이동, 동작, 활동, 동향, 발전, 진행

The politician **emerged** from the scandal with his reputation intact. 그 정치인은 자신의 명성이 손상되지 않은 채 스캔들을 피할 수 있었다.

reputation n. 명성, 평판, 소문, 호평

intact adj. 변하지 않은, 온전한, 손상되지 않은

accrete
v. **일체가 되다**

accretion

n. 1_융합

accumulation ≠ separation

2_증대

addition, augmentation

≠diminution, shrinkage,

reduction, decrease

It is now generally assumed that the planets were formed by the **accretion** of gas and dust in a cosmic cloud.
행성은 우주 구름 속에서 가스와 먼지의 융합으로 형성된다는 것이 요즘의 일반적인 생각이다.

assume v. 생각하다, 가정하다, 떠맡다, 인수하다, 취하다

planet n. 행성, 혹성

form v. 형성하다, ~을 이루다, 생각해내다, 만들다   n. 모양, 몸매, 형식, 종류

cosmic adj. 우주의, 무한한, 조화되어 있는

wildlife
n. **야생 동물** animal, game, creatures

wildlife preserves

야생 동물 보호 지구

The conservation research project will concentrate on the **wildlife** habitats in the forest. 보호 연구 계획은 숲의 야생 동물 서식지에 집중될 것이다.

research n. 연구, 조사 탐구, 탐색   v. ~을 조사(연구)하다

project n. 계획, 기획, 연구 과제   v. 예상하다, 튀어나오다=protrude

concentrate v. 집중시키다, 모으다, 응축하다, 전념하다   n. 응축물, 농축 음료

habitat n. 서식지, 거주 장소=dwelling

jurisdiction

n. **1_재판권** authority

2_권력 power, command

3_관할구역 domain, district

Justices of the peace have **jurisdiction** over the trials of some civil suits and of criminal cases involving minor offenses. 치안 판사는 일부 민사 소송과 경범죄와 관련된 범죄 사건 재판에 대한 재판권을 갖는다.

justice n. 판사, 정의, 공정, 처벌, 정당성, 사법

trial n. 재판, 시험, 실험=experiment, 시련, 고난, 고통 adj. 시험적으로 행해지는

civil adj. 민간의, 시민의, 국가의, 문명화된=civilized, 예의 바른

suit n. 소송, 재판, 양복 v. 만족할 만하다, ~을 맞추다, 적합하다, 어울리다

criminal adj. 형사상의 ≠civil, 범죄의, 죄가 되는, 부당한

case n. 사건, 재판=trial, suit, 경우=instance, 사정, 문제=problem, 그릇, 덮개, 상자

offense n. 범죄, 위반, 모욕, 공격=attack, assault

theme

n. **1_주제** subject, topic

2_화제 focus, point

3_주제곡

The medieval legend of Dr. Faust has been a recurrent **theme** in Western literature. 파우스트 박사에 대한 중세의 전설은 서양 문학에서 주기적으로 반복되는 주제다.

medieval adj. 중세의, 중세적인

legend n. 전설, 기호의 설명표

recurrent adj. 주기적으로 일어나는, 재발하는, 빈발하는

western adj. 서양의, 미국 서부의, 서향의 n. 서부극

inborn

adj. **1_타고난** inbred, inherent, natural

2_선천성의 congenital, innate, inherited

≠acquired, nurtured, extrinsic

Psychologists still wonder if some personality traits are **inborn**. 심리학자들은 일부 성격의 특성은 선천적으로 타고난다는 것에 대해 여전히 기이하게 여기고 있다.

psychologist   n. 심리학자

still   adv. 여전히, 아직도, 그래도   adj. 정지한=motionless, 조용한, 평온한

wonder   v. 기이하게 여기다, 감탄하다=mavel, 의심하다, 놀라다   n. 불가사의한 것

trait   n. 특성, 특징, 습성

breed

v. **1_낳다** give birth, reproduce

2_생산하다 generate

3_기르다 raise, rear, nurture

n. **1_종류** species

2_혈통 race

Hard work **breeds** success. 열심히 일하면 성공할 수 있다.

The Chukchi of the Siberian Arctic **bred** reindeer as a source of food. 시베리아 북극의 추크치 부족은 식용으로 순록을 길렀다.

This dog is very expensive because it's a pure **breed**. 이 개는 순종 혈통이기 때문에 아주 비싸다.

pure   adj. 순종의, 순수한≠mixed, 깨끗한=clear, 전적인=absolute

subsequent(ly)

adj.(adv.)

1_뒤의, 차후의 later, following, succeeding

≠preceding, previous, antecedent, prior

2_다음의 next

3_계속해서 일어나는 sequent, consequent

A **subsequent** action has to be taken in order to completely solve the problem. 그 다음 행동은 문제를 완전히 해결하기 위해 행해져야 한다.

Vice-President Lyndon Johnson became President of the United States following the death of John F. Kennedy and was **subsequently** elected to a full term in 1964. 부통령 린든 존슨은 존 에프 케네디 대통령의 사망으로 잔여 기간 동안 미국 대통령직을 이었으며 1964년에 차기 대통령으로 당선되었다.

elect v. 당선되다, 선거하다, 선임하다, 결정하다, 선택하다 adj. 선출된, 당선된

vulnerable

adj. **1_공격받기 쉬운** unprotected

2_노출되어 있는 susceptible, subject

3_약한 weak

≠strong, invincible, unconquerable

Young people are **vulnerable** to the influence of radio and television. 젊은이들은 라디오나 텔레비전의 영향을 받기 쉽다.

influence v. ~에 영향을 주다(미치다), 감화를 주다 n. 영향, 작용

major

adj. **1_ 중요한** important, principal, significant, main

2_ 매우 큰 sizable

n. **전공** specialty

v. **전공하다** specialize

Glassmaking was the first **major** industry in the United States. 유리 제조업은 미국에서 최초의 대규모 산업이었다.

industry n. 산업, 사업, 근면, 노력, 분야

Car manufacturing is considered to be the **major** industry in the United States. 자동차 제조업은 미국에서 주요한 산업으로 여겨진다.

manufacturing n. 제조 공업 adj. 제조(업)의, 제조업에 종사하는

Lesson 07 Review Test

01 Structurally, the **inside** of early Christian churches was simple.

    ⓐ layout   ⓑ design

    ⓒ interior   ⓓ content

02 It is now generally assumed that the planets were formed by the **accretion** of gas and dust in a cosmic cloud.

    ⓐ separation   ⓑ reaction

    ⓒ accumulation   ⓓ motion

03 Young people are **vulnerable to** the influence of radio and television.

    ⓐ persuaded by   ⓑ appeased by

    ⓒ programmed to   ⓓ susceptible to

04 Positions as teaching assistants **call for** good writing and speaking skills.

    ⓐ require   ⓑ produce

    ⓒ question   ⓓ sharpen

05 Glassmaking was the first **major** industry in the United States.

    ⓐ profitable   ⓑ productive

    ⓒ sizable   ⓓ specialized

06 The conservation research project will concentrate on the **wildlife** habitats in the forest.

    ⓐ tropical   ⓑ animal

    ⓒ regional   ⓓ biological

07 Justices of the peace have **jurisdiction** over the trials of some civil suits and of criminal cases involving minor offenses.

    ⓐ supremacy   ⓑ authority

    ⓒ guidance   ⓓ obedience

08 The medieval legend of Dr. Faust has been a recurrent **theme** in Western literature.

    ⓐ issue   ⓑ tale

    ⓒ discussion   ⓓ subject

09 Vice-President Lyndon Johnson became President of the United States following the death of John F. Kennedy and was **subsequently** elected to a full term in 1964.

    ⓐ duly   ⓑ finally

    ⓒ later   ⓓ therefore

10 Amelia Earhart, an American **aviator**, was the first woman to make a solo flight across the Atlantic Ocean.

    ⓐ stewardess   ⓑ adventuress

    ⓒ conductor   ⓓ pilot

11 **Unlike** gases, liquids are difficult to compress because there is practically no free space between molecules.

    ⓐ In contrast to   ⓑ Similar to

    ⓒ More than   ⓓ Just as

12 The **source** of the Mississippi River is located more than two thousand miles from its mouth.

    ⓐ seaport   ⓑ origin

    ⓒ purest water   ⓓ longest tributary

13 The Abstract Expressionist movement **emerged** in New York City in the 1940's.

ⓐ was severely criticized   ⓑ came into prominence

ⓒ left no impression   ⓓ was labeled

14 Psychologists still wonder if some personality traits are **inborn**.

ⓐ interminable   ⓑ inadvertent

ⓒ innate   ⓓ inevitable

15 The Chukchi of the Siberian Arctic **bred** reindeer as a source of food.

ⓐ chased   ⓑ raised

ⓒ trapped   ⓓ tamed

01	c	ⓐlayout=n. 설계 ⓑdesign=n. 디자인 ⓓcontent=n. 내용물
02	c	ⓐseparation=n. 분리 ⓑreaction=n. 반응 ⓓmotion=n. 운동, 동작
03	d	ⓐpersuade=v. 설득하다 ⓑappease=v. 달래다 ⓒprogram=v. 계획하다
04	a	ⓑproduce=v. 생산하다 ⓒquestion=v. 질문하다 ⓓsharpen=v. 뾰족하게 하다
05	c	ⓐprofitable=adj. 유리(유익)한 ⓑproductive=adj. 생산적인 ⓓspecialized=adj. 전문의
06	b	ⓐtropical=adj. 전형적인 ⓒregional=adj. 지역의 ⓓbiological=adj. 생물학(상)의
07	b	ⓐsupremacy=n. 최고, 주권 ⓒguidance=n. 안내 ⓓobedience=n. 복종
08	d	ⓐissue=n. 논(쟁)점 ⓑtale=n. 이야기 ⓒdiscussion=n. 토론
09	c	ⓐduly=adv. 정식으로 ⓑfinally=adv. 마침내 ⓓtherefore=adv. 그러므로
10	d	ⓐstewardess=n. 스튜어디스 ⓑadventuress=n. 여성모험가 ⓒconductor=n. 안내자, 지휘자
11	a	ⓑSimilar to=~와 유사한 ⓒMore than=~ 이상의 ⓓJust as=꼭 ~와 마찬가지로
12	b	ⓐseaport=n. 항구 ⓒpurest water=가장 깨끗한 물 ⓓtributary=n. 지류
13	b	ⓐbe severely criticized=심하게 비난받다 ⓒleave no impression=아무런 효과도 남기지 않다 ⓓbe labeled= ~라고 불리다
14	c	ⓐinterminable=adj. 끝없는 ⓑinadvertent=adj. 부주의한 ⓓinevitable=adj. 피할 수 없는
15	b	ⓐchase=v. 뒤쫓다 ⓒtrap=v. 덫을 놓다, 속이다 ⓓtame=v. 길들이다

L e s s o n 08

quantity

region

sharp

possess

tough

make up

precise

wild

reasonable(ly)

mammoth

allocate

fowl

gregarious

striking(ly)

tool

quantity

n. **양, 분량, 수량** amount

Home economists recommend buying basic food items in large **quantities**. 가정 경제학자들은 기본적인 식품은 대량으로 구매하기를 권한다.

home   adj. 가정의, 자기 집의, 본국의   n. 가정, 집, 수용시설, 서식지

economist   n. 경제학자

recommend   v. 권하다, 추천하다, 충고하다, 마음에 들게 하다

basic   adj. 기초의, 근본의, 알칼리성의, 초보의   n. 기초, 근본

Some people believe that quality is more important than cost or **quantity** of a product. 어떤 사람들은 상품의 가격이나 양보다는 질이 더 중요하다고 여긴다.

product   n. 생산품, 성과, 결과

quality   n. 품질, 특성, 속성, 성질   adj. 양질의, 사회적 지위가 높은

region

n. **지역** area, place, district, province

The polar **regions** are generally covered with ice and snow. 극지방은 일반적으로 얼음이나 눈으로 덮여 있다.

polar   adj. 극의, 정반대인, 중심적인

cover   v. 덮개를 하다, 씌우다, 포함하다, 감당하다   n. 덮개, 보호=protection

regional

adj. 지역적인 sectional, parochial, provincial

In order to enter the national tournament, the team has to win the **regional** tournament first. 내셔널 토너먼트에 들기 위해, 그 팀은 먼저 지역 토너먼트에서 이겨야 한다.

enter   v. 들어가다, 떠오르다, 가담하다, 참가하다

national   adj. 전국(민)적인, 국가의, 국립의, 국내적인   n. 국민, 교포, 전국대회

sharp	adj.	**1_날카로운** pointed, edged≠blunt, dull
		2_예리한 perceptive, keen≠slow, absentminded, quick
		3_격심한 harsh, stinging≠bland
		4_명확한, 뚜렷한 clear, distinct≠vague, ambiguous

He felt a **sharp** pain in his chest which turned out to be a mild heart attack. 그는 가슴 부위에 예리한 통증을 느꼈는데 그것은 경미한 심장마비로 밝혀졌다.

turn out ~으로 판명되다, 결과로 되다, 참석하다

mild adj. 경미한, 유순한, 상냥한, 온화한, 자극성이 적은, 가벼운

heart attack 심장마비

Cameras take the **sharpest** pictures when they are held still. 카메라는 정지 상태에 있을 때 가장 뚜렷한 사진을 찍을 수 있다.

possess	v.	**1_소유하다** have, own
		2_(자격/능력을) 지니다 hold
		3_~의 마음을 사로잡다 obsess

Snakes do not **possess** legs; many lizards do. 뱀은 다리를 가지고 있지 않으며, 많은 도마뱀들은 가지고 있다.

An ideal leader should **possess** the qualities of honesty, integrity, and decisiveness. 이상적인 지도자는 정직, 청렴 그리고 결단력과 같은 자질을 가지고 있어야 한다.

honesty n. 정직, 고결, 성실함   **integrity** n. 청렴, 정직, 고결, 흠없는 상태

decisiveness n. 결단성, 단호함

I don't know what **possessed** me to agree to work Sundays. 일요일마다 일을 하도록 내 마음을 사로잡는 것이 무엇인지 모르겠다.

tough

adj. **1_강(인)한, 단단한** strong, hard

≠brittle, fragile

2_튼튼한 resilient

≠weak, frail

3_어려운, 고달픈 difficult, arduous

≠easy, fortunate

Oaks are strong, long-lived trees with **tough** wood. 참나무는 강하며, 단단한 목질을 가진 장수하는 나무다.

long-lived adj. 장수의, 오래의

It will be really **tough** for him to accept the news. 그로서는 그 소식을 받아들이기가 아주 어려울 것이다.

really adv. 아주, 실제로는, 사실상

accept v. 받아들이다, 진실하다고 믿다, 수용하다

make up

phr-v. **1_성립되다, 구성되다** constitute, compose

2_고안하다 cook up, fabricate

n. **1_구성**

2_보강

3_재시험

＊명사로 쓸 때는 makeup으로 붙여서 쓴다.

Texas **makes up** one-twelfth of the continental land mass of the United States. 텍사스는 미국 대륙 전체의 12분의 1을 구성하고 있다.

continental adj. 북미 대륙의, 대륙(성)의

mass n. 전체, 덩어리, 집단, 넓이, 부피

There will be a **makeup** class next week. 다음주에 보충 수업이 있을 것이다.

precise

adj. **1_ 정밀한, 정확한** exact, accurate

≠vague, hazy, ambiguous

2_ 바로 그 very

3_ 명확한

4_ 엄격한 rigid

Annie Oakley became famous as one of the world's most
precise sharpshooters. 애니 오크레이는 세계에서 가장 정확한
명사수 중의 한 명으로 유명해졌다.

sharpshooter n. 명사수, 저격자

wild

adj. **1_ 야생의** untamed, uncultivated

≠tamed, cultivated

2_ 거친, 사나운 savage, barbarous, violent

≠calm

3_ 야단법석 떠는 ≠sane, sober

North America has the world's best climate for **wild** grapes.
북미는 세계에서 야생 포도에 가장 좋은 기후 조건을 갖추고 있다.

climate n. 기후, 지방, 지역, 사조, 경향

He gets really **wild** when he is mad. 그는 화가 나면 정말
거칠어진다.

Last night's party was really **wild**. 어젯밤 파티는 정말
야단법석이었다.

# reasonable(ly)
adj.(adv.)

1_분별 있는 rational ≠ irrational, illogical

2_정당한 justifiable

3_적당한 moderate ≠ extreme, excessive

4_비싸지 않은 economical, cheap ≠ expensive

His excuse for coming to the class late was **reasonable**.
수업에 지각한 것에 대한 그의 변명은 적당했다.

excuse   n. 변명, 핑계, 나쁜 본보기   v. 용서하다, 변명하다

Many businesses have turned to automation in order to produce goods more **reasonably**. 많은 비즈니스가 상품을 보다 저렴하게 생산하기 위해 자동화로 바뀌고 있다.

goods   n. 재산, 상품, 직물

mammoth
adj. **거대한** gigantic, vast, huge, enormous, immense
≠ tiny, minute, minuscule, microscopic

The construction of **mammoth** shopping malls has contributed to the decline of small stores in neighboring towns. 거대한 쇼핑몰의 건설은 주변 도시에 있는 작은 상점들의 몰락을 가져왔다.

construction   n. 건설, 건축(물), 해석, 구조

mall   n. 쇼핑 센터, 나무 그늘진 (산책)길, (고속 도로의) 중앙 분리대

contribute   v. 기부하다, 기고하다, 공헌하다

decline   n. 몰락, 약화, 쇠퇴, 종말   v. 거절하다, 기울이다

neighboring   adj. 주변의, 근처에 사는, 인접한

allocate

v. **1_ 할당하다, 배분하다** set aside, assign, distribute, allot

2_ 배치하다 designate

During the Second World War, all important resources in the United States were **allocated** by the federal government.
제2차 세계대전 중에 미국에서 중요한 모든 것은 연방정부에 의해 배분되었다.

federal adj. 연방의, 연합의, 동맹의   n. 연방주의자

fowl

n. **1_ 닭, 가금** poultry

2_ 닭고기, 새고기

3_ 조류

Farmers in eastern Maryland and on Long Island specialize in raising **fowl**. 동부 메릴랜드와 롱아일랜드의 농부들은 닭을 전문적으로 키운다.

specialize v. 전문적으로 연구(취급)하다, 특수화하다, 전문화하다

raise v. 사육하다, 들어올리다, 세우다, 재배하다

gregarious

adj. **사교적인** friendly, outgoing, sociable

≠solitary, reclusive, private, reserved

Reindeer are highly **gregarious** and travel in herds. 순록은 매우 사교적이며 무리를 지어 이동한다.

reindeer   n. 순록

highly   adv. 매우, 대단히, 높이, 고귀하게

travel   v. 이동하다, 가다, 여행하다   n. 여행, 이동

herd   n. 떼, 민중, 대량, 목동   v. 떼지어 가다, 모으다

striking(ly)

adj.(adv.) **1_현저한, 두드러진** notable, outstanding, remarkable

2_인상적인 conspicuous, impressive

≠unimpressive, indifferent, commonplace

The wind chill factor, the combination of low temperature and wind speed, **strikingly** increases the degree of cold felt by a person who is outdoors. 낮은 온도와 바람 세기의 결합물인 풍속 냉각 지수는 실외에 있는 사람이 느끼는 추위 정도를 현저하게 증가시킨다.

wind chill factor   풍속 냉각 지수

combination   n. 결합, 합동, 연합, 조합

degree   n. 한 단계, 신분, 계급, 정도, (각도 단위의) 도

tool

n. **연장, 기구** equipment, instrument, apparatus, utensil, device, implement

The operation of simple **tools** is readily understood by children. 간단한 기구의 작동은 아이들도 쉽게 이해할 수 있다.

operation n. 작동, 기능, 시행, 작업 과정, 작전, 수술

readily adv. 쉽사리, 즉시, 당장

understand(과거형 understood) v. 이해하다, 알다, 해석하다

Lesson 08 Review Test

01 Reindeer are highly **gregarious** and travel in herds.

ⓐ insecure   ⓑ sociable

ⓒ intelligent   ⓓ sought after

02 North America has the world's best climate for **wild** grapes.

ⓐ inedible   ⓑ sweet

ⓒ uncultivated   ⓓ seedless

03 Many businesses have turned to automation in order to produce goods more **reasonably**.

ⓐ perfectly   ⓑ speedily

ⓒ economically   ⓓ simply

04 The wind chill factor, the combination of low temperature and wind speed, **strikingly** increases the degree of cold felt by a person who is outdoors.

ⓐ effectively   ⓑ remarkably

ⓒ certainly   ⓓ unquestionably

05 Home economists recommend buying basic food items in large **quantities**.

ⓐ stores   ⓑ amounts

ⓒ bags   ⓓ boxes

06 The polar **regions** are generally covered with ice and snow.

ⓐ areas   ⓑ rocks

ⓒ mountains   ⓓ famous

07 The construction of **mammoth** shopping malls has contributed to the decline of small stores in neighboring towns.

     ⓐ modern   ⓑ numerous

     ⓒ gigantic   ⓓ separate

08 During the Second World War, all important resources in the United States were **allocated** by the federal government.

     ⓐ nationalized   ⓑ commandeered

     ⓒ taxed   ⓓ distributed

09 Cameras take the **sharpest** pictures when they are held still.

     ⓐ clearest   ⓑ fastest

     ⓒ most interesting   ⓓ most beautiful

10 Snakes do not **possess** legs; many lizards do.

     ⓐ retain   ⓑ develop

     ⓒ utilize   ⓓ have

11 Oaks are strong, long-lived trees with **tough** wood.

     ⓐ hard   ⓑ rough

     ⓒ dark   ⓓ heavy

12 The operation of simple **tools** is readily understood by children.

     ⓐ playthings   ⓑ implements

     ⓒ machinery   ⓓ equations

13 Texas **makes up** one-twelfth of the continental land mass of the United States.

     ⓐ generates   ⓑ demands

     ⓒ constitutes   ⓓ governs

14 Annie Oakley became famous as one of the world's most **precise** sharpshooters.

    ⓐ formidable   ⓑ logical

    ⓒ independent   ⓓ accurate

15 Farmers in eastern Maryland and on Long Island specialize in raising **fowl**.

    ⓐ beans   ⓑ hay

    ⓒ poultry   ⓓ shellfish

01	b	ⓐinsecure=adj. 불안정한 ⓒintelligent=adj. 지적인 ⓓseek after= ~을 추구하다
02	c	ⓐinedible=adj. 먹을 수 없는 ⓑsweet=adj. 단 ⓓseedless=adj. 씨가 없는
03	c	ⓐperfectly=adv. 완전히 ⓑspeedily=adv. 빨리 ⓓsimply=adv. 간단히
04	b	ⓐeffectively=adv. 효과적으로 ⓒcertainly=adv. 확실히 ⓓunquestionably=adv. 분명히
05	b	ⓐstore=n. 가게 ⓒbag=n. 가방 ⓓbox=n. 박스
06	a	ⓑrock=n. 바위 ⓒmountain=n. 산 ⓓfamous=adj. 유명한
07	c	ⓐmodern=adj. 현대적인 ⓑnumerous=adj. 다수의 ⓓseparate=adj. 따로따로의
08	d	ⓐnationalize=v. 국민으로(독립국가로) 만들다 ⓑcommandeer=v. 징집하다 ⓒtax=v. 과세하다
09	a	ⓑfastest=adj. 가장 빠른 ⓒmost interesting=adj. 가장 재미있는 ⓓmost beautiful=adj. 가장 아름다운
10	d	ⓐretain=v. 계속 유지하다 ⓑdevelop=v. 발전시키다 ⓒutilize=이용하다
11	a	ⓑrough=adj. 거칠거칠한 ⓒdark=adj. 어두운 ⓓheavy=adj. 무거운
12	b	ⓐplaything=n. 장난감 ⓒmachinery=n. 기계류 ⓓequation=n. 균등화
13	c	ⓐgenerate=v. 발생시키다 ⓑdemand=v. 요구하다 ⓓgovern=v. 통치하다
14	d	ⓐformidable=adj. 무서운 ⓑlogical=adj. 논리적인 ⓒindependent=adj. 독립심이 강한
15	c	ⓐbean=n. 콩 ⓑhay=n. 건초 ⓓshellfish=n. 조개

Lesson 09

emotion

revolutionize

illustrate

growth

compact

affection

sour

weave

valued

aroma

deal

unrestrained

sluggish

resolute

fusion

emotion

n. **감정** passion, feeling, sentiment

Failure to express **emotions** may actually cause illness.
감정을 표현하지 못하면 실제로 병이 날 수도 있다.

actually adv. 실제로≠probably, 현실로, 사실로

illness n. 병=disease, 불쾌

emotional

adj. 1_감정적인 sensitive

2_감동하기 쉬운

thrilling, dramatic

≠ unmoved, apathetic

The candidate was known to give **emotional** speech during the campaign. 그 후보자는 캠페인 동안 감동적인 연설을 한 것으로 알려졌다.

speech n. 연설=address, 말하는 능력, 말투

campaign n. 캠페인, 전투 v. ~의 운동을 일으키다, 선거 운동을 하다, 종군하다

revolutionize

v. **혁명을 일으키다** completely changed, transform, refashion
≠conserve, preserve, maintain

The invention of the computer **revolutionized** business procedures. 컴퓨터의 발명은 상거래 과정에 혁명을 불러일으켰다.

invention n. 발명, 창출, 고안, 발명품, 꾸며낸 이야기

business adj. 상업의 n. 상업, 장사, 사무, 영업, 거래, 일, 사건=affair

procedure n. 절차, 순서, 방법, 조치=measure

illustrate

v. **1_보여주다** depict, portray, represent

2_설명하다 explain, demonstrate

In economics, graphs are used to **illustrate** functions.

경제학에서 도표는 작용을 보여주기 위해 사용된다.

graph   n. 그래프, 도표   v. ~을 그래프로 나타내다

use   v. ~을 이용하다, 사용하다   n. 사용량, 효과

illustration

n. 예해, 실례, 예증 picture,

depiction, example

illustrative

adj. 설명의

growth

n. **1_성장, 발육** development

2_발전, 발달 development, evolution, advance

≠deterioration, degeneration, regression,

decay

3_증가, 확장

4_산출

In structure and **growth**, rye resembles wheat.

구조와 성장면에서 호밀은 밀과 유사하다.

rye   n. 호밀   adj. 호밀가루로 만든

resemble   v. ~을 닮다, ~과 비슷하다

wheat   n. 밀

compact

adj. 1_**빽빽하게 찬, 밀집한** dense, succinct

≠foamy, discursive

2_꽉 짜인

v. **압축하다** condense, compress, pack

≠expand, disperse, inflate

n. **계약, 맹약** contract, covenant, agreement

In mountainous regions, much of the snow that falls is **compacted** into ice. 산악 지역에서는 내리는 눈의 많은 양이 압축되어 얼음이 된다.

mountainous adj. 산이 많은, 산악성의, 거대한

affection

n. **애정, 호의** tenderness, fondness, attachment

≠coldness, antipathy, detachment

People usually think of their hometown with **affection**. 사람들은 일반적으로 자신들의 고향에 대해서는 애정을 가지고 생각한다.

hometown n. 고향

affectionate(ly)

adj.(adv.) 애정 깊은 loving, tender, warm, doting ≠distant, uncaring, apathetic

The stuffed toy bears belonging to Theodore Roosevelt's children were **affectionately** called Teddy bears. 시어도어 루스벨트의 자녀들이 가지고 놀던 곰인형은 사랑스럽게 '테디 베어'라고 불렸다.

stuff v. 속을 채우다, 막히게 하다, 배불리 먹다 n. 물질, 재료, 가치가 없는 것

belong v. 속하다, 소속하다, 일원이다, 자격이 있다

sour

adj. **1_시큼한, 신** lemony, vinegary

$\neq$ sweet

2_불쾌한 $\neq$ cheerful, affable, pleasant

3_썩은 spoiled, bad $\neq$ fresh

v. **썩히다, 못쓰게 하다** spoil

Generally, a material with a **sour** taste, such as vinegar or lemon juice, contains an acid. 일반적으로 식초나 레몬 주스와 같이 신맛을 가진 물질은 산을 포함하고 있다.

material n. 원료, 재료, 구성 요소, 자료, 소재, 직물

vinegar n. 식초 v. ~에 식초를 섞다

contain v. ~을 포함하다, 억제하다

acid n. 산, 산성 물질 adj. 매서운

weave

v. **1_짜다, 뜨다, 엮다** create, produce, make

2_좌우로 흔들리다

weaver

n. 짜는 사람, 직공

weaving

n. 섬유업 cloth making

Weaving is an art among the Navaho of Arizona and New Mexico. 섬유업은 뉴멕시코와 애리조나의 나바호에서는 일종의 예술이다.

among prep. ~중에(서), ~에 섞여서, ~사이에서 각자에게

valued

adj. **1_귀중한, 소중한** precious, invaluable

2_값진 worthy

≠cheap, worthless

3_평가된 estimated

Good health is a family's most **valued** possession. 건강은 가정의 가장 값진 재산이다.

family n. 가정, 가족, 일가, 가문, 집단 adj. 가족의

health n. 건강, 활력, 보건, 위생

possession n. 재산, 소유, 소지=ownership, 소유권, 자제

aroma

n. **향기** fragrance, scent, smell, odor, incense

He enjoys the **aroma** of freshly brewed coffee. 그는 방금 끓인 커피의 향을 즐긴다.

freshly adv. 새롭게, 최근에, 생생하게

brew 끓이다, 양조하다, (음모 등을) 꾸미다

aromatic

adj. 향기로운 fragrant, savory

≠foul

Mint is an herb that is well known for the **aromatic** oil distilled from all parts of the plant. 민트는 모든 부분에서 뽑아낸 향기로운 기름으로 유명한 풀의 일종이다.

herb n. 약초, 풀

distill v. ~을 증류하다, ~을 거르다, ~의 정수를 뽑다

plant n. 식물, 농작물=crop, 공장=factory, 시설 v. 심다, 든든하게 세우다

deal

v. **1_분배하다** distribute, disseminate

2_다루다 cope, treat, handle, manage

n. **1_거래** transaction

2_타협, 협상 contract, pact

3_다량

The United States is trying to **deal** with the serious problems brought on by the energy crisis. 미국은 에너지 위기로 야기된 심각한 문제들을 다루기 위해 노력하고 있다.

serious adj. 심각한, 진지한, 엄숙한=solemn, 중요한=important

problem n. 문제, 귀찮은 사람, 곤란한 일 adj. 다루기 어려운=unruly

bring on 나게 하다, 가져오다, 일으키다, ~을 향상시키다

energy n. 에너지, 활력, 기력, 능력

unrestrained

adj. **억제되지 않은, 자유로운** unconstrained, unchecked, uncontrolled, unconfined

≠inhibited, controlled, repressed, disciplined, checked

Scientists speculate that **unrestrained** population growth and dwindling resources may force humans to look to the sea for food. 과학자들은 억제되지 않은 인구 증가와 자원의 감소로 인류가 식량을 구하기 위해 바다로 시선을 돌릴 수밖에 없을 것이라고 추측하고 있다.

speculate v. 추측하다, 심사숙고하다, 투기하다

dwindle v. 줄어들다=decrease, 쇠퇴하다, (가치 등이) 없어지다

sea n. 바다, 대양=ocean, (바다처럼) 넓은 범위, 다량(의~) adj. 바다의

sluggish

adj. **1_게으른** lazy, indolent

≠industrious

2_ 동작이 느린 lethargic

≠active, brisk, energetic

3_ 부진한

The lizard called the Gila monster is ordinarily **sluggish** and clumsy. '힐러 몬스터'라고 불리는 도마뱀은 통상적으로 동작이 느리고 서툴다.

monster　n. 괴물, 정상이 아닌 생물, 잔인한 사람, 악한, 초인적인 사람

　　　　　adj. 괴물 같은

ordinarily　adv. 일반적으로=usually, 보통 정도로

clumsy　adj. (동작, 말들이) 서투른, 손재주가 없는≠skillful

---

resolute

adj. **1_ 굳게 결심한** ≠aimless

2_ 완고한, 단호한 determined, firm, decisive, unyielding

≠weak, unsteady, faltering

As governor of Massachusetts, Calvin Coolidge became a national figure because of his **resolute** opposition to the 1919 police strike. 매사추세츠 주지사로서, 캘빈 쿨리지는 1919년의 경찰 파업에 대해 완고한 반대 입장을 취함으로써 전국적으로 알려진 인물이 되었다.

figure　n. 인물, 도형, 그림, 숫자, 가격, 체격=body　v. 계산하다, 생각하다=regard

opposition　n. 반대(자), 저항, 적의, 야당, 대립

strike　n. 파업, 때리기, 공격　v. ~을 치다, 찌르다, 파업하다, 마음에 떠오르다

fusion

n. **1_퓨전** blend, mixture

2_연합, 합동 coalition, alliance, union

≠split, division, factionalism

A major characteristic of parliamentary government is the
fusion of executive and legislative powers in one body.

의회 정치의 가장 주요한 특성은 행정부와 입법부 권한이 하나의 형태로
합쳐진 것이다.

characteristic n. 특징=feature, 특성 adj. 특유한, 독특한=peculiar

parliamentary adj. 의회의, 의회에서 제정한, 의회법에 의한

executive adj. 행정상의 n. 행정부, 집행부, 행정관, 경영간부, 이사

legislative adj. 입법(상)의, 입법부의 n. 입법권, 입법부

power n. 권한, 능력, 힘, 권력, 동력 v. ~에 동력을 공급하다, ~에 힘을 주다

body n. 단체, 모임, 몸, 신체, 시체, 본체, 본문, 본론

Lesson 09 Review Test

01 As governor of Massachusetts, Calvin Coolidge became a national figure because of his **resolute** opposition to the 1919 police strike.

ⓐ firm ⓑ careful

ⓒ restrained ⓓ prompt

02 In structure and **growth**, rye resembles wheat.

ⓐ color ⓑ maturity

ⓒ development ⓓ height

03 A major characteristic of parliamentary government is the **fusion** of executive and legislative powers in one body.

ⓐ fixing ⓑ strength

ⓒ union ⓓ alignment

04 In mountainous regions, much of the snow that falls is **compacted** into ice.

ⓐ broken down ⓑ embedded

ⓒ compiled ⓓ compressed

05 The stuffed toy bears belonging to Theodore Roosevelt's children were **affectionately** called Teddy bears.

ⓐ lovingly ⓑ appropriately

ⓒ unwittingly ⓓ ironically

06 **Weaving** is an art among the Navaho of Arizona and New Mexico.

ⓐ Pottery making ⓑ Jewelry making

ⓒ Doll making ⓓ Cloth making

07 Good health is a family's most **valued** possession.

    ⓐ noticeable   ⓑ useful

    ⓒ costly   ⓓ precious

08 Mint is an herb that is well known for the **aromatic** oil distilled from all parts of the plant.

    ⓐ valuable   ⓑ fragrant

    ⓒ medicinal   ⓓ flavorful

09 Generally, a material with **a sour** taste, such as vinegar or lemon juice, contains an acid.

    ⓐ a tart   ⓑ an oily

    ⓒ a fruity   ⓓ a bland

10 Failure to express **emotions** may actually cause illness.

    ⓐ troubles   ⓑ pains

    ⓒ movements   ⓓ feelings

11 The invention of the computer **revolutionized** business procedures.

    ⓐ greatly simplified   ⓑ completely changed

    ⓒ revised   ⓓ radicalized

12 Scientists speculate that **unrestrained** population growth and dwindling resources may force humans to look to the sea for food.

    ⓐ unavoidable   ⓑ unexpected

    ⓒ unchecked   ⓓ unnecessary

13 In economics, graphs are used to **illustrate** functions.

    ⓐ rate   ⓑ list

    ⓒ verify   ⓓ represent

14 The United States is trying to **deal** with the serious problems brought on by the energy crisis.

    ⓐ dispense   ⓑ cope

    ⓒ cooperate   ⓓ interact

15 The lizard called the Gila monster is ordinarily **sluggish** and clumsy.

    ⓐ ludicrous   ⓑ amorphous

    ⓒ lethargic   ⓓ terrifying

01	a	ⓑcareful=adj. 조심성 있는 ⓒrestrained=adj. 삼가는 ⓓprompt=adj. 신속한
02	c	ⓐcolor=n. 색 ⓑmaturity=n. 성숙 ⓓheight=n. 높이, 키
03	c	ⓐfixing=n. 고정 ⓑstrength=n. 힘, 세기 ⓓalignment=n. 정렬
04	d	ⓐbreak down=고장나다 ⓑembed=v. 파묻다, 깊이 간직하다 ⓒcompile=v. 편집, 수집하다
05	a	ⓑappropriately=adv. 적당히 ⓒunwittingly=adv. 무의식적으로 ⓓironically=adv. 반어적으로
06	d	ⓐPottery making=도자기 제조 ⓑJewelry making=보석 제조 ⓒDoll making=인형 제작
07	d	ⓐnoticeable=adj. 눈에 띄는 ⓑuseful=adj. 유용한 ⓒcostly=adj. 값비싼
08	b	ⓐvaluable=adj. 귀중한 ⓒmedicinal=adj. 약의 ⓓflavorful=adj. 맛좋은
09	a	ⓑoily=adj. 기름기 많은 ⓒfruity=adj. 과일 맛이 나는 ⓓbland=adj. 부드러운, 온화한
10	d	ⓐtrouble=n. 곤란, 어려움 ⓑpain=n. 고통 ⓒmovement=n. 운동
11	b	ⓐgreatly simplified=매우 간소화한 ⓒrevise=v. 교정(정정, 수정)하다 ⓓradicalize=v. 급진적으로 하다
12	c	ⓐunavoidable=adj. 불가피한 ⓑunexpected=adj. 예기치 않은 ⓓunnecessary=adj. 불필요한
13	d	ⓐrate=v. 평가하다 ⓑlist=v. 목록에 올리다 ⓒverify=v. 증명(입증)하다
14	b	ⓐdispense=v. 분배하다 ⓒcooperate=v. 협력하다 ⓓinteract=v. 상호작용하다
15	c	ⓐludicrous=adj. 어이없는 ⓑamorphous=adj. 무정형의 ⓓterrifying=adj. 겁나게 하는

L e s s o n 10

abrupt(ly)

record

undoubted(ly)

overturn

habitat

wage

adequate

husk

coat

fire

issue

aspiration

reform

brittle

incorporate

abrupt(ly)

adj.(adv.)
1_**갑작스러운** sudden
≠expected, foreseen
2_**충동적인** impulsive
3_**뜻밖의** unanticipated
4_**짧은** short, blunt

The lecture came to an **abrupt** end because someone yelled "fire". 누군가가 "불이야"라고 소리쳤기 때문에 강의는 갑작스럽게 끝났다.

lecture   n. 강의, 강연, 훈계   v. 강의를 하다, 훈계하다, 꾸짖다=rebuke

yell   v. 소리치다=scream, ~을 소리쳐 말하다   n. 비명=scream

Unlike the common cold, flu tends to start **abruptly**.
일반적인 감기와는 달리, 유행성 감기는 갑자기 시작하는 경향이 있다.

tend   v. ~하는 경향이 있다, 나아가다, 이르다, 보살피다=watch over

record

n. **기록** account, log, report, journal
v. 1_**기록하다** chronicle, preserve, register
2_**측정하다** register, detect

You should keep a **record** of how much you spend in a month. 한 달에 얼마나 쓰는지 기록을 해야 한다.

spend   v. 쓰다, 지내다, 보내다, ~을 낭비하다, (정력·시간 등을) 소비하다

The instrument used to **record** earthquakes is called a seismograph. 지진을 기록하는 데 사용되는 도구를 지진계라고 부른다.

instrument   n. 기구, 도구, 악기, 수단=means, 앞잡이

earthquake   n. 지진=quake, (정치적·사회적) 대변동, 격동

undoubted(ly)
adj.(adv.)

확실한 certain, unquestionable, sure

≠doubted, questionable

He believes that everything will be alright because he has an **undoubted** faith in God. 그는 신에 대한 확실한 믿음이 있기 때문에 모든 것이 잘될 것이라고 여기고 있다.

believe v. 믿다, 생각하다, 신용하다

faith n. 신앙(심), 믿음, 신뢰, 신념

The most prominent characteristics of handwriting are **undoubtedly** letter formation and slant. 육필의 가장 두드러진 특성은 확실한 글자 형성과 기울기에 있다.

prominent adj. 두드러진=conspicuous, 돌출한=projecting, 중요한, 유명한

slant n. 경사 adj. 비스듬한 v. 기울다, ~한 경향이 있다

overturn

v. 1_뒤집어엎다 reverse
2_타도하다 overthrow
3_붕괴하다 collapse

The United States Supreme Court has the power to **overturn** the decisions of lower courts. 미국 대법원은 하위 법원의 판결을 뒤집을 수 있는 권한이 있다.

supreme adj. 최고의, 극도의, 대단한, 최후의

court n. 법원, 법정, 왕궁, 어전 회의, 코트, 안마당, 아첨 v. 환심을 얻으려고 하다

decision n. 판결, 결정, 결단, 결심

lower adj. 하급의, 보다 낮은 v. ~을 내리다

habitat

n. **환경, 주거환경, 서식지** environment, surrounding, dwelling

The long-term threat to the survival of elephants is the loss of their natural **habitat**. 장기적으로 코끼리 생존을 위협하고 있는 것은 자연적인 서식지를 잃어버렸다는 것이다.

long-term adj. 장기의

threat n. 위협=menace, 협박, 공갈, 징조, 조짐

survival n. 생존, 생존자 adj. 긴급 구난용의

natural adj. 자연의, 가공하지 않은, 타고난, 자연스런 n. ~에 꼭 알맞은 사람

wage

n. **임금** salary, income, pay, stipend

v. **수행하다** undertake, carry on, engage

Cesar Chavez successfully used the boycott to improve the **wages** of the members of his union. 시저 샤베즈는 노조원들의 임금을 높이는 데 보이콧을 성공적으로 사용했다.

boycott n. 보이콧, 불매, 배척 운동 v. 배척하다, 참가를 거부하다

improve v. 증대하다, ~을 개선하다, ~을 향상시키다, 가치를 높이다

union n. 노조, 결합, 연합, 연방

The new drug Czar announced that his agency will **wage** war against drugs at all cost. 새로운 마약 단속반장은 무슨 수를 써서라도 마약과의 전쟁을 수행할 것이라고 발표했다.

drug n. 마약, 약, 약품 v. ~에 약을 혼입하다, ~을 마약으로 마비시키다

announce v. 발표하다, 선언하다, (손님·탈것의) 도착을 알리다

agency n. 정부기관, 서비스 제공 기관, ~의 힘

at all cost 무슨 수를 써서라도, 어떤 대가를 치러서라도

adequate

adj. **1_충분한** enough, ample, sufficient

≠insufficient, below, wanting

2_적당한 tolerable

≠substandard

One of California's greatest problems is providing **adequate** water to meet the needs of its expanding populations.
캘리포니아 주에서 가장 큰 문제점 중 하나는 인구 증가에 따른 충분한 물을 공급해야 한다는 것이다.

greatest adj. 제일 대표적인, 제일 위대한, 최고의

provide v. 공급(제공)하다, 주다, 규정하다, 양육(부양)하다=support

meet v. 만족시키다, 만나다, ~에 직면하다, 대전(경쟁)하다 n. 모임, 경기

need n. 생리적 요구, 필요성, 책임=obligation, 빈곤=poverty v. ~이 필요하다

expand v. 늘다, 발전하다, ~을 늘리다, 확대하다

husk

n. **껍데기, 겉껍질** shell, skin, peel

v. **~의 껍질을 벗기다** strip, peel

The nuts of the filbert tree form compact clusters, with each nut encased in its own **husk**. 개암나무 열매는 촘촘하게 열리는데 열매 하나하나가 껍질에 싸여 있다.

nut n. (딱딱한 과피가 있는) 나무 열매, 핵심, ~광, 얼간이

compact adj. 빽빽한, 밀집해 있는, 작고 경제적인, 간결한=concise

v. 튼튼히 하다

cluster n. (꽃, 열매, 털 등의) 송이, 무리

encase v. ~을 ~에 집어넣다, ~을 케이스에 넣다

coat

n. **1_코트**

2_짐승의 외피, 가죽 hide, fur, skin

3_페인트 등의 칠 layer

v. **덮다, 입히다** cover

The **coat** of the galago, a nocturnal African primate, is very soft. 야행성이며, 아프리카에서 서식하는 영장류의 하나인 갈라고의 가죽은 아주 부드럽다.

nocturnal adj. 야행성의, 밤의, 밤에 하는(오는), 밤에 피는   n. 밤을 다룬 작품

primate   n. 영장류의 동물, 주도자

soft   adj. 부드러운, 말랑한, 보들보들한, 포근한, 상쾌한=pleasant

fire

n. **불** flame, blaze

v. **1_~에 불을 붙이다** ignite, light

2_발사하다 shoot, discharge

3_굽다 bake

4_해고하다 let go, dismiss

≠hire, employ

A kiln is a type of oven in which clay is **fired** so that it hardens into a form of ceramic material. 킬른은 가마의 일종인데 그 속에서 진흙을 딱딱한 도자기 형태로 만들기 위해 불로 굽는다.

type   n. 타입, 전형, 활자, (화폐, 메달 등의) 그림, 글자   v. 타자하다, ~을 상징하다

oven   n. 가마, 솥, 아궁이, 오븐

clay   n. 진흙=mud, 흙, 점토   v. ~에 점토를 섞다, ~을 점토로 걸러내다

harden   v. 굳어지다, 단단해지다, 무정해지다, 강인해지다

ceramic   adj. 도자기의, 요업(제품)의   n. 요업 제품

issue

v. **1_(흘러)나오다** flow, emit, discharge

2_발행하다, 출판하다 publish

n. **1_발행물**

2_주제 topic, subject

3_논쟁 argument, controversy

When high voltage is applied to the electrodes of a vacuum tube, a stream of electrons **issues** from the negative electrode. 진공관의 전극에 고압 전류가 흐르면, 음극에서 전자가 흘러나온다.

vacuum adj. 진공의 n. 진공, 공허, 공백, 텅 빔

tube n. 관, 통=cylinder

stream n. 흐름, 연속, 계속, 시내, 동향, 경향 v. 흐르다, 흐르듯이 이어지다

negative adj. 음의, 마이너스의, 부정의≠affirmative n. 거절 v. ~을 부정하다

aspiration

n. **열망, 포부** ambition, hope, goal, yearning, longing

As nineteenth-century American cultural **aspirations** expanded, women stepped into a new role as interpreters of art, both by writing works on art history and by teaching art. 19세기 미국의 문화적인 열망이 확산되고 있을 때, 여성들은 미술사에 대한 작품을 쓰고 미술을 가르치면서 미술 해석자라는 새로운 역할을 맡게 되었다.

aspire

v. 열망하다, 포부를 갖다 strive, aim, wish, hope

step into ~에 돌입하다

role n. 역할, 임무, 구실, 배역=part

interpreter n. 해석자, 통역관, 연출가

aspiring

adj. 포부가 있는 hopeful

She's an **aspiring** actress. 그녀는 포부가 있는 여배우다.

reform

v. **개혁하다** improve, better, regenerate

≠worsen, degenerate, regress

n. **개혁, 개정** correction, reformation, progress, betterment

≠deterioration, corruption

During the 1840's, Dorothea Dix was a leader in the movement for the **reform** of prison conditions. 1840년대에, 도로시 딕스는 교도소 개혁 운동의 선두자였다.

leader n. 지도자, 지휘자, 통솔자

movement n. 운동, 움직임, 동작, 몸짓, 활기

prison n. 감옥=jail, 수감 v. ~을 교도소에 넣다=imprison

condition n. 상태, 상황=circumstance, 처지, 필요조건 v. ~을 조절하다

brittle

adj. **1_부서지기 쉬운** fragile, breakable, delicate

≠hard, tough, solid

2_과민한 tense, rigid, relaxed

≠mellow, easygoing

Galena, the chief ore of lead, is a **brittle**, lead-gray mineral with a metallic luster. 납에서 제일 주요한 광석인 방연광은 부서지기 쉽고 금속성 광택이 나는 납빛의 광물질이다.

chief adj. 제1의, 주된, 주요한 n. 우두머리, 추장

ore n. 광석, 원광

lead n. 납, 총알, 선두, 우세 v. 이끌다, 도달하다, 좌우하다

luster n. 광택, 윤=polish, 영광, 명성

incorporate

v. **1_~을 포함하다** include, contain

2_합체하다, 통합하다 combine, consolidate, blend

3_법인으로 만들다

The idea of time is **incorporated** in all languages of the world. 시간에 대한 개념은 세계의 모든 언어 속에 포함되어 있다.

idea n. 개념, 사상, 착상, 생각, 느낌

time n. 시간, 세월, 때, 시대, 상황 adj. 시간의

v. 시간을 재다, 박자(상황)를 맞추다

language n. 언어, 말, 전문어, 말투

Lesson 10 Review Test

01 Electrodes of a vacuum tube, a stream of electrons **issues** from the negative electrode.

    ⓐ deflects   ⓑ draws

    ⓒ rebounds   ⓓ flows

02 The United States Supreme Court has the power to **overturn** the decisions of lower courts.

    ⓐ criticize   ⓑ reverse

    ⓒ delay   ⓓ inspect

03 The long-term threat to the survival of elephants is the loss of their natural **habitat**.

    ⓐ ivory   ⓑ environment

    ⓒ allies   ⓓ instincts

04 During the 1840's, Dorothea Dix was a leader in the movement for the **reform** of prison conditions.

    ⓐ unification   ⓑ creation

    ⓒ revival   ⓓ betterment

05 Galena, the chief ore of lead, is a **brittle**, lead-gray mineral with a metallic luster.

    ⓐ petrified   ⓑ dense

    ⓒ breakable   ⓓ sparkling

06 The idea of time is **incorporated** in all languages of the world.

    ⓐ assigned   ⓑ contained

    ⓒ indicated   ⓓ evidenced

07 Cesar Chavez successfully used the boycott to improve the **wages** of the members of his union.

ⓐ fringe benefits   ⓑ working conditions

ⓒ pay   ⓓ prestige

08 One of California's greatest problems is providing **adequate** water to meet the needs of its expanding populations.

ⓐ sufficient   ⓑ palatable

ⓒ suitable   ⓓ unpolluted

09 The nuts of the filbert tree form compact clusters, with each nut encased in its own **husk**.

ⓐ shell   ⓑ flower

ⓒ root   ⓓ cone

10 The **coat** of the galago, a nocturnal African primate, is very soft.

ⓐ suit   ⓑ stole

ⓒ fur   ⓓ tail

11 Unlike the common cold, flu tends to start **abruptly**.

ⓐ mysteriously   ⓑ seasonally

ⓒ repeatedly   ⓓ suddenly

12 The instrument used to **record** earthquakes is called a seismograph.

ⓐ conceal   ⓑ register

ⓒ resist   ⓓ predict

13 The most prominent characteristics of handwriting are **undoubtedly** letter formation and slant.

    ⓐ presumably   ⓑ in many cases

    ⓒ surely   ⓓ without bias

14 A kiln is a type of oven in which clay is **fired** so that it hardens into a form of ceramic material.

    ⓐ repaired   ⓑ baked

    ⓒ melted   ⓓ lightened

15 As nineteenth-century American cultural **aspirations** expanded, women stepped into a new role as interpreters of art, both by writing works on art history and by teaching art.

    ⓐ patronage   ⓑ imagination

    ⓒ ambitions   ⓓ opportunities

01	d	ⓐdeflect=v. 빗나가다 ⓑdraw=v. 끌다 ⓒrebound=v. 되튀다
02	b	ⓐcriticize=v. 비평하다 ⓒdelay=v. 미루다 ⓓinspect=v. 면밀히 살피다, 검사하다
03	b	ⓐivory=n. 상아(색) ⓒally=n. 동맹국(자) ⓓinstinct=n. 본능, 직감
04	d	ⓐunification=n. 통일, 단일화 ⓑcreation=n. 창조 ⓒrevival=n. 재생
05	c	ⓐpetrified=adj. 술 취한 ⓑdense=adj. 밀집한(빽빽한) ⓓsparkling=adj. 불꽃을 튀기는
06	b	ⓐassign=v. 할당하다, 지정하다 ⓒindicate=v. 나타내다 ⓓevidence=v. 증명하다
07	c	ⓐfringe benefit= (연금, 유급휴가, 보험급여 등의) 부가 급부
		ⓑworking conditions= 노동조건 ⓓprestige=n. 위신, 명성
08	a	ⓑpalatable=adj. 맛 좋은 ⓒsuitable=adj. 적당한 ⓓunpolluted=adj. 오염되지 않은
09	a	ⓑflower=n. 꽃 ⓒroot=n. 뿌리 ⓓcone=n. 원뿔
10	c	ⓐsuit=n. 정장 한 벌 ⓑstole=n. (여자용 모피 등의) 어깨걸이 ⓓtail=n. 꼬리
11	d	ⓐmysteriously=adv. 신비하게 ⓑseasonally=adv. 계절(주기)적인 ⓒrepeatedly=adv. 되풀이하여
12	b	ⓐconceal=v. 숨기다 ⓒresist=v. 저항하다 ⓓpredict=v. 예언하다
13	c	ⓐpresumably=adv. 생각컨대, 아마 ⓑin many cases=여러 면에서
		ⓓwithout bias=편견 없이
14	b	ⓐrepair=v. 수리하다 ⓒmelt=v. 녹다 ⓓlighten=v. 밝게 하다
15	c	ⓐpatronage=n. 보호 ⓑimagination=n. 상상 ⓓopportunity=n. 기회

L e s s o n 11

occupation

segment

venom

stern

ignite

sensational

output

dormant

germinate

mimic

pursue

antagonistic

haul

domesticate

tier

occupation

n. **1_직업** job, vocation, work, profession, employment
2_점령

Alice Hamilton was one of the first doctors to study the relation between one's health and one's **occupation**.
앨리스 해밀턴은 인간의 건강과 직업의 관계에 대해 연구한 최초의 의사들 중 한 명이었다.

study v. 연구하다, 공부하다, 주의 깊게 관찰하다 n. 공부, 연구, 학문, 서재

relation n. 관계=connection, 관련=reference, 인척

W.W. II began with Germany's **occupation** of Poland.
제2차 세계대전은 독일의 폴란드 점령으로 시작되었다.

segment

n. **1_단편**
2_조각 piece, slice
3_부분 section, portion, sector, fragment
≠whole, entirety, all, totality
4_한 프로
v. **나누다** divide

The community college is the most rapidly growing **segment** of higher education in the United States. 2년제 대학은 미국 고등교육 중에서 가장 빨리 성장하는 부분이다.

community college 2년제 대학교

rapidly adv. 빨리, 급속히, 서둘러

grow v. 성장하다, 자라다=develop, ~으로 되다=become, turn into, 기르다

higher education 고등교육

venom

n. **1_독** poison

2_악의 ill will, malice

3_원한 ill will, spite, hatred

≠good will, charity, kindness, mercy

The rattlesnake uses its **venom** to stun or paralyze its victims. 방울뱀은 먹이를 기절시키거나 마비시키기 위해 독을 사용한다.

stun v. 기절시키다, 실신케 하다, 놀라게 하다, 멍하게 하다 n. 기절시키는 것

paralyze v. 마비시키다, 무기력하게 하다, 무효로 만들다

There was no mistaking the **venom** in his voice. 그의 목소리에는 원한이 서려 있었다.

voice n. 목소리, 음성, 의견, 발언권, 대변자 v. 말로 나타내다, 조율하다

stern

adj. **1_엄격한** strict≠lenient, gentle

2_단호한 resolute, firm, adamant≠hesitant, faltering, equivocal

3_엄숙한

4_황량한 harsh, austere

Psychologists have found that **stern** disciplinary measures do not always make a child more well behaved. 심리학자들은 엄격한 징계 처분이 항상 아이들을 잘 처신하도록 만드는 것은 아니라는 것을 알게 되었다.

disciplinary adj. 징계적인, 훈련의, 규율상의

measure n. 처분, 조치, 크기, 넓이, 측정, 단위 v. 재다, 측정하다, 평가하다

behave v. 행동하다, 처신하다, 작용하다

The teacher gave his student a **stern** warning not to be late again. 선생님은 학생에게 다시는 늦지 않도록 단호하게 경고했다.

warning n. 경고, 주의, 훈계, 통지

ignite

v. **1_불을 붙이다** catch fire, light, kindle, burn

≠extinguish, put out

2_흥분시키다 excite, agitate, stir up

A burning match applied to paper will make it **ignite**.
불타는 성냥을 종이에 대면 불이 붙을 것이다.

match n. 성냥, 대등한 사람, 경쟁 상대, 시합

v. 필적하다, 어울리다, 꼭 들어맞게 하다

The last minute goal **ignited** the crowd into a frenzy.
마지막 순간의 골이 관중들을 흥분으로 몰아넣었다.

last minute 마지막 순간

frenzy n. 극도의 흥분, 열광, 광란

sensational

adj. **1_선풍적 인기의** exciting

≠dull

2_놀라운 shocking, startling

≠routine

3_선정적인 electrifying, dramatic

≠bland

Kit Carson, an American frontiersman, was one of the most **sensational** heroes of the Old West. 미국의 변경 개척민이었던 킷 카슨은 옛날 서부 시대의 가장 인기있는 영웅들 중의 한 명이었다.

frontiersman n. 국경지대의 주민, 변경 개척자

hero n. 영웅, 주인공

output

n. **산출, 생산** production, yield

v. **산출하다** manufacture, produce, yield

Normally, division of labor leads to increased **output** of goods, making possible an increase in the standard of living of great numbers of people. 일반적으로, 분업은 상품의 생산량을 증가시키며 많은 사람들의 생활 수준을 향상시킨다.

division n. 분할, 구분, 부분, 분열

labor n. 노동(력), 노동자, 일, 진통 v. 일하다, 애쓰다, 고생하다, 애써 나아가다

standard n. 기준, 규범 adj. 표준의, 정평있는, 보통의, 규격에 맞는

The file is too big to **output** to the printer. 그 파일의 양이 너무 방대해서 프린터로 출력할 수 없다.

file n. 파일, 정리 보존 기구

v. 파일에 철하다, 정리하다, 제출하다, 일렬 종대로 행진하다

dormant

adj. **1_잠자는(듯한)** sleeping, slumbering

≠alert, vigorous

2_동면의 hibernate

3_잠복의 inactive, suspended, potential

≠functioning, operative, working

Many cold-blooded animals are **dormant** during the winter. 많은 냉혈동물들은 겨울철에 동면한다.

cold-blooded adj. 냉혈의≠warm-blooded, 냉혹한

The virus remains **dormant** in nerve tissue until activated. 바이러스는 활성화될 때까지는 신경세포에 잠복하고 있다.

nerve tissue 신경세포

activate v. 활성화하다, 활동적이게 하다

germinate

v. **1_ 싹트다** sprout, bud

≠wither, wilt

2_ 자라기 시작하다 develop, grow

≠fade, decay, decline

The dodder seed **germinates** in the ground, producing only a short root to anchor the stem. 도더 식물의 씨앗은 줄기를 지탱해줄 짧은 뿌리만을 내리면서 땅속에서 싹을 틔운다.

seed n. 종자, 씨, 근원, 자손 v. 씨를 뿌리다, 살포하다, 결실을 맺다

root n. 뿌리, 근본, 조상 v. 뿌리박게 하다

anchor n. 닻, 고정 장치 v. 닻으로 고정시키다, 단단히 달라붙어 있다

stem n. 줄기, 대 v. 줄기를 달다, 시작하다, 억지하다, 자제하다, 거슬러 나아가다

mimic

n. **모방자** copycat, imitator, mime

≠inventor, creator

v. **흉내내다** imitate, copy

Researchers have discovered that dolphins are able to **mimic** human speech. 연구원들은 돌고래가 인간의 말을 흉내낼 수 있다는 것을 알게 되었다.

discover v. 발견하다, 깨닫다

He often as a joke **mimicked** his wife's Southern accent. 그는 장난삼아 종종 아내의 남부 사투리를 흉내내었다.

accent n. 사투리, 악센트, 음조, 어조, 말투 v. 강하게 발음하다, 강조하다

pursue

v. **1_뒤쫓다, 추적하다** chase, follow, trail, tail

2_추구하다 long for, yearn, desire

3_수행하다 proceed, practice, conduct

The falcon is a type of hawk that is trained to **pursue** game in the sport called falconry. 팰컨은 매의 일종으로 팰컨리라는 스포츠에서 사냥감을 뒤쫓도록 훈련받는다.

hawk n. 매, 사기꾼 v. 매처럼 날다, 호전적으로 되다, 팔러 다니다, 가래를 뱉다

train v. 훈련시키다, 익숙해지도록 하다, 단련하다 n. 열차, 기차, 열

game n. 사냥감, 경기, 놀이, 운동회

Eager to succeed, he has aggressively **pursued** his new business venture. 성공하려는 열망으로 그는 자신의 새로운 사업에 적극적으로 덤벼들고 있다.

aggressively adv. 적극적으로, 침략적으로

venture n. 모험적 기도, 투기, 위험 v. 위험에 내맡기다, 감히 표명하다

antagonistic

adj. **1_적대의, 반대하는** hostile, quarreling

≠supportive, congenial, harmonious

2_상반되는 clashing, antithetical

Public elections are sometimes held to settle differences between **antagonistic** groups in a government body. 공개 선거는 때때로 정부에서 상반되는 단체들간의 이견을 해결하기 위해 열린다.

public adj. 공개의, 공공의, 공중의, 공적인, 종합 대학의 n. 일반 사람들, 대중, 계층

settle v. 해결하다=decide, 정착하다, ~을 확정하다, 안정시키다

difference n. 차이, 다름, 중대한 변화, 특징

haul

v. **1_잡아끌다** drag

2_끌어당기다 pull, tug

3_운반하다 transport

n. **1_어획량**

2_수송량

Raised for its milk, meat, and hide, the reindeer is also used to **haul** things from place to place. 우유, 고기, 가죽을 위해 사육되는 순록은 여기저기 물건을 끄는 데에도 사용된다.

hide n. 가죽, 피혁, 피부, 핸드백, 경주마

v. 매질하다, 가죽을 벗기다, 숨기다

domesticate

v. **1_길들이다** tame

2_(습관 등을) 도입하다

domesticated

adj. 길들여진 tame ≠ wild, savage

Of all the wild dogs, none is more closely related to the **domesticated** dog than the wolf. 야생개 중에서, 늑대가 길들여진 개와 가장 밀접한 관계가 있다.

wild adj. 야생의, 황량한, 야만의, 맹렬한, 난폭한, 무모한 adv. 무턱대고 n. 황야

relate v. 관계가 있다, ~을 이야기하다, ~을 관련시키다

tier

n. **1_층** level, layer, stratum

2_계급 rank, class

An avalanche is most likely to occur when uneven **tiers** of various snow types are placed under stress. 눈사태는 다양한 종류의 눈으로 이루어진 불균일한 눈층이 압력을 받을 때 쉽게 발생한다.

occur v. 일어나다=happen, take place, 나타나다, 문득 생각나다=come to mind

various adj. 다양한, 서로 다른, 여러 가지의, 다방면의, 다수의=many

uneven adj. 고르지 않은, 불규칙한, 평평하지 않은, 홀수의, 일방적인

place v. ~을 두다, 임명하다, 평가하다=estimate, (시험, 경주 등에서) ~등을 하다

n. 장소, 공간=space, 어떤 자리=spot, 입장, 위치=position, 환경

stress n. 스트레스, 강세, 압력 v. 강조하다, 악센트를 두다

Lesson 11 Review Test

01 Raised for its milk, meat, and hide, the reindeer is also used to **haul** things from place to place.

    ⓐ pull   ⓑ push

    ⓒ direct   ⓓ send

02 An avalanche is most likely to occur when uneven **tiers** of various snow types are placed under stress.

    ⓐ slopes   ⓑ clumps

    ⓒ flakes   ⓓ layers

03 Alice Hamilton was one of the first doctors to study the relation between one's health and one's **occupation**.

    ⓐ heredity   ⓑ job

    ⓒ happiness   ⓓ childhood

04 Kit Carson, an American frontiersman, was one of the most **sensational** heroes of the Old West.

    ⓐ exciting   ⓑ distracting

    ⓒ enigmatic   ⓓ ostentatious

05 Of all the wild dogs, none is more closely related to the **domesticated** dog than the wolf.

    ⓐ ordinary   ⓑ tame

    ⓒ faithful   ⓓ hunting

06 Normally, division of labor leads to increased **output** of goods, making possible an increase in the standard of living of great numbers of people.

ⓐ advertising   ⓑ profit

ⓒ export   ⓓ production

07 Many cold-blooded animals are **dormant** during the winter.

ⓐ freeze   ⓑ starve

ⓒ migrate   ⓓ hibernate

08 The rattlesnake uses its **venom** to stun or paralyze its victims.

ⓐ rattles   ⓑ teeth

ⓒ coils   ⓓ poison

09 Psychologists have found that **stern** disciplinary measures do not always make a child more well behaved.

ⓐ excessive   ⓑ consistent

ⓒ strict   ⓓ vindictive

10 The dodder seed **germinates** in the ground, producing only a short root to anchor the stem.

ⓐ rots   ⓑ rotates

ⓒ sprouts   ⓓ shrinks

11 Public elections are sometimes held to settle differences between **antagonistic** groups in a government body.

ⓐ quarreling   ⓑ unyielding

ⓒ military   ⓓ partisan

12 The community college is the most rapidly growing **segment** of higher education in the United States.

    ⓐ core   ⓑ sector

    ⓒ idea   ⓓ problem

13 A burning match applied to paper will make it **ignite**.

    ⓐ heat up   ⓑ catch fire

    ⓒ disintegrate   ⓓ glow

14 Researchers have discovered that dolphins are able to **mimic** human speech.

    ⓐ ignore   ⓑ imitate

    ⓒ hear   ⓓ understand

15 The falcon is a type of hawk that is trained to **pursue** game in the sport called falconry.

    ⓐ mislead   ⓑ join

    ⓒ chase   ⓓ identify

01	**a**	ⓑpush=v. 밀다 ⓒdirect=v. 지도하다 ⓓsend=v. 보내다
02	**d**	ⓐslope=n. 비탈, 경사 ⓑclump=n. 수풀 ⓒflake=n. 얇은 조각
03	**b**	ⓐheredity=n. 유전 ⓒhappiness=n. 행복 ⓓchildhood=n. 어린 시절
04	**a**	ⓑdistracting=adj. 혼란시키는 ⓒenigmatic=adj. 수수께끼 같은 ⓓostentatious=adj. 자랑삼아 드러내는
05	**b**	ⓐordinary=adj. 보통의 ⓒfaithful=adj. 성실(충실)한 ⓓhunting=n. 수렵(사냥)
06	**d**	ⓐadvertising=n. 광고 ⓑprofit=n. 이익 ⓒexport=n. 수출
07	**d**	ⓐfreeze=v. 얼다 ⓑstarve=v. 굶어죽다 ⓒmigrate=v. 이주하다
08	**d**	ⓐrattle=n. 덜커덕거리는 소리 ⓑtooth=n. 이 ⓒcoil=n. 코일
09	**c**	ⓐexcessive=adj. 지나친 ⓑconsistent=adj. 일관된 ⓓvindictive=adj. 복수심 있는
10	**c**	ⓐrot=v. 썩다 ⓑrotate=v. 회전(순회)하다 ⓓshrink=v. 오그라들다
11	**a**	ⓑunyielding=adj. 유연성이 없는, 완고한 ⓒmilitary=adj. 군(대)의 ⓓpartisan=adj. 당파심이 강한
12	**b**	ⓐcore=n. 핵심 ⓒidea=n. 생각 ⓓproblem=n. 문제
13	**b**	ⓐheat up=데우다 ⓒdisintegrate=v. 붕괴(분해)되다 ⓓglow=v. 빛을 내다
14	**b**	ⓐignore=v. 무시하다 ⓒhear=v. 듣다 ⓓunderstand=v. 이해하다
15	**c**	ⓐmislead=v. 잘못 인도하다 ⓑjoin=v. 참가(가담)하다 ⓓidentify=v. 확인하다, 동일시하다

Lesson 12

end

shy

material

sensation

apparent(ly)

coverage

gain

warrior

incessant(ly)

arouse

heyday

witness

shrink

vague

imprudent

end

n. **1_끝** termination, conclusion

2_멸망 doomsday

3_목적 goal, purpose

adj. **최후의** final, ultimate

v. **끝나다** close, finish, terminate, conclude

The **end** of the movie brought tears to everyone in the theater. 그 영화의 끝은 영화관에 있던 모든 사람들이 눈물을 흘리게 했다.

movie n. 영화, 영화관 adj. 영화의

tear n. 눈물, 물방울, 비애 v. 찢다, 벗기다, 쥐어뜯다

In masculine rhyme, the **end** sounds of stressed syllables are repeated. 힘센 운에서, 강한 어절의 끝소리는 반복된다.

masculine adj. 힘센, 남자의, 남성의 n. 남성, 남자

shy

adj. **1_소심한** timid, reserved

≠adventurous, bold

2_수줍어하는

3_조심성이 많은 cautious

≠active

Bats are extremely **shy** creatures and avoid humans if at all possible. 박쥐는 매우 조심성이 많은 동물이며 가능하면 인간을 피한다.

extremely adv. 매우, 몹시, 극단적으로, 극히

creature n. 동물, 생물, 인간, 산물

avoid v. 피하다, 비키다, 무효로 하다, 취소하다

material

adj. **1_물질의**

2_육체상의 bodily, corporeal

n. **1_재료, 요소**

2_물질 matter, substance

Ammonia, one of the earliest known nitrogen compounds, was originally produced by distilling organic **materials**.
가장 빨리 알려진 질소 화합물 중의 하나인 암모니아는 원래 유기물을 증류할 때 만들어진다.

earliest adj.(adv.) 가장 빠른, 최초의

compound n. 합성물, 혼합물 adj. 합성의, 복합의 v. 혼합하다, 도를 더하게 하다

originally adv. 원래, 처음에는, 처음부터, 독창적으로

sensation

n. **1_느낌** feeling, perception, impression

2_감각

3_마음

The **sensation** of a lump in one's throat arises from an increased flow of blood into the tissues of the pharynx and larynx. 목구멍에 덩어리가 걸려 있을 때의 느낌은 인두와 후두로 흐르는 혈액이 증가하기 때문에 일어난다.

lump n. 덩어리, 혹, 한 무더기, 다수 v. 한 덩어리로 만들다, 일률적으로 다루다

throat n. 목구멍, 목의 앞부분, 좁은 통로 v. ~에 홈을 파다

arise v. 일어나다, 발생하다, 생기다, 비롯되다, 기상하다

flow n. 흐름, 유입, 홍수, 밀물 v. 흐르다, 범람하다=flood, 밀려들어오다

apparent(ly)

adj.(adv.)

1_ 명백한 obvious
2_ 외관상의 seeming

The **apparently** homogeneous Dakota grasslands are actually a botanical garden of more than 400 types of grasses. 언뜻 보기에 같은 종류의 풀만 있는 것처럼 보이는 다코타 목초지는 사실상 400종류가 넘는 풀로 이루어진 식물 정원이다.

homogeneous adj. 동종의, 등질의

grassland n. 목초지=plain, prairie

botanical adj. 식물의, 식물학의, 식물에서 채취한

coverage

n. **1_ 적용**
2_ 보도 reportage
3_ 보험 계약

Photojournalist Margaret Bourke White became famous for her **coverage** of significant events during the Second World War. 보도 사진가인 마가렛 버크 화이트는 제2차 세계대전 동안에 중요한 사건의 보도 때문에 유명해졌다.

significant adj. 중요한, 의미 있는, 뜻깊은, 상당한

event n. 사건=incident, 행사, 종목

during prep. ~동안, ~사이에, ~하는 중에

gain

v. **1_얻다, 획득하다** earn, attain, profit

2_증대하다 put on weight

3_향상되다 progress

n. **1_이익, 이득** profit, benefit

2_증가 increase

I should stop eating late dinners because I **gained** ten pounds since last year. 밤늦게 저녁 먹는 것을 그만 두어야겠다. 왜냐하면 작년에 비해 10파운드나 늘었기 때문이다.

dinner n. 저녁 식사, 만찬, 오찬

Almost all economists agree that nations **gain** by trading with one another. 거의 모든 경제학자들은 국가들간의 무역으로 이익을 얻어야 한다는 데 의견을 같이한다.

warrior

n. **1_전사** combatant, fighter

2_무사

3_용기와 투지가 많은 사람

adj. **1_전투적인**

2_무인다운

The Cheyenne Indians were considered spectacular riders and fierce **warriors**. 샤이엔 인디언들은 탁월한 기수였으며 용맹한 전사였다.

spectacular adj. 탁월한, 눈부신, 장관의, 호화스러운, 극적인

rider n. 기수, 차를 모는 사람, 승객, 타는 사람

# incessant(ly)
adj.(adv.)

끊임없는, 그치지 않는 endless, uninterrupted, ceaseless, constant

The mother finally got tired of her son's **incessant** complaining. 그 어머니는 마침내 아들의 끊임없는 불평에 싫증이 났다.

finally   adv. 마침내, 최후로, 최종적으로, 결정적으로

complain   v. 불평하다, 푸념하다, 한탄하다, 하소연하다, 고소하다

It has been suggested that people who watch television **incessantly** may become overly passive. 끊임없이 TV를 보는 사람은 지나치게 수동적이 될 수 있다는 의견이 나오고 있다.

overly   adv. 지나치게, 몹시

passive   adj. 수동적인, 무저항의, 활동적이 아닌=inactive   n. 수동태

arouse
v.

1_깨우다 awake

2_자극하다 excite

3_각성하다 realize

4_분기하다

In a bullfight, it is the movement, not the color, of objects that **arouses** the bull. 투우에서 소를 자극시키는 것은 색깔이 아니라 물체의 움직임이다.

color   n. 색, 빛깔, 안색, 특색   v. 채색하다, ~을 특징짓다

bull   n. 황소, 억센 사람, 허풍, 허튼 소리   v. 밀고 나아가다, 위협하다, 허풍떨다

heyday

n. **1_ 한창(때)**

2_ 전성(기) prime, golden age

3_ 절정 prime, height, peak

During their **heyday**, showboats were popular and generally prosperous. 순항 연예선의 전성기 때는 인기도 많았고 대체로 번성했다.

showboat n. 연예선, 눈길을 끌고 싶어하는 사람 v. 자랑해 보이다, 과시하다

popular adj. 인기 있는, 대중적인, 민중의 n. 대중

prosperous adj. 번성(영)하는=thriving, 부유한, 성공한, 잘 되어가는

witness

n. **1_ 증언** testimony

2_ 증인 eyewitness

v. **1_ 목격하다** see, observe

2_ 증언하다 attest

Francis Scott Key wrote the words to "The Star-Spangled Banner" after **witnessing** the unsuccessful attack on Fort McHenry. 프랜시스 스콧 키는 맥헨리 요새에서의 공격 실패를 목격한 후 "스타 스팽글드 배너(성조기여 영원하라)"에 가사를 붙였다.

word n. 가사, 단어, 기별, 소식, 약속, 서언, 지시, 명령

fort n. 요새=post, garrison, station

shrink

v. **1_줄어들다** contract, diminish, compress, reduce, decrease

≠expand, increase

2_움츠러지다

3_피하다

If wool is submerged in hot water, it tends to **shrink**. 양모를 뜨거운 물에 담그면 줄어들게 된다.

wool n. 양모, 털실, 모직물 adj. 모직물의

submerge v. 물에 담그다, 잠수하다, 덮어 가리다, 몰두하다

vague

adj. **1_막연한** imprecise

2_애매한 unclear, obscure

3_희미한 blurred

≠defined

The Constitution's **vague** nature has given it the flexibility to be adapted when circumstances change. 헌법의 막연한 성질은 상황의 변화에 적절하게 적용될 수 있는 융통성을 준다.

constitution n. 헌법, 구성, 구조, 체질, 성격

nature n. 성질, 자연, 자연계, 자연물, 본질

flexibility n. 유연성, 다루기 쉬움, 적응성, 융통성, 탄력성

adapt v. 적용하다, 익숙해지다, 개조하다

circumstance n. 상황, 환경, 사건, 사태, 사실

imprudent

adj. **1**_뻔뻔스러운 careless, foolish

2_현명하지 않은 unwise

≠prudent, wise

By today's standards, early farmers were **imprudent**
because they planted the same crop repeatedly,
exhausting the soil after a few harvest. 오늘날의 기준으로 보면
초기의 농부들은 현명하지 못했다. 그들은 같은 작물을 되풀이하여
심었는데 그것은 몇 차례의 수확 후에 땅을 고갈시키는 결과를 낳았다.

repeatedly adv. 되풀이하여, 재삼재사, 여러 차례

exhaust v. 고갈시키다, 소모하다=consume, 다 써버리다, 지치다, 속속들이 규명하다

soil n. 흙, 땅, 지면, 토질, 국토, 농토, 오물 v. 더럽히다

crop n. 농작물, 수확물 v. 자르다, 짧게 깎다

Lesson 12　Review Test

01 In masculine rhyme, the **end** sounds of stressed syllables are repeated.

    ⓐ dominant　　　　　　　　ⓑ vowel

    ⓒ hard　　　　　　　　　　ⓓ final

02 Bats are extremely **shy** creatures and avoid humans if at all possible.

    ⓐ timid　　　　　　　　　　ⓑ clean

    ⓒ private　　　　　　　　　ⓓ noisy

03 Ammonia, one of the earliest known nitrogen compounds, was originally produced by distilling organic **materials**.

    ⓐ masses　　　　　　　　　ⓑ substances

    ⓒ liquids　　　　　　　　　ⓓ fabrics

04 The **sensation** of a lump in one's throat arises from an increased flow of blood into the tissues of the pharynx and larynx.

    ⓐ explanation　　　　　　　ⓑ disease

    ⓒ feeling　　　　　　　　　ⓓ unpleasantness

05 The **apparently** homogeneous Dakota grasslands are actually a botanical garden of more than 400 types of grasses.

    ⓐ seemingly　　　　　　　　ⓑ comparatively

    ⓒ dazzlingly　　　　　　　　ⓓ strangely

06 Photojournalist Margaret Bourke White became famous for her **coverage** of significant events during the Second World War.

    ⓐ usage　　　　　　　　　　ⓑ camouflage

    ⓒ collage　　　　　　　　　ⓓ reportage

07 Almost all economists agree that nations **gain** by trading with one another.

    ⓐ cooperate   ⓑ profit

    ⓒ become more stable   ⓓ become more dependent

08 The Cheyenne Indians were considered spectacular riders and fierce **warriors**.

    ⓐ hunters   ⓑ defenders

    ⓒ enemies   ⓓ fighters

09 It has been suggested that people who watch television **incessantly** may become overly passive.

    ⓐ seriously   ⓑ skeptically

    ⓒ constantly   ⓓ arbitrarily

10 In a bullfight, it is the movement, not the color, of objects that **arouses** the bull.

    ⓐ confuses   ⓑ excites

    ⓒ scares   ⓓ diverts

11 During their **heyday**, showboats were popular and generally prosperous.

    ⓐ golden age   ⓑ infancy

    ⓒ summer voyages   ⓓ revivals

12 Francis Scott Key wrote the words to "The Star-Spangled Banner" after **witnessing** the unsuccessful attack on Fort McHenry.

    ⓐ participating in   ⓑ observing

    ⓒ hearing about   ⓓ resisting

13 If wool is submerged in hot water, it tends to **shrink**.

    ⓐ smell   ⓑ fade

    ⓒ unravel   ⓓ contract

14 The Constitution's **vague** nature has given it the flexibility to be adapted when circumstances change.

ⓐ imprecise

ⓑ diffuse

ⓒ unpolished

ⓓ elementary

15 By today's standards, early farmers were **imprudent** because they planted the same crop repeatedly, exhausting the soil after a few harvest.

ⓐ unwise

ⓑ stubborn

ⓒ tiresome

ⓓ unscientific

01	d	ⓐ dominant=adj. 지배적인 ⓑ vowel=adj. 모음의 ⓒ hard=adj. 어려운, 딱딱한
02	a	ⓑ clean=adj. 깨끗한 ⓒ private=adj. 사적인 ⓓ noisy=adj. 시끄러운
03	b	ⓐ mass=n. 질량 ⓒ liquid=n. 액체 ⓓ fabric=n. 구조, 직물(천)
04	c	ⓐ explanation=n. 설명 ⓑ disease=n. 질병 ⓓ unpleasantness=n. 불쾌함
05	a	ⓑ comparatively=adv. 비교적 ⓒ dazzlingly=adv. 눈부시게 ⓓ strangely=adv. 이상하게
06	d	ⓐ usage=n. 사용 ⓑ camouflage=n. 위장(카무플라주) ⓒ collage=n. 콜라주(기법)
07	b	ⓐ cooperate=v. 협력하다 ⓒ become more stable=더욱더 안정되다
		ⓓ become more dependent=더욱 의존하게 되다
08	d	ⓐ hunter=n. 사냥꾼 ⓑ defender=n. 방어(옹호)자 ⓒ enemy=n. 적
09	c	ⓐ seriously=adv. 진지하게 ⓑ skeptically=adv. 의심 많게 ⓓ arbitrarily=adv. 제멋대로
10	b	ⓐ confuse=v. 혼란시키다 ⓒ scare=v. 깜짝 놀라게 하다 ⓓ divert=v. 전환하다
11	a	ⓑ infancy=n. 유년(초기) ⓒ voyage=n. 항해 ⓓ revival=n. 재생
12	b	ⓐ participate in= ~에 참가하다 ⓒ hear about= ~에 관해서 듣다
		ⓓ resist=v. 저항하다
13	d	ⓐ smell=v. ~의 냄새가 나다 ⓑ fade=v. (빛깔이) 바래다 ⓒ unravel=v. 풀다, 해결하다
14	a	ⓑ diffuse=v. 흐트러뜨리다, 퍼뜨리다 ⓒ unpolished=adj. 닦지 않은 ⓓ elementary=adj. 초보의
15	a	ⓑ stubborn=adj. 고집센 ⓒ tiresome=adj. 귀찮은 ⓓ unscientific=adj. 비과학적인

L e s s o n 13

aid

erupt

therefore

dispensary

subterranean

somewhat

sway

tale

contagious

itinerant

handy

modulate

apparel

foe

indemnify

aid

v. **1_돕다** help, assist ≠ hinder, impede, obstruct

2_ ~을 거들다 accommodate

n. **1_원조**

2_도움 assistance, help ≠ impediment, obstacle

Foxes **aid** the farmer by attacking destructive rodents. 여우들은 해를 끼치는 설치류 동물을 공격함으로써 농부들을 돕는다.

destructive adj. 해를 끼치는, 파괴적인 ≠ constructive

rodent n. 쥐, 설치 동물 adj. 설치류의

The federal government allots millions of dollars for emergency **aids**. 연방정부는 긴급 원조용으로 수백만 달러를 할당해놓고 있다.

allot v. 할당하다, 충당하다

emergency adj. 비상용의, 긴급한 n. 비상 사태, 위급

erupt

v. **1_분출하다** burst

2_폭발하다 explode, discharge

3_발진하다

Mount St. Helens **erupted** in March 1980 after one hundred twenty-three years of silence. 세인트 헬렌 산은 123년의 침묵 후, 1980년 3월에 폭발했다.

mount n. 산 v. 오르다, 타다, 앉히다, 설치하다

silence n. 잠잠함, 침묵, 정숙, 무소식

therefore
adv. **1_그러므로** so

2_따라서 accordingly

3_그 결과(로서) consequently, thus, as a result

In Europe tea drinking and **therefore** tea tables were innovations of the late 1600's. 유럽에서는 차 마시는 것과 그 결과로서의 차 테이블은 1600년대 후기에 새로 도입된 것이었다.

drink v. 마시다, 마셔 없애다 n. 음료, 주류, 한모금

table n. 테이블, 일람표, 목록 adj. 테이블의 v. 탁상에 놓다, 전시하다

innovation n. 새로 도입한 것, (기술) 혁신, 쇄신

late adj. 후기의, 근래의, 최근의, 늦은, 죽은 adv. 늦게, 최근에

dispensary
n. **1_(공장, 학교 등의) 의무실** clinic, infirmary

2_약국 pharmacy, drugstore

3_조제실

Benjamin Rush established the first free **dispensary** in the United States. 벤저민 러시는 미국에서 최초의 무료 약국을 설립했다.

establish v. 설립하다, 제정하다, 자리잡게 하다

first adj. 최초의, 맨 처음의, 첫째의

free adj. 무료의, 자유로운, 외부의 간섭에 얽매이지 않는, ~가 없는, 해방된, 막힘이 없는 adv. 자유롭게, 공짜로 v. 해방하다, 제거하다

subterranean

adj. **1_지하의**

2_지중의 underground

≠surface

Subterranean streams have cut through limestone to form miles of passages and caves, such as Kentucky's Mammoth Cave. 지하수는 석회석을 뚫고 지나가면서 수마일에 달하는 통로를 만들기도 하고 켄터키의 매머드 케이브와 같은 동굴을 만들기도 한다.

through prep. 꿰뚫어, 지나서, ~에 의하여 adv. 관통하여, 끝까지
　　　　 adj. 뚫려 있는, 직행의

passage n. 통로, 한 단락, 경과, 통행(권), 도로, 항해 v. 나아가다, 통과하다

mammoth adj. 거대한 n. 매머드, 거대한 것

cave n. 굴 v. 굴을 파다, 움푹 들어가게 하다, 약화되다

---

somewhat

adv. **1_얼마간** for some time

2_얼마쯤

3_어느 정도 to some degree

4_약간

Lampreys and hagfish have slimy, scaleless bodies shaped **somewhat** like the bodies of eels. 칠장어와 먹장어는 점액성의 비늘이 없는 몸통을 하고 있는데 어느 정도는 뱀장어와 유사한 모습이다.

slimy adj. 점액성의, 진흙투성이의, 끈적끈적한, 불쾌한, 치사한, 비굴한

shape v. 형성하다, 구체화하다, 표현하다 n. 모양, 형태, 모습, 외양

sway

v. **1_흔들다** swing, fluctuate

2_움직이다, 좌우하다 persuade, influence, affect, induce

The trees were **swaying** gently in the wind. 나무들이 바람에 부드럽게 흔들리고 있었다.

gently adv. 부드럽게, 친절하게

wind n. 바람, 강풍, 관악기 v. 바람에 쐬다, 알아채다

Salesmanship is the ability to **sway** people to willingly buy products or support new ideas. 판매 수완이라는 것은 흔쾌히 물건을 사거나 새로운 아이디어에 지지를 보내도록 사람을 움직이는 능력을 말한다.

ability n. 능력, 수완, 재능

willingly adv. 기꺼이, 자진해서, 쾌히

tale

n. **1_이야기, 설화** story, narrative, legend

2_소문 gossip, rumor

Paul Bunyan has been the subject of numerous **tales**.
폴 버니언은 수많은 이야기의 주제가 되고 있다.

subject n. 주제, 과제, 테마, 백성, 학과, 주어, 주체 adj. 지배를 받는, 영향을 받기 쉬운, 조건으로 ~을 필요로 하는 v. 복종시키다, 겪게 하다, 제시하다, 위임하다

Men who served in the army tend to exaggerate when they tell **tales** about their army years. 군에서 복무를 한 사람들은 자신들의 군대 시절 이야기를 할 때 과장하는 경향이 있다.

serve v. 복무하다, 봉사하다, 임무를 다하다, 시중을 들다, 쓸모 있다, 알맞다

exaggerate v. 과장해서 말하다, 악화시키다

contagious

adj. **전염성의** transmissible, communicable, catching, infectious

Influenza is an acute viral disease of the respiratory tract that is extremely **contagious** and often reaches epidemic proportions. 유행성 감기는 전염성이 강하고 때로는 전염성 치수까지 도달하는 호흡기 기관의 급성 바이러스성 질병이다.

influenza n. 유행성 감기, 독감

disease n. 병, 질병, 불건전 상태, 분해, 변질

respiratory adj. 호흡(용)의, 호흡 기관의

tract n. 관, 큰 넓이, 지역, 시간의 경과

reach v. 도달하다, 도착하다, 내밀다, 접촉을 가지다

　　　　 n. 뻗치기, 범위, 넓이, 직선유역

proportion n. 치수, 비, 비율, 바른 관계, 면적, 부분 v. 적합하게 하다, 조화시키다

itinerant

adj. **순회하는** wondering, migratory, nomadic, traveling

≠settled, fixed, rooted

Itinerant preachers played an important role in the United States religious history. 순회 설교자들은 미국 종교 역사에서 중요한 역할을 담당했다.

preacher n. 설교자, 목사, 전도사

play v. 배역을 맡다, 상연하다, 놀다, 승부를 겨루다, 연주하다, 처신하다, 행동하다

　　　 n. 극, 연극, 놀이, 오락, 농담, 경기, 시합, 도박, 내기

religious adj. 종교에 관한, 신앙심 깊은, 정직한, 수도의

　　　　　 n. 수도회원, 수녀, 독실한 신자

handy

adj. **편리한** convenient, accessible, useful, helpful

≠inconvenient, useless

Grouping stars by constellations is a **handy** way of mapping the sky. 별자리로 별을 분류하는 것은 하늘을 측량하는 편리한 방법이다.

group v. 무리로 만들다, 분류하다 n. 무리, 모임, 그룹, 집단

star n. 별, 운수, 운명, 별모양(의 것) adj. 탁월한, 인기 배우의

　　 v. 별을 흩뿌리다, 주연을 시키다, 별표를 달다, 반짝이다, 눈에 띄다

constellation n. 별자리, 성좌, 화려한 무리

way n. 길, 거리, 인생의 길, 방향, 진행, 방법

map v. 지도를 만들다, 측량하다, 위치하다 n. 지도

modulate

v. **1_조정하다** regulate, adjust

2_변화시키다 temper

3_변조하다 modify

Because noises **modulate** radio frequency, radio stations use a band of frequencies to prevent interference with other stations. 소음이 라디오 진동수를 변화시키기 때문에 라디오 방송국들은 다른 방송국에 의한 방해를 막기 위하여 한 무리의 진동수를 사용한다.

noise n. 소리, 잡음 v. 시끄럽게 지껄여 대다, 떠들고 다니다

frequency n. 진동수, 자주 일어나기, 빈도

station n. 방송국, 장소, 위치, 역, 정거장, 지역 본부, 신분 v. 배치하다

band n. 한 무리, 일행, 음악대, 밴드

prevent v. 막다, 방해하다

interference n. 방해, 훼방, 간섭

apparel

n. **의복, 의상** garments, attire, wardrobe, costume, outfit, clothes

When apprentices in colonial America satisfactorily completed their training periods, each received two sets of **apparel** as a graduation gift. 식민지 시절 미국에서 견습공들이 훌륭하게 훈련 기간을 끝냈을 때 졸업 선물로 2벌의 의복을 받았다.

apprentice n. 견습공, 실습생 v. 견습공으로 내보내다

satisfactorily adv. 만족할 만하게, 훌륭히, 더할 나위 없이

complete v. 완전하게 하다, 끝내다, 완투하다 adj. 완전한, 철저한, 완벽한

training n. 훈련, 양성, 좋은 컨디션 adj. 훈련의, 연습용의

period n. 기간, 시대, 세월 adj. 어떤 시대의

foe

n. **적** enemy, opponent, adversary, antagonist
≠ally, friend, comrade, associate

One type of cobra sprays venom into the eyes of a **foe** instead of biting it. 코브라 중에 한 종류는 적을 깨무는 대신 눈에 독을 뿜는다.

spray v. 뿌리다 n. 물보라, 분무

instead of ~대신에

bite v. 깨물다, 스며들다, 맞물다 n. 물어뜯기, 상처, 한 조각, 걸림

indemnify

v. **〜에게 배상하다** compensate, repay, reimburse, remunerate

Insurance companies in certain states do not have to **indemnify** a driver who causes an accident. 어떤 주에서는 보험회사들이 사고를 일으킨 운전자에게 배상할 필요가 없다.

insurance   n. 보험(업), 보험금, 보험 계약 adj. 승리를 확실하게 하는

certain   adj. 어떤, 확신하여, 틀림없는, 정해진

accident   n. 사고, 재난, (토지의) 고저

Lesson 13 Review Test

01 Foxes **aid** the farmer by attacking destructive rodents.

    ⓐ abandon   ⓑ inspire

    ⓒ elude   ⓓ help

02 Mount St. Helens **erupted** in March 1980 after one hundred twenty-three years of silence.

    ⓐ exploded   ⓑ split

    ⓒ roared   ⓓ disintegrated

03 In Europe tea drinking and **therefore** tea tables were innovations of the late 1600's.

    ⓐ consequently   ⓑ curiously

    ⓒ subsequently   ⓓ predictably

04 Benjamin Rush established the first free **dispensary** in the United States.

    ⓐ clinic   ⓑ school

    ⓒ library   ⓓ university

05 **Subterranean** streams have cut through limestone to form miles of passages and caves, such as Kentucky's Mammoth Cave.

    ⓐ Secondary   ⓑ Underground

    ⓒ Unharnessed   ⓓ Miniscule

06 Lampreys and hagfish have slimy, scaleless bodies shaped **somewhat** like the bodies of eels.

    ⓐ to some degree   ⓑ at some times

    ⓒ in some cases   ⓓ for some reason

07 Salesmanship is the ability to **sway** people to willingly buy products or support new ideas.

    ⓐ educate   ⓑ expect

    ⓒ allow   ⓓ persuade

08 Paul Bunyan has been the subject of numerous **tales**.

    ⓐ stories   ⓑ statues

    ⓒ songs   ⓓ speeches

09 Influenza is an acute viral disease of the respiratory tract that is extremely **contagious** and often reaches epidemic proportions.

    ⓐ communicable   ⓑ dangerous

    ⓒ prevalent   ⓓ toxic

10 **Itinerant** preachers played an important role in the United States religious history.

    ⓐ Protestant   ⓑ Evangelical

    ⓒ Unofficial   ⓓ Traveling

11 Grouping stars by constellations is a **handy** way of mapping the sky.

    ⓐ nice   ⓑ funny

    ⓒ manual   ⓓ convenient

12 Because noises **modulate** radio frequency, radio stations use a band of frequencies to prevent interference with other stations.

    ⓐ govern   ⓑ adapt

    ⓒ temper   ⓓ renovate

13 When apprentices in colonial America satisfactorily completed their training periods, each received two sets of **apparel** as a graduation gift.

    ⓐ clothes   ⓑ credentials

    ⓒ wages   ⓓ tools

14 One type of cobra sprays venom into the eyes of **a foe** instead of biting it.

    ⓐ an adversary   ⓑ a mouse

    ⓒ a mongoose   ⓓ a victim

15 Insurance companies in certain states do not have to **indemnify** a driver who causes an accident.

    ⓐ locate   ⓑ compensate

    ⓒ prosecute   ⓓ penalize

01	d	ⓐabandon=v. 포기하다 ⓑinspire=v. 고무(격려)하다 ⓒelude=v. 피하다
02	a	ⓑsplit=v. 쪼개다 ⓒroar=v. 으르렁거리다 ⓓdisintegrate=v. 붕괴(분해)시키다
03	a	ⓑcuriously=adv. 호기심에서 ⓒsubsequently=adv. 그 후에 ⓓpredictably=adv. 예상대로
04	a	ⓑschool=n. 학교 ⓒlibrary=n. 도서관 ⓓuniversity=n. 대학
05	b	ⓐSecondary=adj. 제2위의 ⓒUnharness=v. 마구를 풀다 ⓓMiniscule=n. 소문자
06	a	ⓑat some times=어느 때는 ⓒin some cases=어떤 경우에는 ⓓfor some reason=어떤 이유로
07	d	ⓐeducate=v. 교육하다 ⓑexpect=v. 기대하다 ⓒallow=v. 허락하다
08	a	ⓑstatue=n. 상(像) ⓒsong=n. 노래 ⓓspeech=n. 연설
09	a	ⓑdangerous=adj. 위험한 ⓒprevalent=adj. 만연한 ⓓtoxic=adj. 유독한
10	d	ⓐProtestant=adj. 신교도의 ⓑEvangelical=adj. 복음 전도의 ⓒUnofficial=adj. 비공식적인
11	d	ⓐnice=adj. 좋은 ⓑfunny=adj. 재미있는 ⓒmanual=adj. 손의(수동의)
12	c	ⓐgovern=v. 다스리다 ⓑadapt=v. 적응시키다 ⓓrenovate=v. ~을 새롭게 하다
13	a	ⓑcredential=n. 신임장 ⓒwage=n. 임금 ⓓtool=n. 연장
14	a	ⓑmouse=n. 쥐 ⓒmongoose=n. 몽구스(독사의 천적) ⓓvictim=n. 희생자
15	b	ⓐlocate=v. 위치를 ~에 정하다 ⓒprosecute=v. 수행하다, 기소하다 ⓓpenalize=v. 벌을 주다

L e s s o n 14

considerable

touchdown

polish

foolish

gem

coordinate

outstretched

applaud

liquid

cave

compulsory

withhold

ferocious

summit

feeble

considerable

adj. **1_중요한** significant≠insignificant, trivial, trifling

2_무시할 수 없는 notable≠nondescript

3_상당한 great≠minuscule

Mary Mapes Dodge exercised **considerable** influence on children's literature in the late nineteenth century. 메리 맵스 도지는 19세기 후반 어린이 문학에 상당한 영향을 미쳤다.

exercise v. (영향 등을) 미치다, ~을 이용하다, 완수하다, 훈련하다, 연습하다

　　　　n. 운동, 훈련, 연습, 교습, 실습

A **considerable** number of people went to the last night's concert. 상당히 많은 사람들이 어젯밤에 열린 음악회에 갔다.

concert n. 음악회, 연주회, 콘서트, 일치, 조화=harmony, 협동, 협력=agreement

　　　　adj. 음악회용의, 음악회에서 연주되는

touchdown

n. **착륙** landing, arrival

After thirty-six orbits, the first flight of the space shuttle Columbia was brought to a smooth **touchdown** at Edwards Air Force Base in California. 36회의 궤도 비행 후에 최초의 우주 왕복선 컬럼비아 호는 캘리포니아에 있는 에드워즈 공군 기지에 원활한 착륙을 했다.

orbit n. 궤도, 행로, 활동 범위, 세력권

　　　v. 주위를 궤도를 그리며 돌다, ~을 선회하다

shuttle n. 우주 왕복선, 정기 왕복 교통 기관 v. 실어 나르다 adj. 근거리 왕복의

smooth adj. 원활히 움직이는, 순조롭게 나아가는, 반들반들한, 매끄러운≠rough,

　　　　평탄한, 조용한=tranquil

base n. 기지, 토대, 기초, 근거 v. ~의 기초를 쌓다, 기초를 두다, ~을 주둔시키

　　　다, 배치하다 adj. 상스러운≠noble

polish

v. **1_ 닦다, ~의 윤을 내다** gloss, shine, varnish

≠dull, dim

2_ ~을 다듬다 refine, cultivate

≠vulgarize, cheapen

n. **광택** luster, elegance

adj. **닦여진**

Boxwood is close-grained, hard, and **polishes** nicely when waxed. 회양목은 나무결이 좁고 딱딱하며 왁스칠을 했을 때 윤이 잘 난다.

You'll need to **polish** your English before you go off to the United States. 미국 가기 전에 영어를 다듬을 필요가 있다.

foolish

adj. **1_ 미련한, 어리석은** unwise, imprudent

≠wise, sensible, reasonable

2_ 바보 같은 stupid

≠intelligent

3_ 우스운 ridiculous

It was commonly felt that the purchase of Alaska by the United States in 1867 was **foolish**. 1867년 미국이 알래스카를 구입한 것은 대체로 어리석은 행동이라고 여겨졌었다.

purchase n. 구매, 구매품 v. ~을 사다, 얻다, 쟁취하다, ~을 사기에 충분하다

It would be **foolish** to spend that much money on a car. 차에다 그렇게 많은 돈을 소비하는 것은 바보 같은 짓이다.

gem

n. **1_보석, 주옥** jewel, precious stone

2_귀중품, 일품 masterpiece, marvel, treasure

He is considered to be a real **gem** by many people. 많은 사람들이 그를 진정한 보석으로 여겼다.

real adj. 진짜의, 참된, 정말의=true, 현실의, 실제의=actual

The emerald, a rich green variety of beryl, is prized as a **gem**. 풍부한 녹색빛을 가진 에메랄드는 보석으로 평가되고 있다.

prize v. ~을 평가하다, ~을 소중히 하다, 귀중히 하다 n. 상, 귀중한 것

coordinate

adj. **동등한** equal, parallel, equivalent

n. **1_동등한 것**

2_동격자

3_좌표

v. **1_통합하다** integrate

2_조화시키다 harmonize

The cerebellum is the section of the brain that **coordinates** the movements of voluntary muscles. 소뇌는 수의근의 움직임을 통합시키는 뇌의 한 부분이다.

section n. 부분, 구역, 절단, 계층, (신문 등의) 난, 단면

brain n. 뇌, 골, 이해력, 지력, 수재, 두뇌 부분, 전자 장치

voluntary adj. 자진하여 하는, 자연히 일어나는

outstretched

adj. **펼친, 뻗친** spread

To the Sioux, the symbol of a cross represented a
dragonfly with its wings **outstretched**. 수족에게 있어, 십자가
의 상징은 날개를 활짝 편 잠자리를 나타낸다.

symbol n. 상징, 표상, 부호, 기호

cross n. 십자가, X표, 교차점, 이종 교배

　　　　v. 교차시키다, 십자가를 굿다, 건너다, 횡단하다, 거역하다

represent v. 나타내다, 상징하다, 대표하다, 상연하다, 표본이 되다

wing n. 날개, 팔, 좌우 배경, 좌·우익

applaud

v. **1_박수 갈채를 보내다** clap, cheer ≠boo

2_성원하다 hail, laud≠denounce, condemn

3_칭찬하다 acclaim, praise≠criticize, knock

The ideal listener has been humorously described as a
person who **applauds** vigorously. 이상적인 청중이란 열성적으
로 박수 갈채를 보내는 사람이라고 익살스럽게 표현한다.

ideal adj. 이상적인, 상상적인, 가공의, 이상주의의 n. 이상, 궁극의 목적, 공상

describe v. 표현하다, ∼이라고 말하다, 도형으로 설명하다

vigorously adv. 활력에 넘치게, 강하게, 힘차게

People **applaud** the President's decision to veto the bill.
사람들은 그 법안에 거부권을 행사하겠다는 대통령의 결정에 성원을 보
낸다.

liquid

adj. **1_ 액체의, 유동체의** wet, moist, damp≠hard, solid, dry

2_ 유동적인

3_ 현금으로 바꾸기 쉬운

n. **액체** fluid, solution, juice

Some people prefer a **liquid** soap to a bar of soap. 어떤 사람들은 고형 비누보다는 액체 비누를 더 선호한다.

prefer v. ~보다 더 좋아하다, 차라리 ~하기를 좋아하다

bar n. (막대기 모양의) 덩어리, 빗장, 판매대, 변호사단 v. 금지하다

Mechanics is the study of the effects of forces on bodies or **liquids** at rest or in motion. 기계학은 쉬고 있을 때와 움직이고 있을 때의 동체 혹은 액체에 대한 힘의 영향에 대한 학문이다.

rest n. 휴식, 해방, 정지, 쉼, 숙박소, 나머지 v. 쉬게 하다, 놓다, 보내다

motion n. 움직임, 운동, 동의, 제의, 제안, 내적 충동 v. 지시하다

cave

n. **굴, 동굴** cavern, tunnel

v. **1_ ~에 굴을 파다**

2_ 양보하다, 굴복하다 yield, retreat, give up

Many **caves** are formed by the pounding of ocean waves on the coastline. 많은 동굴들이 파도가 해안 지대를 반복적으로 세게 침으로써 형성된다.

pound v. 여러 번 세게 두들기다, 갈아 부수다, 치다 n. 파운드, 어망

coastline n. 해안지대

The United States' stand on terrorism is not to **cave** in at any cost. 테러리즘에 대한 미국의 입장은 어떠한 경우에도 굴복하지 않는 것이다.

stand n. 태도, 시기, 정지, 방어, 장소, 증인석, 관람석, 노점

at any cost 어떤 대가를 치러서라도, 무슨 수를 써서라도

compulsory

adj. **1_강제된** coercive

2_의무적인 obligatory, mandatory, binding

3_필수의 required

≠optional, voluntary, elective

After 1850, various states in the United States began to pass **compulsory** school attendance laws. 1850년 이후, 미국의 여러 주에서는 의무 교육 법안을 통과시키기 시작했다.

pass v. 통과하다, 지나가다, 합격하다, 눈감아주다, 초월하다, 경험하다, 건네주다

attendance n. 출석, 참석, 봉사, 시중, 간호

withhold

v. **1_보류하다** hold back, retain

2_억누르다 restrain≠promote, advance, release

A portion of an employee's wages is **withheld** by the employer for income taxes. 고용인들 임금의 일부는 소득세 때문에 고용주에 의해 보류되어 있다.

wage n. 임금, 급료 v. (전쟁, 투쟁, 토론 등을) 하다

He was found guilty of **withholding** information about the terrorist offences from the authority. 그는 테러범의 범죄에 대한 정보를 상부에 보고하지 않은 것으로 유죄 처분을 받았다.

guilty adj. 유죄의, 죄를 범한, 죄의

authority n. 정부, 권력, 직권, 근거

ferocious

adj. **1_사나운** savage, fierce

≠tame, docile, mild

2_잔인한 cruel

≠humane

When cornered, a bobcat is **ferocious**. 살쾡이가 구석에 몰리면 사나워진다.

corner v. ~을 구석으로 몰다 n. 구석, 가장자리, 길모퉁이, 궁지, 난처한 입장

summit

n. **1_정상, 꼭대기** top, peak, apex

≠bottom, foot

2_정상회담

The Argentine mountain named Aconcagua is the highest **summit** outside Central Asia. 아콩카과 산이라고 불리는 아르헨티나의 산은 중앙 아시아를 제외하고서는 가장 높은 꼭대기이다.

highest adj. 가장 높은, 최상의

outside prep. ~의 밖에, 범위를 넘어서, 제외하고 adj. 외부의, 옥외의

feeble

adj.

1_약한 weak

2_허약한 ailing, frail, fragile

3_부족한 inadequate, paltry

By **feeble** contractions, the jellyfish propels itself along, buoyed up by the surrounding water. 수축이 약하기 때문에, 해파리는 주위의 물로 인해 띄워져 주변을 떠다닌다.

contraction n. 수축, 단축, 절감, 제한, 축소

propel v. 추진시키다, 몰아대다

buoy v. 띄워놓다, 부표로 표시하다, 뜨다 n. 부이, 부표

surrounding adj. 둘러싸는, 주위의 n. 둘러싸고 있는 것, 포위

water n. 물, 광천수, 수량, 수위, 영해, 근해, 체액

Lesson 14 Review Test

01 Mary Mapes Dodge exercised **considerable** influence on children's literature in the late nineteenth century.

    ⓐ stylistic   ⓑ great

    ⓒ personal   ⓓ exclusive

02 After thirty-six orbits, the first flight of the space shuttle Columbia was brought to a smooth **touchdown** at Edwards Air Force Base in California.

    ⓐ conclusion   ⓑ crash

    ⓒ victory   ⓓ landing

03 Boxwood is close-grained, hard, and **polishes** nicely when waxed.

    ⓐ carves   ⓑ bleaches

    ⓒ shines   ⓓ wears

04 It was commonly felt that the purchase of Alaska by the United States in 1867 was **foolish**.

    ⓐ ridiculous   ⓑ excessive

    ⓒ necessary   ⓓ timely

05 The emerald, a rich green variety of beryl, is prized as a **gem**.

    ⓐ souvenir   ⓑ reward

    ⓒ jewel   ⓓ gift

06 The cerebellum is the section of the brain that **coordinates** the movements of voluntary muscles.

    ⓐ executes   ⓑ integrates

    ⓒ differentiates   ⓓ activates

07 To the Sioux, the symbol of a cross represented a dragonfly with its wings **outstretched**.

    ⓐ rising   ⓑ spread

    ⓒ torn   ⓓ missing

08 The ideal listener has been humorously described as a person who **applauds** vigorously.

    ⓐ plays   ⓑ attends

    ⓒ responds   ⓓ claps

09 Mechanics is the study of the effects of forces on bodies or **liquids** at rest or in motion.

    ⓐ atoms   ⓑ objects

    ⓒ gases   ⓓ fluids

10 Many **caves** are formed by the pounding of ocean waves on the coastline.

    ⓐ cavalries   ⓑ caverns

    ⓒ shells   ⓓ beaches

11 After 1850, various states in the United States began to pass **compulsory** school attendance laws.

    ⓐ harsh   ⓑ diversified

    ⓒ mandatory   ⓓ complicated

12 A portion of an employee's wages is **withheld** by the employer for income taxes.

    ⓐ borrowed   ⓑ retained

    ⓒ guaranteed   ⓓ paid

13 When cornered, a bobcat is **ferocious**.

    ⓐ careful   ⓑ fierce

    ⓒ frustrated   ⓓ trapped

14 The Argentine mountain named Aconcagua is the highest **summit** outside Central Asia.

    ⓐ volcano   ⓑ range

    ⓒ refuge   ⓓ peak

15 By **feeble** contractions, the jellyfish propels itself along, buoyed up by the surrounding water.

    ⓐ weak   ⓑ rhythmic

    ⓒ deliberate   ⓓ automatic

01	b	ⓐstylistic=adj. 문체(양식)의 ⓒpersonal=adj. 개인의 ⓓexclusive=adj. 배타적인
02	d	ⓐconclusion=n. 결말(결론) ⓑcrash=n. 추락 ⓒvictory=n. 승리
03	c	ⓐcarve=v. 베다 ⓑbleach=v. 표백하다 ⓓwear=v. 입다
04	a	ⓑexcessive=adj. 과도의 ⓒnecessary=adj. 필요한 ⓓtimely=adj. 때에 알맞은
05	c	ⓐsouvenir=n. 기념품 ⓑreward=n. 보수(보상) ⓓgift=n. 선물
06	b	ⓐexecute=v. 실행하다, 사형을 집행하다 ⓒdifferentiate=v. 구별짓다 ⓓactivate=v. 활성화하다
07	b	ⓐrising=adj. 떠오르는 ⓒtorn=tear(v. 찢다)의 과거분사 ⓓmissing=adj. 분실한
08	d	ⓐplay=v. 놀다 ⓑattend=v. ~에 참석하다 ⓒrespond=v. 대답하다
09	d	ⓐatom=n. 원자 ⓑobject=n. 대상 ⓒgas=n. 기체, 가스
10	b	ⓐcavalry=n. 기병(대) ⓒshell=n. 조가비 ⓓbeach=n. 바닷가
11	c	ⓐharsh=adj. 거친, 가혹한 ⓑdiversified=adj. 변화가 많은 ⓓcomplicated=adj. 복잡한
12	b	ⓐborrow=v. 빌리다 ⓒguarantee=v. 보증하다 ⓓpay=v. 지불하다
13	b	ⓐcareful=adj. 조심성 있는 ⓒfrustrated=adj. 좌절감을 느낀 ⓓtrap=v. 덫을 놓다, 속이다
14	d	ⓐvolcano=n. 화산 ⓑrange=n. 산맥, 범위 ⓒrefuge=n. 피난(처)
15	a	ⓑrhythmic=adj. 율동적인 ⓒdeliberate=adj. 고의의 ⓓautomatic=adj. 자동의

L e s s o n 15

eminence
receive
forecast
fidelity
ratify
improve
particularly
organization
accelerate
surpass
acrid
draw
wrath
isolate
barter

eminence

n. **1_고위, 높음**

2_명성 fame, renown, celebrity

Duke Ellington achieved **eminence** in the late 1920's. 듀크
엘링턴은 1920년대 후기에 명성을 얻었다.

achieve v. 달성하다, 얻다, 획득하다, 성과를 올리다

eminent

adj. 저명한

renowned, distinguished,
esteemed, noted ≠obscure,
mediocre, unknown

The students in the class were surprised when they found
out that such an **eminent** writer was coming to speak to
them. 교실에 있는 학생들은 그렇게 유명한 작가가 자신들에게 연설하
기 위해 왔다는 것을 알고서는 놀랐다.

speak v. 연설하다, 말하다, 담화하다, 변호를 하다

receive

v. **받다** get, accept

≠reject, refuse

In North America deciduous trees grow best on warmer
southern slopes that **receive** the most direct rays from the
sun. 북미에서 낙엽수는 태양으로부터 가장 직접적인 광선을 받는, 보다
따뜻한 남쪽 비탈에서 제일 잘 자란다.

deciduous adj. 낙엽성의, 일시적인

slope n. 경사지, 비탈, 경기의 후퇴 v. 경사지다

direct adj. 똑바른, 최단 거리의, 직계의, 직접의, 솔직한, 순전한

ray n. 한 줄기의 빛, 반지름 v. 빛을 발하다, 번쩍이다, 방사하다

forecast

v. **~을 예상하다, 예측하다** predict, foretell, foresee, prophesy

Large passenger planes often carry weather instruments with which to **forecast** storms. 커다란 여객기는 폭풍우를 예측하기 위해 종종 기상 기구를 휴대하고 다닌다.

passenger n. 승객, 여객

carry v. 지니다, 나르다, 가지고 가다, 전달하다, 통과시키다

weather n. 기상, 날씨, 일기, 악천후

storm n. 폭풍우, 세찬 비, 맹공격, 빗발, 격동

fidelity

n. **충실, 성실** faithfulness, loyalty, honesty, integrity
≠disloyalty, treachery, faithlessness, infidelity

The rosemary plant is an emblem of **fidelity** and remembrance. 로즈마리는 성실과 기억의 상징이다.

emblem n. 상징, 표상, 전형, 표지 도안 v. ~의 상징이 되다

remembrance n. 기억, 인상, 추억

ratify

v. **1 _ 허가하다** sanction, endorse

≠veto, oppose

2 _ 확인하다 confirm

3 _ 확증하다, 인증하다 approve, validate

≠repudiate

Before an amendment can be added to the Constitution, it must be **ratified** by three-fourths of the state legislatures. 헌법에 수정 조항이 추가되기 전에는 주의회의 4분의 3의 인증이 있어야만 한다.

amendment n. 수정, 개정, 수정조항, 개심

add v. 첨가하다, ~을 더하다, 합계하다

legislature n. 의회, 입법부

improve

v. **1 _ 개선하다** better, reform

≠impair, worsen, weaken, damage

2 _ 향상(발달)시키다 enhance, advance

≠deteriorate, decline

Although originally a German innovation, kindergarten got its real start in the United States as a movement to provide an **improved** learning environment for children. 유치원은 원래 독일에서 고안된 제도였지만, 미국에서 어린이들을 위해 개선된 교육 환경을 제공하기 위한 움직임의 하나로 진정한 출발을 하게 되었다.

kindergarten n. 유치원

particularly

adv. **1_특히** especially

2_현저하게 remarkably

3_상세히 specifically

4_면밀하게 in detail

Medicine depends on other fields of knowledge for basic information, **particularly** in some of its specialized branches. 의약은 기본 정보를 위한 지식의 분야에 따라 달라지는데 특히 전문화된 분야의 일부에서 더 그렇다.

field n. 활동 범위, 벌판, 땅, 산지, 경기장, 전투 지역

branch n. 분야, 부문, 가지, 분지, 분가, 지점

organization

n. **1_조직(체)** association, affiliation, corporation, club

≠disorder, chaos, confusion

2_협회

One needs to be careful when joining an unknown **organization**. 잘 알려지지 않은 조직체에 가입할 때는 조심해야 한다.

organizational

adj. 조직의

organize

v. 조직하다

We're very fortunate that we were able to spot John's **organizational** skill, otherwise we'd have fired him. 우리가 존의 조직적인 기술을 알아볼 수 있어서 정말 다행이다. 그렇지 않았으면 그를 해고했을 것이다.

organizer

n. 조직자 planner

Augusta Savage was one of the principal **organizers** of the Harlem Artists Guild. 아우구스타 새비지는 할렘 아티스트 길드의 중심적인 조직자 중의 한 명이었다.

accelerate

v. 1_**～을 촉진하다** hasten, quicken, expedite

빠르게 하다, 앞당기다 ≠slow down, delay

2_**～을 가속하다** speed

≠brake, decelerate,

The scientist's main goal was to **accelerate** the growth process. 과학자들의 주요한 목표는 성장 과정을 가속시키는 것이었다.

accelerated

adj. 속도가 붙은, 가속된 rapid

Current demographic trends, such as the fall in the birth rate, should favor **accelerated** economic growth in the long run. 출생률 감소처럼 현재의 인구 통계 흐름은 결국에는 가속된 경제 성장에 더 유리할 것이다.

surpass

v. **～을 능가하다, 넘다** exceed, excel, overpass

There is always excitement at the Olympic games when a previous record of performance is **surpassed**. 이전의 기록을 능가하게 될 때 올림픽 게임에서는 항상 흥분이 따른다.

excitement n. 흥분, 동요, 자극

previous adj. 이전의, 앞의, 시기 상조의, 조급한

record n. 기록, 최고 기록, 등록, 공식 문서, 성적, 경력, 음반 v. 기록하다

performance n. 성과, 연주, 상연, 흥행, 행위

acrid

adj. **1_쓴** bitter ≠ sweet

2_톡 쏘는 sharp, pungent, biting
≠ soft

Wild raspberries have a more **acrid** flavor than do cultivated raspberries. 야생 나무 딸기는 재배된 나무 딸기보다 더 신맛을 가지고 있다.

flavor n. 맛, 풍미, 향신료, 정취, 특색

cultivate v. 재배하다, 양식하다, 경작하다, 개척하다, 기르다, 즐기다

draw

v. **1_~을 끌다** pull, haul, drag, tow
≠ push, thrust, shove

2_매혹하다 attract, allure, entice
≠ repulse, dispel

3_스케치하다 sketch

4_작성하다 write

5_(결론 등을) ~에서 얻다 derive

Immigrants were **drawn** to the United States by the growing cities and industries. 이민자들은 성장하는 도시와 산업 때문에 미국으로 이끌려 왔다.

immigrant n. 이민, 이주자, 외래 동물 adj. 이민에 관한

growing adj. 성장의, 커지는, 증대하는

wrath

n. **분노** rage, anger, fury, resentment

≠pleasure, delight

In the ancient civilizations of Greece and Rome, thunder was believed to be a manifestation of the **wrath** of the gods. 그리스와 로마의 고대 문명에서, 천둥은 신들이 분노를 표현하는 것이라고 여겼다.

civilization n. 문명, 문명국, 문명인, 개화, 세련

thunder n. 천둥, 우레, 위협

manifestation n. 표현, 징후, 명시, 표명, 정견 발표, 시위

god n. 신, 창조주, 신상, 우상

isolate

v. **1_~을 떼어놓다** separate, set apart, detach

≠unite, attach, combine

2_고립시키다 segregate, sequester, seclude

3_~을 격리하다 quarantine

His political stands **isolated** him from his peers. 그의 정치적 입장은 동료들로부터 그를 고립시키는 결과를 가져왔다.

isolated

adj. 고립된, 격리된 solitary

isolation

n. 1_고립 seclusion, solitude

2_분리 separation, detachment

Many of novelist Carson McCuller's characters are **isolated**, disappointed people. 소설가 카슨 매컬러스의 소설에 나오는 많은 등장인물은 고립되고, 좌절한 사람들이다.

barter

v. **물물교환을 하다** trade, exchange

n. **물물교환**

By producing an excess amount of some household articles, a New England colonial family could **barter** with other families. 일부 가정용 물품을 초과 생산하게 되어, 뉴잉글랜드 식민지 지역 가족은 다른 가족들과 물물교환을 할 수 있었다.

excess   n. 초과, 지나침, 무절제

amount   n. 양, 총액, 결과   v. ~에 이르다, 결과적으로 ~이 되다

household   n. 가족, 세대   adj. 가족의, 가정의, 보통의, 흔한

Lesson 15 Review Test

01 Duke Ellington achieved **eminence** in the late 1920's.

    ⓐ fame   ⓑ leadership

    ⓒ experience   ⓓ wealth

02 In North America deciduous trees grow best on warmer southern slopes that **receive** the most direct rays from the sun.

    ⓐ touch   ⓑ get

    ⓒ greet   ⓓ hold

03 Large passenger planes often carry weather instruments with which to **forecast** storms.

    ⓐ impede   ⓑ divert

    ⓒ diagram   ⓓ predict

04 The rosemary plant is an emblem of **fidelity** and remembrance.

    ⓐ thoughtfulness   ⓑ tenderness

    ⓒ faithfulness   ⓓ happiness

05 Before an amendment can be added to the Constitution, it must be **ratified** by three-fourths of the state legislatures.

    ⓐ discussed   ⓑ proposed

    ⓒ endorsed   ⓓ revised

06 Although originally a German innovation, kindergarten got its real start in the United States as a movement to provide **an improved** learning environment for children.

    ⓐ an easy   ⓑ a playful

    ⓒ an open   ⓓ a better

07 Medicine depends on other fields of knowledge for basic information, **particularly** in some of its specialized branches.

    ⓐ conventionally   ⓑ obviously

    ⓒ especially   ⓓ inevitably

08 Augusta Savage was one of the principal **organizers** of the Harlem Artists Guild.

    ⓐ planners   ⓑ employees

    ⓒ actors   ⓓ recipients

09 Current demographic trends, such as the fall in the birth rate, should favor **accelerated** economic growth in the long run.

    ⓐ fashionable   ⓑ rapid

    ⓒ modern   ⓓ contemporary

10 There is always excitement at the Olympic games when a previous record of performance is **surpassed**.

    ⓐ exceeded   ⓑ matched

    ⓒ maintained   ⓓ announced

11 Wild raspberries have a more **acrid** flavor than do cultivated raspberries.

    ⓐ defined   ⓑ gratifying

    ⓒ recognizable   ⓓ bitter

12 Immigrants were **drawn** to the United States by the growing cities and industries.

    ⓐ drafted   ⓑ transported

    ⓒ attracted   ⓓ ordered

13 In the ancient civilizations of Greece and Rome, thunder was believed to be a manifestation of the **wrath** of the gods.

    ⓐ spirit   ⓑ voice

    ⓒ power   ⓓ anger

14 Many of novelist Carson McCuller's characters are **isolated**, disappointed people.

    ⓐ solitary   ⓑ grumpy

    ⓒ feeble   ⓓ frugal

15 By producing an excess amount of some household articles, a New England colonial family could **barter** with other families.

    ⓐ share   ⓑ trade

    ⓒ repair   ⓓ sell

01	a	ⓑleadership=n. 지도(권) ⓒexperience=n. 경험 ⓓwealth=n. 부, 재산
02	b	ⓐtouch=v. 대다, 만지다 ⓒgreet=v. 인사하다 ⓓhold=v. 잡다
03	d	ⓐimpede=v. 방해하다 ⓑdivert=v. 전환하다 ⓒdiagram=v. 그림(도표)으로 나타내다
04	c	ⓐthoughtfulness=n. 사려 깊음 ⓑtenderness=n. 유연함 ⓓhappiness=n. 행복
05	c	ⓐdiscuss=v. 논의하다 ⓑpropose=v. 제의하다 ⓓrevise=v. 교정(수정, 개정)하다
06	d	ⓐeasy=adj. 쉬운 ⓑplayful=adj. 놀기 좋아하는 ⓒopen=adj. 열린
07	c	ⓐconventionally=adv. 인습적으로, 진부하게 ⓑobviously=adv. 분명히 ⓓinevitably=adv. 피할 수 없는
08	a	ⓑemployee=n. 피고용인 ⓒactor=n. 배우(남) ⓓrecipient=n. 수령인
09	b	ⓐfashionable=adj. 최신 유행의 ⓒmodern=adj. 현대의 ⓓcontemporary=adj. 현대의, 최신의
10	a	ⓑmatch=v. 조화하다(어울리다) ⓒmaintain=v. 유지하다 ⓓannounce=v. 알리다
11	d	ⓐdefine=v. 정의를 내리다 ⓑgratifying=adj. 만족한 ⓒrecognizable=adj. 인식(분간)할 수 있는
12	c	ⓐdraft=v. 기초(기안)하다 ⓑtransport=v. 수송(운송)하다 ⓓorder=v. 명령(주문)하다
13	d	ⓐspirit=n. 정신 ⓑvoice=n. 목소리 ⓒpower=n. 힘
14	a	ⓑgrumpy=adj. 성미 까다로운 ⓒfeeble=adj. 연약한 ⓓfrugal=adj. 절약하는
15	b	ⓐshare=v. 나누다 ⓒrepair=v. 수리하다 ⓓsell=v. 팔다

L e s s o n 16

Fourth Week

tradition

sphere

faith

autocrat

immense

magnificent(ly)

claw

supplant

fury

apt

remedy

investigate

notion

nomadic

abuse

tradition

n. **1_전통** practice, custom

2_전설 folklore

Voluntarism is a **tradition** in the United States, but how many people realize that up to fifty-two percent of the adult population is engaged in some kind of volunteer service? 자원봉사제는 미국의 전통이다. 그러나 성인 인구의 52퍼센트 정도가 어떤 종류로든 자원봉사와 관련되어 있다는 사실을 인식하고 있는 사람이 과연 얼마나 될까?

realize v. 인식하다, 확실히 이해하다, 깨닫다, 실현하다

adult n. 성인, 어른 adj. 성인의, 어른의

traditional

adj. 1_전통(적)의 conventional, customary

2_전설의

engage v. 관여시키다, 끌어들이다, 고용하다, 사로잡다, 교전시키다, 약속하다, 약혼하다

service n. 봉사, 공헌, 활약, 공급, 서비스, 손님 시중

sphere

n. **1_구체** ball, globe

2_영역, 범위 province, range, scope

The porcupine fish, a tropical marine puffer fish found worldwide, gulps air and then swells up to the shape of a **sphere**. 전 세계적으로 발견되는 열대 해양 복어인 가시복어는 공기를 한 입에 들이마시고 몸이 둥근 형태가 될 때까지 부풀린다.

tropical adj. 열대의, 몹시 더운, 열렬한

marine adj. 해양용의, 바다의, 항해의 n. 해병, 선박

gulp v. 한 입에 삼키다, 목을 꿀꺽하다 n. 꿀꺽꿀꺽, 한 입에 삼키는 양

swell v. 부풀다, 팽창하다, 증대하다

Some are worried that the government is extending its **sphere** of influence to cover all parts of our lives. 일부에서는 정부가 우리 삶의 모든 분야에 이르도록 그 영향력을 확대하고 있다고 걱정하고 있다.

faith

n. **1_신뢰** trust, confidence

2_신앙 belief, creed

3_신념

It was through his **faith** that he was able to overcome the most difficult time in his life. 그가 자신의 인생에서 가장 힘든 시기를 극복할 수 있었던 것은 바로 그의 신념을 통해서였다.

overcome v. 극복하다, 압도하다, 이기다, 억누르다

difficult adj. 힘드는, 어려운, 성미 까다로운, 불리한, 고통스러운

faithful

adj. 1_성실한 trustworthy

2_충실한 loyal, devoted

≠faithless

A married couple is bound by law to be **faithful** to each other. 결혼한 사람들은 법적으로 서로에게 성실해야 할 의무가 있다.

bound adj. 묶인, 가두어진, 구속된 n. 구역, 범위=limit, 한계 v. bind(묶다)의 과거형

Feudal society depended on the existence of **faithful** vassals. 봉건 사회는 충실한 가신들이 있었기에 가능했다.

vassal n. (봉건 시대의) 가신, 봉신, 부하, 종복

autocrat

n. **독재(자), 군주** dictator, tyrant, authoritarian, totalitarian

Within their courtrooms, judges are virtual **autocrats**.
자신들의 법정 내부에서 재판관은 사실상 독재자들이다.

within prep. ~의 내부에, ~이내에, 범위 내에, ~의 안쪽에

courtroom n. 법정

judge n. 재판관, 심사원, 감정가 v. 재판하다, 판결을 내리다, 판정하다

virtual adj. 사실상의, 실질상의, 효과적인

immense

adj. **막대한, 무한한, 끝없는** huge, vast, great, enormous, massive, tremendous, gigantic

≠small, tiny, minute

Cowboy films traditionally open with a view of an **immense** spread of rugged terrain. 카우보이 영화는 전통적으로 바위투성이 지형이 끝없이 펼쳐진 광경으로 시작한다.

film n. 영화 산업, 얇은 층, 가는 실 v. 얇은 껍질로 덮다

open v. 시작하다, 열다, 뜨다, 펼치다, 개발하다, 장애물을 제거하다, 폭로하다

view n. 광경, 경치, 전망, 보기, 시각, 조망, 목적, 개론 v. 보다, 바라보다, 고려하다

rugged adj. 바위투성이의, 울퉁불퉁한, 거칠거칠한, 험악한, 어려운, 억센

terrain n. 지형, 지세

---

magnificent(ly)

adj.(adv.)

1_장대한, 장엄한 grand, splendid, grandiose, imposing, superb≠humble, modest, ordinary

2_당당한 stately

3_훌륭한 impressive, outstanding, superb

The Empire State Building is reputed to be one of the **magnificent** buildings constructed in the twentieth century. 엠파이어 스테이트 빌딩은 20세기에 건설된 장엄한 빌딩 중의 하나로 여겨진다.

repute v. ~이라고 생각하다, 간주하다 n. 평판, 세평, 호평

The human brain is the most **magnificently** organized concentration of matter in the known universe. 인간의 뇌는 우주에 알려진 물질 중 가장 훌륭하게 조직된 집합체다.

organize v. 조직하다, 편성하다, 설립하다, 계획하다

concentration n. 집합물, 집중(상태), 전념, 농축, 응축

claw

n. **발톱** nail

v. **손(발)톱으로 할퀴다** scratch, tear, pull

When playing with a cat, beware of its **claw**. 고양이와 놀 때
는 발톱을 조심해.

beware v. 조심하다, 주의하다

A male puma **claws** trees to mark its territory. 수컷 퓨마는
자신의 세력권을 표시하기 위하여 나무를 발톱으로 할퀸다.

mark v. 표시하다, 나타내다, 특징짓다, 채점하다

　　 n. 자국, 표시, 기호, 징조, 감명, 평점

territory n. 세력권, 영역, 지역, 영토, 담당구역

supplant

v. **1_대신하다** replace, displace

2_탈취하다

3_〜에 대신하다 succeed

Penicillin quickly **supplanted** the sulfa drugs in the
treatment of bacterial diseases. 페니실린은 세균성 질병의 치료
에서 술파제 약품을 빠르게 대신해냈다.

quickly adv. 빨리, 서둘러, 신속히

treatment n. 치료, 처치, 대우, 취급

fury

n. **1_격노, 격분** rage, anger, wrath, furor

≠serenity, peace

2_열광 frenzy, rampage

≠calm, self-control, detachment

Music expresses, at different moments, serenity or exuberance, regret or triumph, **fury** or delight. 음악은 매순간 평온함이나 풍부함. 유감이나 승리의 기쁨, 격노나 기쁨을 표현한다.

express v. 표현하다, 나타내다, (물건을) 급송하다, 짜다

adj. 명시된, 특별한, 급행편의 n. 급행, 특사

moment n. 순간, 단시간, 한때, 현재, 시기, 기회

exuberance n. 풍부, 윤택

regret n. 유감, 후회, 슬픔, 낙심, 애도

triumph n. 승리의 기쁨, 승리, 정복, 위업 v. 승리를 거두다, 번성하다

delight n. 기쁨, 즐거움, 유쾌 v. 기쁘게 하다, 즐거워하다

apt

adj. **1_~하기 쉬운** likely

2_~하는 경향이 있는 liable, tending, disposed, likely

≠inapt, slow, difficult

A drastic change in one part of the environment is **apt** to cause an equally drastic, but unexpected, change somewhere else. 환경에서 한 부분의 격렬한 변화는 다른 지역에서는 똑같이 격렬하지만 뜻밖의 변화를 일으키는 경향이 있다.

drastic adj. 격렬한, 강렬한, 과감한

unexpected adj. 뜻밖의, 예기치 않은, 생각지도 않은, 불시의

remedy

n. **1_치료, 의료** treatment, cure

2_교정 correction

v. **1_고치다** correct

2_치료하다 heal, cure

It is widely known that vitamin C is one of the effective **remedies** for the common cold. 비타민 C는 일반적인 감기에 효과적인 치료제의 하나로 널리 알려져 있다.

widely adv. 널리, 광범위하게, 크게, 현저하게

effective adj. 효과적인, 유효한, 감동적인, 실제의

Some of technology's negative aspects are extremely hard to **remedy**. 기술발전의 일부 부정적 측면은 교정하기가 아주 어렵다.

aspect n. 측면, 외관, 모양, 양상, 표정, 국면

investigate

v. **1_조사하다** search, inquire, probe, scrutinize, survey, track, trace

2_연구하다 study, research, examine

The Crab Nebula, a striking formation in the constellation Taurus, may be the most thoroughly **investigated** object of modern astrophysical science. 황소자리에서 인상적인 형태를 하고 있는 게자리는 현대 천체 물리학에서 가장 완전하게 조사된 대상일 것이다.

striking adj. 인상적인, 현저한, 타격의, 치는

object n. 대상, 객체, 목적, 목표, 물건, 물체 v. 반대하다, 싫어하다

astrophysical adj. 천체 물리학의

investigation

n. 조사, 연구, 심사 inquiry, search, examination, inspection, review

notion

n. **1_관념, 개념** conception, belief

2_생각, 의견 idea, thought, opinion,

Biological determinism is a **notion** that has important
philosophical implications and political consequences.
생물학적 결정론은 중요한 철학적 함축과 정치적인 결론을 내포한
개념이다.

biological adj. 생물학의, 생물체의

determinism n. 결정론

implication n. 함축, 포함, 연루, 밀접한 관계

consequence n. 결론, 결과, 중요성, 중대함

nomadic

adj. **유목의, 방랑의** wandering, migrant, migratory, itinerant,
vagabond

≠settled, rooted

Sometime between A.D. 1000 and A.D. 1500, the **nomadic**
Navajo arrived in the American Southwest. A.D. 1000년에서
A.D. 1500년 사이의 어느 시기에, 방랑하던 나바호족은 미남서부에 도착
했다.

arrive v. 도착하다, 이르다, 나타나다, 오다

abuse

v. **1_ 남용하다, 악용하다** misuse, harm

2_ 학대하다 mistreat

n. **1_ 남용, 오용** insult, wrong

2_ 학대 mistreatment

He was very careful about not **abusing** his political power.

그는 자신의 정치적인 힘을 남용하지 않으려고 아주 조심했다.

careful adj. 조심스러운, 주의 깊은, 소중히 하는, 면밀한

power n. 힘, 능력, 특별한 재능, 권력

The Grange, an agrarian organization founded in 1867,

sought to correct economic **abuses** through cooperative

enterprise. 1867년에 설립된 농업 기구인 농민 공제 조합에서는

협동체를 통해 경제적인 남용을 바로잡기 위해 노력했다.

cooperative adj. 협동하는, 협조적인, 협동조합의 n. 협동조합, 조합식 아파트

enterprise n. 사업, 일의 기획, 참가, 종사, 기업

Lesson 16 Review Test

01 Feudal society depended on the existence of **faithful** vassals.

    ⓐ diligent   ⓑ gullible

    ⓒ pious   ⓓ loyal

02 The porcupine fish, a tropical marine puffer fish found worldwide, gulps air and then swells up to the shape of a **sphere**.

    ⓐ spear   ⓑ sponge

    ⓒ ball   ⓓ roll

03 Voluntarism is a **tradition** in the United States, but how many people realize that up to fifty-two percent of the adult population is engaged in some kind of volunteer service?

    ⓐ need   ⓑ business

    ⓒ diversion   ⓓ custom

04 Within their courtrooms, judges are virtual **autocrats**.

    ⓐ automatons   ⓑ dictators

    ⓒ dealers   ⓓ coaches

05 Cowboy films traditionally open with a view of **an immense** spread of rugged terrain.

    ⓐ a beautiful   ⓑ an unsettled

    ⓒ a vast   ⓓ an immediate

06 The human brain is the most **magnificently** organized concentration of matter in the known universe.

    ⓐ strangely   ⓑ superbly

    ⓒ perplexingly   ⓓ completely

07 A male puma **claws** trees to mark its territory.

    ⓐ tears down   ⓑ climbs

    ⓒ leaves its smell on   ⓓ scratches

08 Penicillin quickly **supplanted** the sulfa drugs in the treatment of bacterial diseases.

    ⓐ was added to   ⓑ improved

    ⓒ replaced   ⓓ provided support for

09 Music expresses, at different moments, serenity or exuberance, regret or triumph, **fury** or delight.

    ⓐ darkness   ⓑ grief

    ⓒ disgust   ⓓ anger

10 A drastic change in one part of the environment is **apt** to cause an equally drastic, but unexpected, change somewhere else.

    ⓐ likely   ⓑ necessary

    ⓒ advised   ⓓ rumored

11 Some of technology's negative aspects are extremely hard to **remedy**.

    ⓐ understand   ⓑ identify

    ⓒ utilize   ⓓ correct

12 The Crab Nebula, a striking formation in the constellation Taurus, may be the most thoroughly **investigated** object of modern astrophysical science.

    ⓐ scrutinized   ⓑ admired

    ⓒ repudiated   ⓓ invested

13 Biological determinism is **a notion** that has important philosophical implications and political consequences.

    ⓐ an idea   ⓑ a policy

    ⓒ a commentary   ⓓ an insinuation

14 Sometime between A.D. 1000 and A.D. 1500, the **nomadic** Navajo arrived in the American Southwest.

    ⓐ exotic   ⓑ wandering

    ⓒ flourishing   ⓓ ancient

15 The Grange, an agrarian organization founded in 1867, sought to correct economic **abuses** through cooperative enterprise.

    ⓐ earnings   ⓑ failures

    ⓒ indicators   ⓓ wrongs

L e s s o n 17

differ

contiguous

foot

melodious

serene

prolong

famous

painstaking(ly)

flawless

brink

barely

stockpile

stumble

abhor

caustic

differ

v. **1_다르다** contrast, vary, stand apart

≠match, correspond, coincide

2_견해 차이가 나다 dispute, oppose, contest, deviate, dissent

≠consent, concur, agree

Radishes **differ** in shape, size, and color, according to the type. 무는 종류에 따라 형태, 크기, 색깔이 다르다.

size n. 크기, 대소, 규모, 치수, 형 v. ~을 크기에 따라 분류하다, ~을 어떤 크기로 만들다

according to ~에 따라서

contiguous

adj. **1_접촉하는, 인접하는** touching, adjoining

≠distant, far, remote, removed, detached

2_근접한 immediate, adjacent, neighboring, near

The Pacific Ocean and its **contiguous** seas cover more than one-third of the Earth. 태평양과 그에 인접한 바다는 지구의 3분의 1 이상을 이룬다.

earth n. 지구, 이승, 현세, 지구 표면, 지상, 흙

foot

n. **1_밑부분, 기슭** base, basis, foundation, floor

≠head, summit

2_밑바닥 bottom

≠top

Potholes are scooped-out hollows that often form beneath the rapids of a river or at the **foot** of a waterfall. 팟호울은 움푹 파인 구멍인데 흔히 강의 급류 아래에 혹은 폭포의 밑바닥에 형성된다.

pothole n. 파인 구멍, 깊은 구멍, 구혈 v. 동굴을 탐험하다

hollow n. 구멍, 움푹 들어간 곳, 골짜기 adj. 속이 빈, 표면이 우묵한, 공허한, 내

용이 없는

waterfall n. 폭포, 낙수

melodious

adj. **선율이 아름다운, 곡조가 좋은** tuneful, musical, melodic

≠harsh, cacophonous, noisy

Whippoorwills are shy birds, generally nocturnal, which emit **melodious** calls. 쪽독새는 수줍음이 많은 새로, 일반적으로 야행성이며 선율이 아름다운 소리를 낸다.

shy adj. 부끄럼 타는, 겁많은, 꺼리는, 의심 많은

emit v. 방출하다=discharge, 공포하다, 발행하다

melody

n. 1_멜로디, 선율

2_곡조, 가락

serene   adj. **1_고요한, 잔잔한** calm, tranquil, peaceful
                ≠stormy, cloudy, turbulent

    2_화창한 clear, bright, fair

    3_평화스러운 peaceful, pleasant
                ≠anxious, nervous, disturbed

The forests of the Green Mountains of Vermont are luxuriant, fragrant, and **serene**. 버몬트에 있는 그린 마운틴스의 숲은 울창하고, 향기로우며 고요하다.

luxuriant adj. 울창한, 풍부한, 무성한, 비옥한

fragrant adj. 향기로운, 냄새 좋은, 달콤한

---

prolong   v. **1_늘이다, 연장하다** extend, lengthen, continue
                ≠shorten, abbreviate, limit

    2_오래 끌다 protract, draw out, drag out ≠ curtail, cut short

After having a great time at the resort, the Smiths want to **prolong** their vacation. 휴양지에서 즐겁게 지낸 후, 스미스 씨 가족은 휴가를 연장하기를 원한다.

resort n. 휴양지, 번화가, 의지하기

vacation n. 휴가, 방학, 중지, 비워주기 v. 휴가를 얻다(보내다)

prolonged

adj. 장기의 lengthy

After **prolonged** exertion, it is difficult for the body to continue being active. 오랫동안 고된 일을 한 후, 신체가 계속적으로 활동적인 상태를 유지하는 것은 어렵다.

exertion n. 고된 일, 격심한 활동, 노력, 진력

active adj. 활동적인, 활약하고 있는, 분주한, 진행중인, 민첩한, 재빠른

famous

adj. **유명한, 저명한** renowned, prominent, well-known, celebrated, eminent, acclaimed

≠unknown, obscure, anonymous, unrecognized

Willie Mays, the **famous** American baseball player, hit 660 home runs in his professional career. 미국의 유명한 야구 선수인 윌리 메이스는 그의 프로 선수 경력 동안 660개의 홈런을 쳤다.

hit v. 치다, 때리다, 충돌하다, 부탁하다

professional adj. 직업의, 전문직의, 전문의, 의도적인 n. 직업 선수, 전문가

career n. 직업, 경력, 활동, 성공, 진전, 속력

painstaking(ly)

adj.(adv.)
1_ **성실한** careful, diligent
2_ **정성을 들이는** assiduous, precise≠sloppy, clumsy, careless
3_ **엄밀한** meticulous

n. **수고, 정성, 고심**

Scientists performed a **painstaking** experiment. 과학자들은 정성을 들이는 실험을 행한다.

perform v. 행하다, 상연하다, 연기하다, 연주하다

In order to validate their findings, paleontologists **painstakingly** examine all of the fossils they dig up. 자신들이 발견한 것들을 입증하기 위해, 고생물학자들은 파낸 모든 화석을 정성스럽게 조사한다.

validate v. 입증하다, 실증하다, 유효하게 하다

fossil n. 화석 adj. 화석상의, 발굴된, 시대에 뒤진

dig v. 파다, 파서 찾아내다, 찔러넣다, 감상하다

flawless

adj. **1_흠 없는** unblemished

≠blemished, spotted, flawed

2_완벽한 perfect

≠imperfect, flaw, defect, fault

A **flawless** diamond is worth a great deal more than one with imperfections. 완벽한 다이아몬드는 결함이 있는 것보다 상당한 가치가 있다.

worth adj. 가치가 있는, 재산이 있는

a great deal 상당히, 매우

imperfection n. 결함, 불완전, 불충분

brink

n. **1_가장자리** edge, margin, border

≠center, core

2_~하기 직전 verge

3_(아슬아슬한) 고비

Six of the seven species of sea turtles in the world are being driven to the **brink** of extinction. 세계에 있는 바다거북의 7종 중에서 6종은 멸종 위기에 처해 있다.

world n. (전) 세계, 지구, 인간, 사회, 영역, 우주, 천지

drive to (어떤 상태에) 이르게 하다, 무리하게 (~에) 이르게 하다

extinction n. 멸종, 소화, 소멸, 단절, 폐지

barely

adv. **1_간신히, 가까스로** just, hardly, only, merely, at most
2_거의 ~않다 scarcely
3_빈약하게

In 1920 the number of people living in the United States totaled **barely** 106 million. 1920년에도 미국에 살고 있던 사람의 수는 1억 6백만 명이 간신히 되는 것으로 집계되었다.

live v. 살다, 생존하다 adj. 살아 있는, 생기 있는, 실황인

total v. 합계되다, 합치다 n. 총액, 총량, 전체 adj. 전부의, 완전한, 총력의

stockpile

n. **비축, 재고** stock
v. **비축(저장)하다** store, stock, amass, accumulate
≠deplete, spend, use, exhaust, squander

The United Nations has **stockpiled** supplies of food throughout the world for use in time of emergency. 유엔은 비상시에 사용하기 위해 전 세계에 음식물을 비축하고 있다.

in time of ~의 때에

stumble

v. **1_ 넘어지다, 비틀거리다** trip, fall

2_ 실수하다 blunder, err, fumble

3_ 우연히 발견하다 come upon by chance

The knee-jerk reflex is activated when a person **stumbles**.
무릎 반사는 사람이 넘어질 때 활성화된다.

knee n. 무릎, 무릎 부분 v. ~을 무릎으로 차다, 무릎을 꿇다

jerk n. 갑작스런 움직임, 경련, 반사운동

reflex n. 반사 행동, 그림자 반영된 모습

abhor

v. **1_ 혐오하다** detest, despise, loathe, hate

2_ 거부하다 reject

≠accept, affirm, sanction

3_ 멸시하다 disdain

≠respect, admire

The Shakers, an austere religious community, **abhorred**
ornamentation. 금욕적인 종교 공동체인 셰이커 교도들은 장식을 혐
오한다.

austere adj. 금욕적인, 엄숙한, 진지한, 무거운

ornamentation n. 장식, 장식물

caustic

n. **부식제**

adj. **1_부식성의** corrosive

≠neutral, inactive, inert

2_신랄한 biting, harsh, acrimonious

≠mild, gentle, soothing

The wit of the comedian W. C. Fields was quite **caustic**.

코미디언 필드의 위트는 아주 신랄하다.

quite adv. 아주=very, 완전히

Lesson 17　Review Test

01 The forests of the Green Mountains of Vermont are luxuriant, fragrant, and **serene**.

    ⓐ peaceful   ⓑ vigilant

    ⓒ desolate   ⓓ fanciful

02 In order to validate their findings, paleontologists **painstakingly** examine all of the fossils they dig up.

    ⓐ interestedly   ⓑ meticulously

    ⓒ hopefully   ⓓ miserably

03 **A flawless** diamond is worth a great deal more than one with imperfections.

    ⓐ A dauntless   ⓑ An indivisible

    ⓒ A flashy   ⓓ An unblemished

04 Six of the seven species of sea turtles in the world are being driven to the **brink** of extinction.

    ⓐ verge   ⓑ end

    ⓒ beach   ⓓ height

05 The Pacific Ocean and its **contiguous** seas cover more than one-third of the Earth.

    ⓐ adjoining   ⓑ exquisite

    ⓒ glistening   ⓓ voluminous

06 Potholes are scooped-out hollows that often form beneath the rapids of a river or at the **foot** of a waterfall.

    ⓐ edge   ⓑ boot

    ⓒ toe   ⓓ bottom

07 In 1920 the number of people living in the United States totaled **barely** 106 million.

    ⓐ twice   ⓑ scarcely

    ⓒ beyond   ⓓ approximately

08 The United Nations has **stockpiled** supplies of food throughout the world for use in time of emergency.

    ⓐ sold   ⓑ amassed

    ⓒ traded   ⓓ stockaded

09 After **prolonged** exertion it is difficult for the body to continue being active.

    ⓐ vigorous   ⓑ anticipated

    ⓒ lengthy   ⓓ high-powered

10 Willie Mays, the **famous** American baseball player, hit 660 home runs in his professional career.

    ⓐ confident   ⓑ humble

    ⓒ frank   ⓓ celebrated

11 The knee-jerk reflex is activated when a person **stumbles**.

    ⓐ hits the ground   ⓑ jumps in the air

    ⓒ trips   ⓓ prays

12 The Shakers, an austere religious community, **abhorred** ornamentation.

    ⓐ tolerated   ⓑ criticized

    ⓒ loathed   ⓓ envied

13 The wit of the comedian W. C. Fields was quite **caustic**.

    ⓐ clever   ⓑ subtle

    ⓒ fiery   ⓓ biting

14 Radishes **differ** in shape, size, and color, according to the type.

ⓐ vary ⓑ diffuse

ⓒ disagree ⓓ propagate

15 Whippoorwills are shy birds, generally nocturnal, which emit **melodious** calls.

ⓐ odious ⓑ private

ⓒ tuneful ⓓ raspy

01	a	ⓑvigilant=adj. 자지 않고 지키는, 경계하는 ⓒdesolate=adj. 황량한 ⓓfanciful=adj. 공상에 잠기는
02	b	ⓐinterestedly=adv. 흥미롭게 ⓒhopefully=adv. 희망을 가지고 ⓓmiserably=adv. 비참하게
03	d	ⓐdauntless=adj. 겁이 없는 ⓑindivisible=adj. 불가분의 ⓒflashy=adj. 섬광적인
04	a	ⓑend=n. 끝 ⓒbeach=n. 해변 ⓓheight=n. 길이, 키
05	a	ⓑexquisite=adj. 절묘한 ⓒglistening=adj. 반짝이는 ⓓvoluminous=adj. 부피가 큰
06	d	ⓐedge=n. 가장자리 ⓑboot=n. 장화 ⓒtoe=n. 발가락
07	b	ⓐtwice=n. 두 번 ⓒbeyond=prep. ~을 넘어서 ⓓapproximately=adv. 대략
08	b	ⓐsell=v. 팔다 ⓒtrade=v. 장사하다 ⓓstockade=v. 방책을 치다
09	c	ⓐvigorous=adj. 정력적인 ⓑanticipate=v. 예기하다 ⓓhigh-powered=강력한
10	d	ⓐconfident=adj. 자신만만한 ⓑhumble=adj. 비천한 ⓒfrank=adj. 솔직한
11	c	ⓐhit the ground=땅을 치다 ⓑjump in the air=공중에서 점프하다 ⓓpray=v. 기원하다
12	c	ⓐtolerate=v. 참다 ⓑcriticize=v. 비평(비판)하다 ⓓenvy=v. 부러워하다
13	d	ⓐclever=adj. 영리한 ⓑsubtle=adj. 민감한 ⓒfiery=adj. 불같은
14	a	ⓑdiffuse=v. 흐트러뜨리다, 퍼뜨리다 ⓒdisagree=v. 일치하지 않다 ⓓpropagate=v. 번식(증식)시키다
15	c	ⓐodious=adj. 증오할, 밉살스러운 ⓑprivate=adj. 사적인 ⓓraspy=adj. 삐걱거리는, 신경질적인

L e s s o n 18

leap

choice

oral

enormous(ly)

rough(ly)

collaborate

terminate

withstand

bleach

authentic(al)

pressing

single

unravel

appropriate

amenity

leap

v. **1_뛰다** spring, hop, jump, vault

2_떠오르다

n. **1_뜀** jump

2_도약

3_급변

The grasshopper is an insect that can **leap** about twenty times the length of its own body. 메뚜기는 자신의 몸길이의 약 20배 정도를 뛸 수 있는 곤충이다.

insect n. 곤충, 벌레 adj. 곤충의

length n. 길이, 키, 기간, 범위

There has been a **leap** in sales of sports goods in this week. 이번 주에는 스포츠용품 판매에서 도약이 있다.

choice

n. **1_선택** pick, selection

2_선택권 option, alternative

3_종류 type

adj. **1_뛰어난**

2_까다로운

In violin making, the **choice** of the wood is crucial. 바이올린 제작에서, 나무의 선택은 중요하다.

making n. 제조, 만들기, 구조, 원인, 적성, 재료

crucial adj. 중요한, 결정적인, 힘든, 어려운

oral

adj. **1_ 구두의, 구술의** spoken, verbal

≠ written

2_ 입으로 하는

n. **구술 시험**

Sequoya, a Native American who was born about 1770, formed an alphabet of eighty-six letters that enabled him to put the **oral** Cherokee language into writing. 1770년경에 태어난 인디언 세퀘이아는 86자의 알파벳을 만들었으며, 이로써 구두의 체로키 언어를 쓰기가 가능하도록 했다.

bear(bear-bore-born) v. 낳다, 출산하다, 생기다, 받치다

enable v. 가능하게 하다, 할 수 있게 하다

writing n. 쓰기, 집필, 필적, 저술, 기법

enormous(ly)

adj.(adv.)

거대한, 막대한, 대단한 huge, gigantic, immense, vast, tremendous ≠ diminutive, small, tiny, minuscule, minute

After winning a lottery, he bought an **enormous** house much too big for his family. 복권에 당첨된 후, 그는 거대한 집을 샀는데 그의 가족들이 살기에는 너무 컸다.

lottery n. 복권, 추첨, 제비뽑기, 운명

As photographic techniques have become more sophisticated, the scope of their application has expanded **enormously**. 사진 기법이 더욱 정교해지면서, 적용 범위도 거대하게 확대되고 있다.

technique n. 기법, 기량, 연주법, 기교, 기능, 솜씨

sophisticate v. 정교하게 하다, 세련되게 하다

scope n. 범위, 한계, 시야, 자유, 기회, 넓이

application n. 적용, 이용, 응용, 지원하기, 신청(서), 근면

rough(ly) adj.(adv.)

1_거친, 험악한 jagged, coarse, crude
≠smooth, level, flat

2_가공되지 않은 unprocessed, unrefined
≠cultivated, polish, refined, delicate,
finished

3_고된 uncomfortable

4_대강의, 대략적인 vague, approximate

A cup of whole milk provides **roughly** one hundred sixty-six calories of energy. 우유 한잔 전부는 대략 166칼로리의 에너지를 공급한다.

whole　adj. 전부의, 모든, 총~　n. 전체, 전부, 완전체

collaborate v.

협력하다, 합작하다 cooperate, combine, work together

Honey guides, or indicator birds, **collaborate** with honey badgers in seeking out bee colonies. 일명 '표지 새'라고도 불리는 벌꿀길잡이새는 벌이 모여 있는 곳을 찾을 때 벌꿀오소리와 협력한다.

guide　n. 안내인, 지도자, 선도자, 여행 안내서, 길표지

indicator　n. 지시하는 사람/것, 표시기, 표지

seek out　찾아내다, 주의 깊게 찾다

collaborator
n. 공동 제작자, 합작자, 공저자
collaborative
adj. 협력적인, 공동 제작의

terminate

v. **1_ 끝내다, 종결시키다** finish, stop, end, dismiss

≠start, begin, introduce, inaugurate, open

2_ 해고하다 fire, dismiss

Glaciers **terminate** where the rate of ice loss is equivalent to the forward advance of the glacier. 빙하는 얼음의 손실 비율이 빙하가 앞으로 나아가는 것과 같을 때 끝난다.

glacier n. 빙하

rate n. 비율, 요금, 가격, 속도, 진도, 등급 v. 평가하다, 간주하다, 부과하다

equivalent adj. 같은, 동등한, 상당하는, 대등한 n. 동등한 것, 등량

forward adv. 앞으로, ~이후, 바깥으로 adj. 전진하는, 자진하여 ~하는, 주제넘은

withstand

v. **1_ ~에 저항하다** oppose, resist, hold out

≠falter, retreat, fail

2_ 잘 견디다, 버티다 endure, bear

Because it **withstands** the effects of high temperatures, rhenium is a valuable ingredient in certain alloys. 고온의 영향에도 잘 견디기 때문에, 레늄은 어떤 합금에는 귀중한 구성 요소다.

effect n. 영향, 결과, 발효, 시행

temperature n. 온도, 기온, 체온, 고열, 격렬

valuable adj. 귀중한, 가치 있는, 값비싼, 평가할 수 있는 n. 귀중품

ingredient n. 구성 요소, 성분, 원료, 구성분자

bleach

v. **희게 하다, 표백하다** lighten, wash out, whiten, pale, fade
≠darken, cloud

n. **표백(제)**

The **bleaching** of laundry by sunlight is at least partly a photochemical process. 햇빛에 의한 세탁물 표백은 적어도 부분적인 광화학 과정이다.

laundry n. 세탁물, 세탁소=laundromat, dry cleaner's, cleaner, 세탁실
sunlight n. 햇빛, 태양 광선, 일광, 양지
partly adv. 부분적으로, 어느 정도는, 일부분은
process n. 과정, 전진, 수행, 경과, 방법, 순서

authentic(al)

adj. **1_믿을 만한, 확실한** trustworthy
2_진정한, 진짜의 genuine, real, actual, legitimate, bona fide
≠false, spurious, fictitious, fake, counterfeit

The painting looked so real that many experts believed it was **authentic**. 그 그림이 너무나 진짜 같아서 많은 전문가들은 진짜라고 믿었다.

authentically

adv. 확실히, 진정하게 actually, legitimately, genuinely

The stories of Sarah Orne Jewett are considered by many to be more **authentically** regional than those of Bret Harte. 사라 오른 주잇의 이야기는 브레트 하트의 이야기보다 확실히 더 지역적이라고 여겨진다.

regional adj. 지역의, 특정 지구의, 지방적인 n. 지방판, 지방 본부, 지방 예선

pressing

adj. 1_ **절박한, 긴급한** urgent, imperative, important
≠frivolous, trivial, unnecessary
2_ **간청하는**
n. 1_ **누르기**
2_ **인쇄하기** printing

The most **pressing** problem any economic system faces is how to use its scarce resources. 어떤 경제 체제라도 직면하는 가장 절박한 문제는 고갈되어 가는 자원을 어떻게 사용해야 하는가다.

single

adj. 1_ **단 하나의** one, exclusive≠composite, mixed, conglomerate
2_ **1인용 침대의**
3_ **혼자의** solitary, lone, alone
n. **한 개, 단일**
v. **뽑아내다** pick

The Food and Drug Administration classifies as a cosmetic any product whose **single** purpose is to improve a person's appearance. FDA는 사람들의 외모를 향상시키는 목적만 있는 생산품은 화장품으로 분류한다.

administration n. 관리, 경영, 통치, 지배, 행정기관, 시행

classify v. 분류하다, 구분하다

cosmetic n. 화장품, 결점을 감추는 것 adj. 미용을 위한, 화장용의

purpose n. 목적, 동기, 결과, 결심

appearance n. 외관, 겉보기, 출현, 용모

unravel

v. 1_풀다 unwind

2_해명하다 explain

3_해결하다 solve

Natural silk is obtained by **unraveling** the thin threads of the cocoons spun by the caterpillars of the silk worm moth. 천연 실크는 누에나방의 애벌레가 방적한 고치의 얇은 실을 풀어서 얻을 수 있다.

obtain v. 얻다, 획득하다, 설립하다

thin adj. 얇은, 가느다란, 마른, 드문드문한, 적은, 희박한

thread n. 실, 가는 선, 줄거리, 맥락

spin(spin-spun-spun) v. 방적하다, 잣다, 실을 내다, 전개시키다

worm n. 벌레, 벌레 비슷한 것, 고통, 고뇌 v. 천천히 움직이다

appropriate

v. 1_충당하다 assume

2_책정하다 expropriate

adj. 적합한 proper, suitable

≠inappropriate, improper

appropriation

n. 전유, 지출금, 예산 allocation, funding, budget, expenditure

Samuel Morse requested from the congress of the United States an **appropriation** to construct an experimental telegraph line. 새뮤얼 모스는 미 국회에 시험적인 전선을 가설할 예산을 요청했다.

request v. 요청하다, 원하다 n. 요구, 요청, 간청, 청원서, 수요

congress n. 국회, 의회, 집합, 회합

construct v. 건설하다, 구성하다 n. 구조물, 건축물

experimental adj. 시험적인, 실험의

amenity

n. **1_기분 좋음** ≠discomfort, displeasure, distress

2_쾌적한 설비 comfort, facility

The **amenities** of civilization are left behind when an individual embarks on a camping trip in a remote area. 한 개인이 멀리 떨어진 지역에서 캠핑 여행을 시작할 때는 문명의 안락함은 뒤에 남겨지게 된다.

leave behind ~을 뒤에 남기다, 두고 가다

individual adj. 개인의, 단일의, 별개의, 독자적인 n. 개인, 사람, 개체

embark v. 시작하다, 배에 태우다, 싣다, 적재하다, 탑승하다, 사업에 끌어들이다

remote adj. 멀리 떨어진, 원격의, 훨씬 이전, 관계가 깊지 않은

area n. 지역, 구역, 범위, 영역

Lesson 18 Review Test

01 The **amenities** of civilization are left behind when an individual embarks on a camping trip in a remote area.

    ⓐ activities   ⓑ rules

    ⓒ comforts   ⓓ signs

02 Samuel Morse requested from the congress of the United States **an appropriation** to construct an experimental telegraph line.

    ⓐ a guidance   ⓑ a funding

    ⓒ a property   ⓓ a power

03 As photographic techniques have become more sophisticated, the scope of their application has expanded **enormously**.

    ⓐ diversely   ⓑ flagrantly

    ⓒ appealingly   ⓓ tremendously

04 Because it **withstands** the effects of high temperatures, rhenium is a valuable ingredient in certain alloys.

    ⓐ discharges   ⓑ resists

    ⓒ reduces   ⓓ withholds

05 The **bleaching** of laundry by sunlight is at least partly a photochemical process.

    ⓐ airing   ⓑ drying

    ⓒ whitening   ⓓ scrubbing

06 The stories of Sarah Orne Jewett are considered by many to be more **authentically** regional than those of Bret Harte.

ⓐ blatantly   ⓑ genuinely

ⓒ intentionally   ⓓ thoroughly

07 Honey guides, or indicator birds, **collaborate** with honey badgers in seeking out bee colonies.

ⓐ work together   ⓑ travel north

ⓒ live   ⓓ compete

08 Glaciers **terminate** where the rate of ice loss is equivalent to the forward advance of the glacier.

ⓐ stop   ⓑ turn

ⓒ crack   ⓓ rotate

09 A cup of whole milk provides **roughly** one hundred sixty-six calories of energy.

ⓐ discreetly   ⓑ approximately

ⓒ barely   ⓓ coarsely

10 The most **pressing** problem any economic system faces is how to use its scarce resources.

ⓐ puzzling   ⓑ controversial

ⓒ terrifying   ⓓ urgent

11 The grasshopper is an insect that can **leap** about twenty times the length of its own body.

ⓐ jump   ⓑ see

ⓒ hear   ⓓ call

12 Sequoya, a Native American who was born about 1770, formed an alphabet of eighty-six letters that enabled him to put the **oral** Cherokee language into writing.

ⓐ secret   ⓑ complex

ⓒ spoken   ⓓ ancient

13 The Food and Drug Administration classifies as a cosmetic any product whose **single** purpose is to improve a person's appearance.

ⓐ obvious   ⓑ simple

ⓒ exclusive   ⓓ assumed

14 Natural silk is obtained by **unraveling** the thin threads of the cocoons spun by the caterpillars of the silk worm moth.

ⓐ unwinding   ⓑ unleashing

ⓒ undulating   ⓓ undertaking

15 In violin making, the **choice** of the wood is crucial.

ⓐ grain   ⓑ selection

ⓒ resonance   ⓓ shape

01	c	ⓐactivity=n. 활동 ⓑrule=n. 규칙 ⓓsign=n. 신호(기호)
02	b	ⓐguidance=n. 안내 ⓒproperty=n. 재산 ⓓpower=n. 힘(권력)
03	d	ⓐdiversely=adv. 다양하게 ⓑflagrantly=adv. 악명 높게 ⓒappealingly=adv. 매력적이게
04	b	ⓐdischarge=v. 짐을 내리다 ⓒreduce=v. 줄이다 ⓓwithhold=v. 보류하다
05	c	ⓐair=v. 바람에 쐬다 ⓑdry=v. 말리다 ⓓscrub=v. 북북 문지르다
06	b	ⓐblatantly=adv. 떠들썩하게 ⓒintentionally=adv. 고의로 ⓓthoroughly=adv. 철저히
07	a	ⓑtravel north= 북으로 여행하다 ⓒlive=v. 살다 ⓓcompete=v. 경쟁하다
08	a	ⓑturn=v. 돌리다 ⓒcrack=v. 금이 가다 ⓓrotate=v. 회전(순환)하다
09	b	ⓐdiscreetly=adv. 분별 있게 ⓒbarely=adv. 간신히 ⓓcoarsely=adv. 조잡(야비)하게
10	d	ⓐpuzzling=adj. 당황하게 하는 ⓑcontroversial=adj. 논쟁의 ⓒterrifying=adj. 겁나게 하는
11	a	ⓑsee=v. 보다 ⓒhear=v. 듣다 ⓓcall=v. 부르다(전화하다)
12	c	ⓐsecret=adj. 비밀의 ⓑcomplex=adj. 복잡한 ⓓancient=adj. 고대의
13	c	ⓐobvious=adj. 명백한 ⓑsimple=adj. 단순한 ⓓassumed=adj. 가정한
14	a	ⓑunleash=v. ~의 가죽끈을 끄르다, 자유롭게 하다 ⓒundulate=v. 물결(파동)치다 ⓓundertake=v. (일, 책임 등을) 맡다
15	b	ⓐgrain=n. 곡물 ⓒresonance=n. 공명(울림) ⓓshape=n. 모양

Lesson 19

elect

attractive

academy

cultivate

device

creek

authorize

mount

dawn

acute(ly)

commodity

thrust

suppress

tranquil

overcome

Fourth Week

elect

v. **1_뽑다, 선택하다** select, choose

≠dismiss, discharge, cancel

2_선출하다 vote

adj. **당선된, 선정된** selected, chosen

The shop steward, the first-level officer in a labor union, is **elected** by its members. 노동조합의 일급 임원인 노동조합의 대표자는 조합원들에 의해 선출된다.

steward n. 간사, 재산 관리인

officer n. 관리, 공무원, 임원

union n. 조합, 동맹, 연합, 병합, 결합체, 결혼

The president **elect** became busier after the election because of the worsening economic condition. 대통령 당선자는 악화된 경제 사정으로 인해 선거 후 더 바빠졌다.

attractive

adj. **1_매력적인** inviting, appealing, alluring

≠repulsive, repellent

2_관심을 끄는 enticing, engaging

3_아름다운 pretty, pleasing,

≠unattractive, ugly

The flower is the most **attractive**, most colorful, and most fragrant part of many plants. 꽃은 많은 식물들의 가장 아름답고, 다채롭고, 향기로운 부분이다.

colorful adj. 다채로운, 색채가 다양한, 화려한

part n. 부분, 일부, (책의) 부, 권, 지역

academy

n. **1_학회, 학술원, 학원** institute, school, organization

2_사립 중 · 고등학교

Elizabeth Blackwell founded an **academy** to train women physicians in 1868. 엘리자베스 블랙웰은 여성 의료인들을 훈련시키기 위해 1868년에 학원을 창설했다.

found v. 창설하다, 기초를 쌓다, 세우다

physician n. 의사, 내과의사

academic

adj. 1_학원의, 대학의

2_학구적인, 이론적인

---

cultivate

v. **1_(땅을) 갈다, 경작하다**

2_재배하다 grow

3_계발하다 develop, improve, advance, progress

≠stunt, atrophy, neglect

4_장려하다 encourage

≠disregard, discourage

Parsley is **cultivated** throughout much of the world. 파슬리는 세계의 많은 곳에서 재배되고 있다.

device

n. **1_고안, 계획, 방책** plot, scheme, plan, design, ploy

2_장치, 설비 mechanism, implement, tool, apparatus

3_소망, 욕망 desire, inclination, pleasure

Various remote-control **devices**, including automatic valves in pipelines, are activated by radio signals. 수송관의 자동 밸브를 포함해서 다양한 리모컨 장치가 라디오 신호에 의해 활성화되고 있다.

automatic adj. 자동인, 기계적인

valve n. 밸브(장치), 판 v. 밸브로 흐름을 조절하다

signal n. 신호, 계기, 도화선, 조짐, 징후 adj. 신호용의 v. 신호를 보내다

creek

n. **1_시내, 샛강** stream, spring, bayou

2_꼬불꼬불하고 좁은 통로

3_(바다, 강, 호수 따위의) 작은 만

A ford is a place where it is possible to cross a **creek** or river. 여울은 시내나 강에서 건널 수 있는 곳이다.

ford n. 여울, 얕은 곳 v. 얕은 곳을 따라 걸어서 건너다

possible adj. 할 수 있는, 가능한, 있을 수 있는

river n. 강, 흐름

authorize

v. **1_ ~에게 권한을 주다** empower, commission

2_ 위임하다

3_ 인가하다 permit, license, warrant, charter ≠ prohibit, ban, bar

4_ 정당하다고 인정하다 legitimatize

The Morrill Act of 1862 **authorized** the states to use federal lands for the establishment of colleges that would offer programs in agriculture and the mechanical arts. 1862년의 모릴 수정 조항에서는 주에 농업과 기계적인 아트 프로그램을 제공하는 대학의 설립을 위해 연방 영토를 사용할 수 있는 권한을 주었다.

establishment n. 설립, 창설, 입증, 제도, 주거, 세대, 점포

offer v. 제공하다, 말하다, 바치다, 약속하다 n. 제공, 제안, 신청, 구혼

agriculture n. 농업, 농경, 농예

mechanical adj. 기계상의, 기계적인, 소극적인, 물리적인

---

mount

v. **1_ 오르다** ascend, rise, climb ≠ descend, go down

2_ 따다

3_ 공격을 시작하다 attack

4_ 증가하다, 늘다 increase, grow, escalate ≠ lessen, lower, diminish, decline, plunge

n. **산, 언덕**

Mounting evidence indicates that acid rain is damaging historic sites in Boston and Philadelphia. 늘어나는 증거는 산성비가 보스턴과 필라델피아에 있는 역사적인 장소를 훼손시키고 있음을 나타내고 있다.

indicate v. 나타내다, 가리키다, 암시하다, 표현하다

historic adj. 역사상 유명한, 역사에 남는

site n. 장소, 위치, 유적, 자취 v. ~의 위치를 정하다 = locate

dawn

n. **1_새벽, 여명** daybreak, sunrise

≠sunset, twilight, dust

2_처음, 시작 beginning, start, commencement

≠end, finish, close, decline, fall

v. **1_날이 새다, 밝아지다**

2_시작하다 start, commence

With the **dawn** of space exploration, the notion that atmospheric conditions on Earth may be unique in the solar system was strengthened. 우주 탐험의 시작과 함께, 지구의 대기 조건이 태양계에서 유일할 것이라는 생각은 더욱 강화되었다.

exploration n. 탐험, 탐사, 답사, 조사, 연구

notion n. 생각, 개념, 관념, 인식

atmospheric adj. 대기 속의, 대기로 이루어진, 정취 있는

strengthen v. 강화하다, 증강시키다, 힘을 돋우다, 격려하다

acute(ly)

adj.(adv.) **1_날카로운** sharp

≠dull, blunt

2_예리한 keen, discerning, sharp, perceptive

≠dull, stupid, unaware

3_심각한 critical, crucial, severe

≠unimportant, superficial

4_급성의 sudden

≠gradual, progressive

One of California's most **acute** problems is an inadequate water supply. 캘리포니아에서 가장 심각한 문제 중의 하나는 물 공급이 충분하지 못하다는 것이다.

inadequate adj. 불충분한, 부적당한, 부적격한 n. 사회적 부적격자

commodity

n. **1_필수품, 물자** goods, wares, object

2_상품 merchandise, article of trade, goods

Salt has been a respected **commodity** for much of recorded time. 소금은 역사가 기록된 시간 중 오랫동안 존중받아온 필수품이다.

respect v. 존경하다, 존중하다, 고려하다 n. 존경, 존중, 중시, 경의, 세목

recorded time 역사가 기록된 시간

thrust

n. **1_밀기** shove, push

2_찌르기

3_공격 attack, assault

4_요점, 진의, 취지 gist, significance, essence

v. **1_밀다** shove, push

2_찌르다 stab, poke, pierce, puncture

3_강요하다 compel, force

In the Mesozoic period, the upward **thrust** of great rock masses created the Rocky Mountains and the Alps. 중생대에, 거대한 바위 덩어리들의 상승이 로키 산맥과 알프스 산맥을 만들었다.

upward adv. 위쪽으로, 더 높은 지위에

suppress

v. **1_억압하다, 억누르다** subdue, repress, crush, squash

≠encourage, feed, fuel, free

2_ 참다, 감추다 withhold, restrain

≠express

3_ 막다 check, inhibit, limit

≠release

Although poisonous, many alkaloids are valuable as medicines, and some can **suppress** coughing. 독성이 있음에도 불구하고, 많은 알칼로이드가 의약품으로 가치가 있으며 그 중 일부는 기침을 막을 수도 있다.

poisonous adj. 독성의, 유독한, 유해한

cough n. 기침, 헛기침 v. 기침하다

---

tranquil

adj. **조용한, 평온한** calm, relaxed, serene, placid, peaceful

≠agitate, excited, troubled, fuming, noisy, tumultuous, stormy, disturbing

Grandma Moses, a popular painter, spent her life in a **tranquil** little farming community. 인기있는 화가인 그랜드마 모제스는 조용한 작은 농촌 공동체에서 일생을 보냈다.

painter n. 화가, 칠장이

community n. 지역 공동체, 군락, 사회

overcome

v. **1 _ ~을 이겨내다** defeat, triumph
2 _ 극복하다, 정복하다 conquer, surmount, prevail
3 _ 압도하다 overpower

Speech difficulties may sometimes be **overcome** if a person is shown where to place the tongue and teeth to make sounds. 소리를 내기 위하여 혀와 치아를 어디에 두어야 하는지를 보여준다면 언어장애는 때때로 극복될 수도 있다.

tongue n. 혀, 말하는 능력, 말, 언어, 말투

tooth(pl. teeth) n. 이, 치아, 엄함, 격렬함, 기호

sound n. 소리, 음향, 음파, 잡음, 말소리 v. 소리를 내다, 울리다, 들리다

Lesson 19 Review Test

01 The shop steward, the first-level officer in a labor union, is **elected** by its members.

    ⓐ paid   ⓑ advised

    ⓒ consulted   ⓓ chosen

02 The flower is the **most attractive**, most colorful, and most fragrant part of many plants.

    ⓐ prettiest   ⓑ rarest

    ⓒ softes   ⓓ strongest

03 Elizabeth Blackwell founded **an academy** to train women physicians in 1868.

    ⓐ a philosophy   ⓑ a clinic

    ⓒ a school   ⓓ a company

04 Parsley is **cultivated** throughout much of the world.

    ⓐ seen   ⓑ grown

    ⓒ dried   ⓓ cooked

05 Various remote-control **devices**, including automatic valves in pipelines, are activated by radio signals.

    ⓐ mechanisms   ⓑ messages

    ⓒ responses   ⓓ beans

06 A ford is a place where it is possible to cross a **creek** or river.

    ⓐ trench   ⓑ gorge

    ⓒ ravine   ⓓ stream

07 The Morrill Act of 1862 **authorized** the states to use federal lands for the establishment of colleges that would offer programs in agriculture and the mechanical arts.

ⓐ challenged   ⓑ persuaded

ⓒ empowered   ⓓ invited

08 **Mounting** evidence indicates that acid rain is damaging historic sites in Boston and Philadelphia.

ⓐ Hanging   ⓑ Tentative

ⓒ Increasing   ⓓ Irrefutable

09 With the **dawn** of space exploration, the notion that atmospheric conditions on Earth may be unique in the solar system was strengthened.

ⓐ beginning   ⓑ continuation

ⓒ expansion   ⓓ outcome

10 One of California's most **acute** problems is an inadequate water supply.

ⓐ unusual   ⓑ persistent

ⓒ unexpected   ⓓ critical

11 Salt has been a respected **commodity** for much of recorded time.

ⓐ flavoring   ⓑ preservative

ⓒ remedy for illness   ⓓ article of trade

12 In the Mesozoic period, the upward **thrust** of great rock masses created the Rocky Mountains and the Alps.

ⓐ collision   ⓑ angle

ⓒ push   ⓓ erosion

13 Although poisonous, many alkaloids are valuable as medicines, and some can **suppress** coughing.

ⓐ check

ⓑ cause

ⓒ demonstrate

ⓓ worsen

14 Grandma Moses, a popular painter, spent her life in **a tranquil** little farming community.

ⓐ a lovely

ⓑ a serene

ⓒ an isolated

ⓓ a snobbish

15 Speech difficulties may sometimes be **overcome** if a person is shown where to place the tongue and teeth to make sounds.

ⓐ identified

ⓑ minimized

ⓒ surmised

ⓓ surmounted

01	d	ⓐpay=v. 지불하다 ⓑadvise=v. 충고하다 ⓒconsult=v. 상담하다
02	a	ⓑrarest=adj. 가장 드문 ⓒsoftest=adj. 가장 부드러운 ⓓstrongest=adj. 가장 강한
03	c	ⓐphilosophy=n. 철학 ⓑclinic=n. 진료소 ⓓcompany=n. 회사
04	b	ⓐsee=v. 보다 ⓒdry=v. 말리다 ⓓcook=v. 요리하다
05	a	ⓑmessage=n. 전갈 ⓒresponse=n. 응답 ⓓbean=n. 콩
06	d	ⓐtrench=n. 참호 ⓑgorge=n. 골짜기 ⓒravine=n. 좁은 골짜기
07	c	ⓐchallenge=v. 도전하다 ⓑpersuade=v. 설득하다 ⓓinvite=v. 초대하다
08	c	ⓐHanging=adj. 매달린 ⓑTentative=adj. 시험적인(임시의) ⓓIrrefutable=adj. 반박할 수 없는
09	a	ⓑcontinuation=n. 계속됨 ⓒexpansion=n. 확장(팽창) ⓓoutcome=n. 결과(성과)
10	d	ⓐunusual=adj. 보통이 아닌 ⓑpersistent=adj. 고집이 센 ⓒunexpected=adj. 예기치 않은
11	d	ⓐflavoring=n. 조미료 ⓑpreservative=n. 방부제 ⓒremedy for illness=병을 위한 치료(요법)
12	c	ⓐcollision=n. 충돌 ⓑangle=n. 각도 ⓓerosion=n. 부식(침식)
13	a	ⓑcause=v. ~의 원인이 되다 ⓒdemonstrate=v. 논증(증명, 설명)하다 ⓓworsen=v. 악화시키다
14	b	ⓐlovely=adj. 사랑스러운 ⓒisolated=adj. 고립된 ⓓsnobbish=adj. 속물의
15	d	ⓐidentify=v. 확인하다 ⓑminimize=v. 최소화하다 ⓓsurmise=v. 짐작(추측)하다

L e s s o n 20

comic

wed

gather

rehabilitate

pass

embrace

discord

informal(ly)

blunder

substitute

disparage

propel

grueling

penetrate

detrimental(ly)

comic

adj. **1_희극의**

2_우스운 funny, humorous, amusing≠tragic

n. **1_희극 배우** comedian

2_유머 작가 humorist

3_우스운 사람

4_우스움

Clark Gable gave a **comic** performance in the movie *It Happened One Night.* 클라크 게이블은 "어느 날 밤에 생긴 일"이라는 영화에서 우스운 역을 해냈다.

comics

n. (신문 · 잡지 등의) 만화란

His ultimate goal in life is to become a successful **comic**. 그의 인생의 궁극적인 목표는 성공적인 희극 배우가 되는 것이다.

ultimate adj. 궁극의, 가장 먼, 가장 오랜, 최후의, 근본적인, 기본적인

n. 최종단계, 궁극점, 결론

goal n. 목표, 목적, 행선지, 득점 장소, 득점

wed

v. **1_~와 결혼하다** marry, tie the knot, mate

≠divorce, separate

2_~와 융합하다 unite, attach, join, bind

≠sever, divide, split

For most people the decision to **wed** is generally surrounded by social constraints. 대부분의 사람들에게 결혼을 결정하는 것은 일반적으로 사회적인 속박에 둘러싸이게 되는 것이다.

generally adv. 일반적으로, 대개, 대체로

surround v. 둘러싸다, 에워싸다

constraint n. 강제, 속박, 제약, 억제

wedding

n. 결혼식 marriage ceremony

gather

v. **1_모이다** assemble, collect

≠separate, disperse, distribute, spread, scatter

2_점차 늘리다 congregate

3_수확하다 pick, harvest

4_추측하다 conclude, infer, understand

n. **수확** harvest

Moving continuously, a glacier **gathers** the rocks and other materials in its path. 끊임없이 움직이는 빙하는 그 과정에서 바위와 다른 물질들을 끌어모은다.

continuously adv. 끊임없이, 계속하여

path n. 진로, 통로, 궤도, 방향, 길, 산책길, 인생행로

I **gather** that you're going to graduate next semester. 나는 네가 다음 학기에는 졸업할 것이라고 생각하는데.

graduate v. 졸업하다, 학위를 받다, 변화하다 n. 졸업생, 대학원생 adj. 졸업한

semester n. 학기

rehabilitate

v. **1_원 상태로 되돌리다** restore, recover, regenerate

≠do away with, wipe out

2_복원하다 repair, renew

≠throw out, oust, banish

The doctor told him that it would take at least six months to **rehabilitate** his torn knee. 그 의사는 그의 찢어진 무릎이 회복되는 데 적어도 6개월이 걸린다고 말했다.

rehabilitation

n. 회복, 재활 recovery, restoration

Proper exercise plays a significant role in the **rehabilitation** of patients with various back ailments. 적절한 운동은 등에 각종 병이 있는 환자들의 회복에 중요한 역할을 한다.

patient n. 환자 adj. 참을성 있는, 허용하는, 수동적인

back n. 등, 몸의 뒷부분, 등뼈, 후면 v. 후원하다, 후퇴하다, 뒤에 쓰다

ailment n. 병, 질환, 불쾌

pass

v. **1_지나다** go ahead, surpass, exceed≠endure, last, persist
2_~을 통과시키다≠delay, drag　**3_합격하다**≠fail, flunk
4_넘겨주다≠reject　　　　　**5_(시간을) 보내다** spend

n. **1_통행(길)** passage way, route
2_통행 허가증 permit, permission

Hibernation is a state of inactivity in which some animals **pass** the winter. 겨울잠은 일부 동물들이 겨울을 지내기 위해 움직이지 않은 상태로 있는 것을 말한다.

inactivity n. 활동하지 않는 것, 움직이지 않는 것

He was thrilled to learn that he would receive a weekend **pass** for his exemplary behavior in the barracks. 그는 내무반에서의 본보기적인 행동에 대해 1주일간의 통행 허가증을 받을 것이라는 것을 듣고서는 가슴이 설레었다.

thrill v. 가슴 설레게 하다, 오싹하게 하다, 진동시키다, 퍼지다　n. 오싹함, 전율

barrack n. 내무반, 병영　v. 막사에 수용하다

embrace

v. **1_포옹하다** hug
2_포함하다 include, contain, take in≠exclude
3_맞이하다 receive, welcome
4_채택하다 take up, adopt

n. **포옹** hug

Horseback riding **embraces** both the skill of handling a horse and the mastery of diverse riding styles. 말을 타는 것은 말을 조정하는 기술과 다양한 말타는 스타일을 숙달하는 것을 포함한다.

ride v. 말을 타다, 타고 가다　n. 타기, 타는 시간

mastery n. 숙달, 정통, 전문적 기능, 지배　　**diverse** adj. 다양한, 다른, 별개의

The father gave his son a warm **embrace**. 아버지는 아들에게 따뜻하게 포옹을 해주었다.

warm adj. 따뜻한, 훈훈한, 진심 어린, 애정을 품고 있는

discord

n. **1_불화** disagreement, difference≠amity

2_내분 disturbance≠tranquility

3_불협화음, 소음, 잡음 disharmony≠harmony

v. **화합하지 않다** disagree, clash, differ, dissent
≠yield, agree, consent

Using extremely different decorating schemes in adjoining rooms may result in **discord** and a lack of unity in style.
방을 연결할 때 극단적으로 서로 다른 장식 기획을 사용하는 것은 스타일에 있어서 일체성이 없게 만들거나 불협화음을 낳을 수 있다.

decorate v. 장식하다, 꾸미다

scheme n. 기획, 계획, 음모, 구성, 조직

adjoining adj. 인접한, 부근의

informal(ly) adj.(adv.)

1_비공식의, 약식의 unofficial, unceremonious
≠formal, ceremonious

2_스스럼없는 relaxed, free≠constrained, stiff

3_친밀감을 나타내는 casual　　**4_회화체의**

The party is **informal**, so dress casually. 그 파티는 비공식적인 것이다. 그러므로 캐주얼하게 옷을 입어라.

The ice cream cone, the hamburger, and iced tea were all introduced at the 1904 Louisiana Purchase Exposition **informally** known as the St. Louis Fair. 아이스크림 콘, 햄버거, 아이스 티는 비공식적으로는 세인트 루이스 장날로 알려진 1904년 루이지애나 매입 전시회에서 소개되었다.

cone n. 원뿔, 원추체 v. 원뿔 모양으로 만들다

introduce v. 소개하다, 처음으로 경험하게 하다, 발표하다, 시작하다

exposition n. 전시회, 해설, 설명

fair n. 품평회, 장날 adj. 공평한, 정당한, 충분한, 유망한 adv. 공정하게, 제대로

blunder

n. **큰 실수** error, slip, mistake, fumble, bungle, botch, goof*

v. **실수를 하다**

Diplomatic misunderstandings can often be traced back to **blunders** in translation. 외교적인 오해는 종종 번역에서의 큰 실수로 인한 것임을 알 수 있다.

diplomatic adj. 외교의, 외교 수완이 있는, 능란한

misunderstanding n. 오해, 의견의 불일치, 분쟁

translation n. 번역, 해석

＊blunder와 관련된 명사형 유사어(error 제외) 모두 다 동사형으로도 사용될 수가 있다.

substitute

v. **1_대응하다 2_바꾸다** supplant, replace, exchange, switch **3_대신하다**

n. **대역** replacement, substitution

adj. **대리의** alternate, alternative, backup

≠original, first, primary, actual

People buy insurance in order to **substitute** a small, certain, tolerable loss for a large, uncertain, catastrophic one. 사람들은 크고, 불확실한 대참사를 작고 확실하며 견딜 만한 손실로 대신하기 위해 보험에 든다.

tolerable adj. 견딜 만한, 참을 수 있는, 괜찮은 편인, 나쁘지 않은

uncertain adj. 불확실한, 분명하지 않은, 변하기 쉬운

catastrophic adj. 대참사의, 불운의

The **substitute** teacher had a difficult time handling rowdy students. 대리로 오신 선생님은 난폭한 학생들을 다루느라고 힘들었다.

rowdy adj. 난폭한, 툭하면 싸우는 n. 난폭한 사람, 싸움쟁이

disparage

v. **1_~의 명예를 손상시키다** defame, discredit

2_~을 얕보다 belittle

disparaging

adj.1_깔보는 demeaning, belittling

2_비난하는 negative, critical

Many movies receive **disparaging** reviews from film experts and yet become extremely successful. 많은 영화들이 영화 전문가들로부터 비평을 받았지만 아주 성공하고 있다.

review n. 비평기사, 논평, 재고, 복습, 검사, 검열, 보고 v. 복습하다, 검토하다

expert n. 전문가, 권위자 adj. 숙련된=skilled, 전문적인 v. ~을 전문으로 하다

yet conj. 그렇지만, 그럼에도 불구하고=nevertheless, 지금까지 존속하는 adv. 아직

successful adj. 성공한, 출세한, (~와) 잘 지내고 있는

propel

v. **1_추진하다** push, drive for, move

≠retreat, withdraw

2_재촉하다 urge, impel

In North America, the first canoes were constructed from logs and **propelled** by means of wooden paddles. 북미에서 첫 카누는 통나무로 만들어졌고 나무 패달로 움직였다.

log n. 통나무, 장작, 항해(항공) 일지, 운전(실험) 기록

means n. 수단, 방법, 매개

paddle n. 노, 주걱, (탁구 등의) 라켓 v. 젓다, 노상 판매하다

grueling

adj. **1_기진맥진하게 하는** exhausting, arduous, punishing

2_지독한 severe

≠easy, comfortable, restful

n. **가혹한 처사**

The most **grueling** of all Olympic events is the decathlon.
올림픽의 모든 경기 종목 중에서 가장 기진맥진하게 만드는 것은 10종 경기다.

penetrate

v. **1_꿰뚫다, 관통하다** break through, puncture, pierce

≠reflect, deflect

2_통과하다 pass through

3_침투하다 permeate, invade

Automobile experts have shown that halogen headlights **penetrate** thick fog more effectively than traditional incandescent headlights and thus help to reduce accidents.
자동차 전문가들은 전통적인 백열 헤드라이트보다는 할로겐 헤드라이트가 훨씬 효과적으로 짙은 안개를 꿰뚫을 수 있으며 이로써 사고를 줄일 수 있음을 보여주고 있다.

thick adj. 짙은, 두꺼운≠thin, 굵은, 밀집한≠compact, 진한, 걸쭉한

fog n. 안개, 모호함 v. ~을 안개로 뒤덮다, 흐리게 하다, ~을 혼란시키다

thus adv. 그러므로, 따라서=accordingly, 이 정도로

reduce v. ~을 줄이다, ~을 축소하다=lessen, 바꾸다

detrimental(ly)
adj.(adv.)

유해한, 손해 되는 harmful, injurious, unfortunate,
disadvantageous, deleterious
≠beneficial, advantageous, good

While some bacteria are beneficial, others are **detrimental**
in that they cause disease. 일부 박테리아는 이익을 주는 반면에,
다른 것들은 병을 유발한다는 점에서는 유해하다.

bacteria n. 박테리아, 분열균

beneficial adj. ~에 이익이 되는, 유익한, 도움이 되는

Lesson 20 Review Test

01 Proper exercise plays a significant role in the **rehabilitation** of patients with various back ailments.

    ⓐ operation   ⓑ recovery

    ⓒ casting   ⓓ relaxation

02 Using extremely different decorating schemes in adjoining rooms may result in **discord** and a lack of unity in style.

    ⓐ compromise   ⓑ disharmony

    ⓒ disillusion   ⓓ anxiety

03 The ice cream cone, the hamburger, and iced tea were all introduced at the 1904 Louisiana Purchase Exposition **informally** known as the St. Louis Fair.

    ⓐ previously   ⓑ unofficially

    ⓒ incorrectly   ⓓ occasionally

04 Diplomatic misunderstandings can often be traced back to **blunders** in translation.

    ⓐ mistakes   ⓑ attempts

    ⓒ insults   ⓓ arguments

05 Clark Gable gave a **comic** performance in the movie *It Happened One Night.*

    ⓐ sophisticated   ⓑ clever

    ⓒ discreet   ⓓ funny

06 While some bacteria are beneficial, others are **detrimental** in that they cause disease.

    ⓐ harmful   ⓑ prodigious

    ⓒ intrusive   ⓓ mordant

07 For most people the decision to **wed** is generally surrounded by social constraints.

    ⓐ marry   ⓑ emigrate

    ⓒ choose a job   ⓓ have children

08 Moving continuously, a glacier **gathers** the rocks and other materials in its path.

    ⓐ buries   ⓑ crushes

    ⓒ collects   ⓓ freezes

09 People buy insurance in order to **substitute** a small, certain, tolerable loss for a large, uncertain, catastrophic one.

    ⓐ provide   ⓑ return

    ⓒ exchange   ⓓ predict

10 Many movies receive **disparaging** reviews from film experts and yet become extremely successful.

    ⓐ authoritative   ⓑ lengthy

    ⓒ uninteresting   ⓓ negative

11 In North America, the first canoes were constructed from logs and **propelled** by means of wooden paddles.

    ⓐ carved   ⓑ docked

    ⓒ driven forward   ⓓ carried upright

12 The most **grueling** of all Olympic events is the decathlon.

    ⓐ exhilarating   ⓑ gruesome

    ⓒ exhausting   ⓓ creative

13 Hibernation is a state of inactivity in which some animals **pass** the winter.

    ⓐ prepare for   ⓑ wait for

    ⓒ miss   ⓓ spend

14 Horseback riding **embraces** both the skill of handling a horse and the mastery of diverse riding styles.

    ⓐ fosters   ⓑ emphasizes

    ⓒ exaggerates   ⓓ includes

15 Automobile experts have shown that halogen headlights **penetrate** thick fog more effectively than traditional incandescent headlights and thus help to reduce accidents.

    ⓐ dissolve   ⓑ perceive

    ⓒ touch   ⓓ pierce

01	b	ⓐoperation=n. 수술 ⓒcasting=n. 배역 ⓓrelaxation=n. 편히 쉼
02	b	ⓐcompromise=n. 타협 ⓒdisillusion=v. ~의 환영(환상)을 깨우치다 ⓓanxiety=n. 걱정
03	b	ⓐpreviously=adv. 이전에(미리) ⓒincorrectly=adv. 부정확하게 ⓓoccasionally=adv. 가끔
04	a	ⓑattempt=n. 시도 ⓒinsult=n. 모욕 ⓓargument=n. 논의
05	d	ⓐsophisticated=adj. 세련된 ⓑclever=adj. 영리한 ⓒdiscreet=adj. 사려(분별) 있는
06	a	ⓑprodigious=adj. 거창(막대)한 ⓒintrusive=adj. 침입적인 ⓓmordant=adj. 비꼬는(신랄한)
07	a	ⓑemigrate=v. 이민 가다 ⓒchoose a job=직업을 고르다 ⓓhave children=아이들을 가지다
08	c	ⓐbury=v. 파묻다 ⓑcrush=v. 눌러 부수다 ⓓfreeze=v. 얼다
09	c	ⓐprovide=v. 주다 ⓑreturn=v. 되돌아가다(오다) ⓓpredict=v. 예언하다
10	d	ⓐauthoritative=adj. 권한이 있는 ⓑlengthy=adj. 긴, 오랜 ⓒuninteresting=adj. 재미없는
11	c	ⓐcarve=v. 베다, 새기다 ⓑdock=v. (배를) 부두에 대다 ⓓcarry upright=똑바로 나르다
12	c	ⓐexhilarating=adj. 기분을 돋우는 ⓑgruesome=adj. 소름끼치는 ⓓcreative=adj. 창조적인
13	d	ⓐprepare for= ~을 준비하다 ⓑwait for=~을 기다리다 ⓒmiss=v. ~을 놓치다
14	d	ⓐfoster=v. 기르다 ⓑemphasize=v. 강조하다 ⓒexaggerate=v. 과장하다
15	d	ⓐdissolve=v. 용해하다, 녹이다 ⓑperceive=v. 지각(인지)하다 ⓒtouch=v. 대다(만지다)

L e s s o n 21

highly

growth

seldom

youth

dwell

comprehensible

bulk

devise

conflict

win

undertake

rise

desolate

stun

woo

highly

adv. **1_높은 위치에**

2_대단히, 매우 very, greatly, extremely, vastly, intensely

≠little, slightly, barely, scarcely, hardly

3_크게 칭찬하여 favorably, warmly

≠critically, disparagingly, coldly

Tolerance for noise is a **highly** individual matter. 소음에 대한 참을성은 매우 개인적인 문제다.

matter n. 문제, 일, 사건, 물질, 성분

growth

n. **1_성장, 발육** development, evolution, advance

≠deterioration, degeneration, regression, decay

2_증가, 확장 increase, surge, rise, expansion

≠decrease, diminution, descent

The **growth** of the pharmaceutical industry during the twentieth century has been astonishing. 20세기 동안 제약산업의 성장은 놀랍다.

pharmaceutical adj. 약학의, 약제의, 약국의 n. 조제약, 제약

astonishing adj. 놀라운, 깜짝 놀라게 하는

seldom

adv. **좀처럼 ~않게, 드물게** rarely, infrequently, hardly, scarcely, sporadically, occasionally

≠often, frequently, usually, regularly, always

A number of mammals live in trees and only **seldom** descend to the ground. 많은 포유류는 나무 위에 살고 있으며 땅으로 거의 내려오지 않는다.

mammal n. 포유동물

descend v. 내려오다, 미치다, 전해지다

ground n. 땅, 지면, 흙, 토양, 장소, 근거, 이유

youth

n. **1_젊음**

2_초기 infancy, beginning

3_미성년자 youngster, minor, child

Little Lord Fauntleroy is the tale of a **youth** who inherits a fortune. 『소공자』는 큰 돈을 물려받은 아이에 대한 이야기다.

tale n. 이야기, 허위, 거짓말

inherit v. 재산을 물려받다, 상속분으로 나누다, 뒤를 잇다

fortune n. 큰 돈, 부, 자산, 운명, 운수

dwell

v. **1_ 살다, 거주하다** reside, live, inhabit, stay, remain, settle

≠go away, depart, leave

2_ 머무르다

3_ ~을 생각하다 ponder, consider

≠ignore, overlook, disregard

As early as the eleventh century, the Pueblo people **dwelt** in large cities that were constructed from boulders and mud bricks. 이미 11세기부터, 푸에블로 사람들은 둥근 돌과 진흙 벽돌로 건설된 큰 도시에 살았다.

boulder n. 둥근 돌, 큰 자갈

mud n. 진흙, 가치 없는 것, 쓰레기

brick n. 벽돌, 벽돌 모양의 덩어리

comprehensible

adj. **이해할 수 있는** intelligible, understandable, distinct, clear, knowable, lucid

≠unfathomable, puzzling, incomprehensible, abstruse, ambiguous

The ballet's visual message is **comprehensible** to almost everyone. 발레의 시각적인 메시지는 거의 모든 사람들이 이해할 수 있다.

visual adj. 시각의, 눈에 보이는

message n. 메시지, 전언, 통신, 교서, 교훈, 사명

bulk

n. **1_체적**

　　2_크기, 부피 mass, volume, weight, size, amount

　　3_대부분 majority, most

v. **1_커지다, 증대하다**

　　2_무겁게 하다

It is now common for physically disabled individuals to receive the **bulk** of their education in regular school programs. 육체적으로 장애가 있는 사람들은 교육의 대부분을 이제는 정규적인 학교 프로그램 속에서 받는 것이 일반적이다.

disabled adj. 신체에 장애가 있는, 불구의

regular adj. 정규의, 순서가 잡힌, 보통의, 일정한, 완전한

program n. 프로그램, 계획, 행동 계획

devise

v. **1_궁리하다** form, plan, fashion, concoct, establish

　　2_발명하다 invent, create, establish

n. **(부동산의) 유증**

　　(유언장의) 증여 조항

Astronauts are subjected to the most rigorous training that has ever been **devised** for human beings. 우주 비행사는 인간을 위해 발명된 것 중에서 가장 엄격한 훈련을 필요로 한다.

astronaut n. 우주 비행사

subject to ~을 필요로 하는, 조건으로 하는, 지배하에 있는, 받기 쉬운

rigorous adj. 엄격한, 엄중한, 정확한, 면밀한

conflict

v. **1_충돌하다, 모순되다** oppose, clash, disagree, collide

2_다투다 argue, fight

n. **1_투쟁, 다툼** dissention, struggle

2_싸움 battle, combat*

3_논쟁, 불일치 antagonism, discord

conflicting

adj. 모순되는, 서로 다투는

incompatible

Different biologists, analyzing the same data, may arrive at wholly different and sometimes **conflicting** interpretations. 같은 데이터를 분석하면서도, 생물학자들은 완전히 다른, 때로는 모순되는 해석에 도달하기도 한다.

analyze v. 분석하다, 분석하여 조사하다, 해석하다

interpretation n. 해석, 해명, 설명, 이해

＊conflict에서 싸움이라는 뜻의 유사어들은 동사형으로도 사용된다.

win

v. **1_이기다** triumph, conquer, prevail, defeat

≠fail, lose, fall

2_～을 얻다, 획득하다 get, achieve, attain, earn, acquire, reach, gain

≠miss, lose

3_설득시키다 persuade, convince

Most people know that George Washington Carver was an acclaimed scientist, but how many realize that he also **won** recognition for his talent as a painter. 대부분의 사람들은 조지 워싱턴 카버가 박수 갈채를 받는 과학자라고 알고 있다. 하지만 그가 화가로서도 재능을 인정받았다는 사실을 아는 사람이 얼마나 될까.

recognition n. 인정, 승인, 인식, 평가, 표창, 사례

talent n. 재능, 소질, 탤런트, 특수한 재능을 지닌 사람들

undertake

v. **1_맡다, 의무를 지다** attempt, take on, assume

≠abstain, avoid, refuse

2_시작하다, 나서다 set about, engage in

3_~을 관리하다 manage

During her husband's presidency, Jacqueline Kennedy
undertook the coordination of the White House restoration.
남편의 재임시절, 재클린 케네디는 백악관을 복구하는 데 조정 역할을
맡았다.

coordination n. 조정, 일치, 공동작용, 대등 관계

restoration n. 복구, 복원, 회복, 부흥

rise

v. **1_뜨다** ascent, soar

≠descend, drop, fall, plunge

2_발전하다 progress, advance, improve, develop

≠decline, fall, depreciate, deteriorate

3_증가하다 increase

4_폭동을 일으키다 rebel, revolt

5_나타나다 emerge, appear

n. **출현** emergence, ascent

With the **rise** of the "theater of the absurd," trends in
scenery design have become eclectic, ranging from realism
to surrealism. '부조리 연극'의 출현과 함께 배경 디자인의 경향은
현실주의에서 초현실주의까지 폭이 넓어졌다.

scenery n. 경치, 풍경, 무대 장치, 배경

realism n. 현실주의 ≠surrealism(n. 초현실주의)

desolate

adj. **1_황폐한, 인기척이 없는** deserted, uninhabited, barren

≠inhabited, populated, bustling

2_내버려진 forsaken, abject, dejected

≠popular, well-liked

v. **황폐시키다**

Large areas of Alaskan land remain **desolate** due to harsh climate. 알래스카의 넓은 지역이 거친 기후로 인해 황폐한 채로 남아 있다.

remain v. 여전히 ~상태이다, 머무르다, 잔류하다

due to ~때문에

stun

v. **1_기절시키다** pass out

≠awaken

2_멍하게 하다 daze

≠arouse, stir, excite, animate

3_대경실색케 하다 astonish, bewilder, astound

A serious burn can **stun** and weaken the victim. 심한 화상은 희생자를 멍하게 하고 약화시킬 수 있다.

burn n. 화상, 구워 만들기

weaken v. 약하게 하다, 무력해지다

victim n. 희생자, 피해자, 속는 사람

WOO

v. **1_구애하다** court, pay suit, pursue

2_얻으려고 노력하다 cajole, fatter, coax

3_지지를 얻으려고 애쓰다 court

4_간청하다 solicit

Politicians are often said to **woo** voters. 정치인들은 종종 유권자들을 끌어들이려고 한다고들 한다.

politician n. 정치가, 행정관, 권력주의자

often adv. 종종, 자주, 대개

voter n. 유권자, 투표자

Lesson 21 Review Test

01 A number of mammals live in trees and only **seldom** descend to the ground.

    ⓐ sadly   ⓑ rarely

    ⓒ quietly   ⓓ briefly

02 *Little Lord Fauntleroy* is the tale of a **youth** who inherits a fortune.

    ⓐ cousin   ⓑ servant

    ⓒ child   ⓓ peasant

03 It is now common for physically disabled individuals to receive the **bulk** of their education in regular school programs.

    ⓐ majority   ⓑ assignments

    ⓒ tests   ⓓ rest

04 Astronauts are subjected to the most rigorous training that has ever been **devised** for human beings.

    ⓐ demanded   ⓑ created

    ⓒ diagnosed   ⓓ allowed

05 A serious burn can **stun** and weaken the victim.

    ⓐ injure   ⓑ infuriate

    ⓒ daze   ⓓ exhaust

06 Politicians are often said to **woo** voters.

    ⓐ intrigue   ⓑ court

    ⓒ think little of   ⓓ try to avoid

07 Different biologists, analyzing the same data, may arrive at wholly different and sometimes **conflicting** interpretations.

ⓐ unsuitable　　　　　　　ⓑ invalid

ⓒ unintelligible　　　　　ⓓ incompatible

08 Most people know that George Washington Carver was an acclaimed scientist, but how many realize that he also **won** recognition for his talent as a painter?

ⓐ sought　　　　　　　　ⓑ deserved

ⓒ achieved　　　　　　　ⓓ anticipated

09 During her husband's presidency, Jacqueline Kennedy **undertook** the coordination of the White House restoration.

ⓐ took on　　　　　　　　ⓑ underestimated

ⓒ took down　　　　　　　ⓓ underplayed

10 Tolerance for noise is **a highly** individual matter.

ⓐ a basically　　　　　　ⓑ an unusually

ⓒ a loudly　　　　　　　ⓓ an extremely

11 The **growth** of the pharmaceutical industry during the twentieth century has been astonishing.

ⓐ furor　　　　　　　　　ⓑ nurturing

ⓒ expansion　　　　　　　ⓓ patenting

12 With the **rise** of the "theater of the absurd", trends in scenery design have become eclectic, ranging from realism to surrealism.

ⓐ drama　　　　　　　　　ⓑ improvisation

ⓒ criticism　　　　　　　ⓓ emergence

13 Large areas of Alaskan land remain **desolate** due to harsh climate.

    ⓐ inaccessible   ⓑ immature

    ⓒ parched   ⓓ barren

14 As early as the eleventh century, the Pueblo people **dwelt in** large cities that were constructed from boulders and mud bricks.

    ⓐ longed for   ⓑ resided in

    ⓒ planned for   ⓓ worshipped in

15 The ballet's visual message is **comprehensible** to almost everyone.

    ⓐ acceptable   ⓑ understandable

    ⓒ interesting   ⓓ pleasing

01	b	ⓐ sadly=adv. 슬프게 ⓒ quietly=adv. 조용히 ⓓ briefly=adv. 간단히
02	c	ⓐ cousin=n. 사촌 ⓑ servant=n. 하인 ⓓ peasant=n. 시골뜨기
03	a	ⓑ assignment=n. 숙제(과제) ⓒ test=n. 시험 ⓓ rest=n. 휴식
04	b	ⓐ demand=v. 요구하다 ⓒ diagnose=v. 진단하다 ⓓ allow=v. 허락하다
05	c	ⓐ injure=v. 상처를 입히다 ⓑ infuriate=v. 격노하게 하다 ⓓ exhaust=v. 다 써버리다(소모하다)
06	b	ⓐ intrigue=v. 음모를 꾸미다 ⓒ think little of=~을 대수롭지 않게 여기다
		ⓓ try to avoid=~을 피하려고 (노력)하다
07	d	ⓐ unsuitable=adj. 부적당한 ⓑ invalid=adj. 병약한 ⓒ unintelligible=adj. 이해할 수 없는
08	c	ⓐ seek=v. 찾다(추구하다) ⓑ deserve=v. ~할(받을) 만하다 ⓓ anticipate=v. 예상(기대)하다
09	a	ⓑ underestimate=v. 과소 평가하다 ⓒ take down=무너뜨리다
		ⓓ underplay=v. 소극적으로 연기하다
10	d	ⓐ basically=adv. 원래 ⓑ unusually=adv. 보통과는 달리 ⓒ loudly=adv. 큰 소리로
11	c	ⓐ furor=n. 열광 ⓑ nurture=v. 양육하다 ⓓ patent=v. ~의 특허를 얻다
12	d	ⓐ drama=n. 희곡(연극) ⓑ improvisation=n. 즉석에서 하기(즉흥) ⓒ criticism=n. 비평
13	d	ⓐ inaccessible=adj. 접근하기(얻기) 어려운 ⓑ immature=adj. 미숙한 ⓒ parched=adj. 바짝 마른
14	b	ⓐ long for=~을 애타게 바라다 ⓒ plan for=~을 계획하다
		ⓓ worship in=예배(숭배)하다
15	b	ⓐ acceptable=adj. 받아들일 수 있는 ⓒ interesting=adj. 흥미 있는 ⓓ pleasing=adj. 유쾌한

L e s s o n 22

sum

flow

inhabitant

matchless

primarily

backbone

moreover

reinforce

urge

reservoir

forestall

deceptive

tamp

graze

flamboyant

sum

n. **1_합계, 총량(금액)** total amount

2_전체 total, whole

3_요점 essence

v. **1_합계하다, 계산하다** calculate, estimate

2_요약하다 summarize

In statistics, the mathematical mean is obtained by dividing the **sum** of a group of scores by the number of scores. 통계학에서 수학적인 산술 평균은 그룹의 득점 합계를 득점수로 나누어서 얻는다.

statistics n. 통계학, 통계, 통계 자료   **mathematical** adj. 수학의, 수학용의

mean n. 산술 평균, 중앙, 중간, 중용

The student was able to **sum** up his point in a clear fashion. 그 학생은 확실한 방법으로 자신의 점수 합계를 낼 수 있었다.

fashion n. 방법, 방식, 종류, 스타일, 유행 v. ~을 만들다, 맞추다

flow

v. **1_흐르다** stream, travel, run

2_통하다

3_순환하다 circulate

n. **1_흐름** river, current

2_홍수 flood

When an electric current **flows** through a wire, a magnetic field appears around the wire. 전류가 전선을 통해 흐를 때, 전선 주변에 자기장이 나타난다.

magnetic adj. 자기의, 자석의, 매력 있는 n. 자석, 자성체

wire n. 전선, 철사, 전화선, 철조망

If you want not to be noticed, you should go with the **flow**. 만약 네가 주목받는 것을 원하지 않는다면, 흐르는 대로 가야 할 것이다.

notice v. 주목하다, 알아차리다, 조심하여 보다, 주의하다

n. 주목, 주의, 통지, 해약 통고, 게시판

inhabitant

n. **1_주민** tenant, resident

2_거주자 dweller, occupant, habitant, settler

3_서식 동물

San Francisco's Chinese community, comprising of 67,000 **inhabitants**, is the largest concentration of Chinese outside of Asia. 67,000명의 주민으로 이루어진 샌프란시스코의 중국인 커뮤니티는 아시아를 벗어나서는 중국인 인구가 가장 집중된 곳이다.

matchless

adj. **1_상대가 없을 만큼** unrivaled, excellent

2_최고의 unparalleled, unequaled, peerless

≠undistinguished, lackluster, second-rate, average, mediocre

Critics have never been able to find adequate praise for Marian Anderson's **matchless** contralto voice. 비평가들은 마리안 앤더슨이 가지고 있는 최고의 콘트랄토 목소리에 걸맞은 칭찬을 찾아내지 못하고 있다.

adequate adj. 알맞은, 충족시키는, 상응하는, 상당한

praise n. 칭찬, 찬미, 찬성 v. 칭찬하다, 찬양하다, 찬미하다

primarily

adv. **1_본질적으로** fundamentally

2_원래, 주로 mostly, principally

≠secondarily

Steel is an alloy composed **primarily** of iron and carbon.
강철은 주로 철과 탄소로 구성된 합금이다.

steel n. 강철, 강철 제품, 검, 칼 adj. 강철의, 강철로 만든

v. 강철을 달다, 강철 비슷하게 만들다.

alloy n. 합금, 비금속, 불순물 v. 섞다, 섞어서 합금을 만들다, 완화하다

iron n. 철, 단단하고 강한 것, 철로 만든 기구 adj. 철제의, 불굴의, 확고한

v. 철을 입히다, 다림질하다

carbon n. 탄소, 카본지

backbone

n. **1_등뼈** spine, vertebrae

2_주력 mainstay, support, pillar

3_강한 정신력 courage, resolution, firmness

≠ weakness, timidity, spinelessness,
cowardice

The common characteristic of fish, amphibians, reptiles,
birds, and mammals is that all have **backbones**. 어류, 양서
류, 파충류, 조류, 포유류의 공통적인 특성은 모두 등뼈를 가지고 있다
는 것이다.

common adj. 공통의, 널리 퍼진, 흔히 볼 수 있는 n. 공유지, 평민

amphibian n. 양서 동물, 이중 인격자 adj. 양서류의

moreover

adv. **1_게다가** in addition

2_더욱이, 또한 furthermore

Concrete is a durable, watertight, and incombustible material that is, **moreover**, inexpensive to make. 콘크리트는 견고하고, 물이 스미지 않으며, 불연성 물질인데, 게다가 만드는 데도 비용이 적게 든다.

watertight adj. 물이 스미지 않는, 완벽한

incombustible adj. 불연성의 (것)

inexpensive adj. 값이 싼, 비용이 안 드는

reinforce

v. **1_보강하다, 늘리다** strengthen, revitalize, invigorate
≠undermine, weaken, debilitate

2_증진시키다 beef up, refresh, augment
≠water down

Monkeys constantly groom one another, thus **reinforcing** the social bonds necessary to their survival. 원숭이들은 끊임 없이 서로의 털을 다듬어준다. 이렇게 해서 자신들의 생존에 필요한 사회적 결속력을 강화시킨다.

groom v. 다듬다, 반듯하게 손질하다 n. 신랑, 마부

bond n. 묶는 것, 줄, 연줄, 동맹, 보증, 보세창고 보관

urge

v. **1_추진하다** stimulate, propel, force, advocate

≠deter, restrain, check, hold back

2_간청하다 advocate, beg, implore

≠discourage, caution, dissuade

n. **추진력, 본능적인 충동** drive, yearning, impulse

Marcus Garvey, who **urged** the back to Africa movement, attempted to establish colonies of Black Americans in Africa. 아프리카로 돌아가기 운동을 추진했던 마르쿠스 가비는 아프리카에 흑인 미국인들의 거주지를 세우려고 시도했다.

attempt v. 시도하다, 공격하다 n. 시도, 기도, 미수, 실패작

reservoir

n. **1_저수지** receptacle, depository

2_축적 reserve, store, supply

Underground storage **reservoirs** are important in the conservation of natural gas. 지하 저장소는 천연 가스의 보존에 중요하다.

underground adj. 지하의, 지하용의, 비밀의 adv. 지하에서, 비밀히

n. 지하도, 지하운동

storage n. 저장, 보관, 저장소, 저장량

forestall

v. **1_선손쓰다** avert, prevent

2_앞질러 방해하다 ward off, frustrate, hinder, deter, hamper

≠encourage, abet, incite, provoke, induce

Strict sanitary procedures help to **forestall** outbreaks of disease. 엄격한 공중 위생 처리는 돌발적인 발병을 막는 데 도움이 된다.

strict adj. 엄중한, 엄격한, 면밀한, 주의 깊은

sanitary adj. (공중) 위생의, 위생적인, 깨끗한

outbreak n. 돌발, 급격한 증가, 폭동

deceptive

adj. **1_남을 속이는** misleading, false, deceitful

2_믿을 수 없는 fake, spurious

≠genuine, real, authentic, true, accurate, verifiable

Deceptive labeling of certain types of merchandise is not allowed under the Pure Food and Drug Act of 1906. 1906년의 PFD 수정 조항에 의해 일부 상품에 소비자를 속이는 라벨 표기를 금지하고 있다.

label v. 라벨을 붙이다, 꼬리표를 달다

merchandise n. 상품, 물품, 재고품 v. 매매하다, 장사하다

allow v. 허락하다, 지급하다, 인정하다

tamp

v. **1_ 흙으로 틀어막다** pack down, press, cram

2_ 다져 굳히다

3_ 담배를 재다

When planting shrubbery, it is advisable to **tamp** the dirt around the roots after covering them. 관목을 심을 때, 뿌리를 덮은 후 주변에 흙을 다져 굳히는 것이 좋다.

advisable adj. 바람직한, 유명한, 현명한, 권할 만한

dirt n. 흙, 토양, 더러움, 먼지, 진흙, 부도덕, 상스러운 말

graze

v. **1_ (가축이) 풀을 뜯어먹다** feed

2_ 가볍게 스쳐 지나가다 skim, brush, touch, glance

Cattle **graze** on the dry uplands of the island of Hawaii. 소들은 하와이 섬의 건조한 고지에서 풀을 뜯는다.

cattle n. 소, 가축

dry adj. 건조한, 마른, 습기가 없는

upland n. 고지, 고산 지방

island n. 섬, 삼림지대, 고립된 언덕

flamboyant   adj. **1_타는 듯한, 눈부신** ornate, vivid, flashy, showy,

2_현란한 bright, loud

≠muted, drab, plain, dull, quiet, colorless,

inconspicuous

Alexander Woollcott's **flamboyant** personality combined
sharpness of wit with sentimentality. 알렉산더 울컷의 눈부신
성격은 위트의 신랄함과 감정적 행위가 결합되어 있다.

combine   v. 결합하여 하나로 하다, 짜맞추다, 연합시키다, 겸비하다

sharpness   n. 예리한 것

sentimentality   n. 감상성, 감정(감상)적 행위

Lesson 22 Review Test

01 When planting shrubbery, it is advisable to **tamp** the dirt around the roots after covering them.

    ⓐ water   ⓑ fertilize

    ⓒ pack down   ⓓ tamper with

02 Cattle **graze** on the dry uplands of the island of Hawaii.

    ⓐ wander   ⓑ breed

    ⓒ feed   ⓓ exercise

03 In statistics, the mathematical mean is obtained by dividing the **sum** of a group of scores by the number of scores.

    ⓐ total   ⓑ square

    ⓒ numerator   ⓓ list

04 When an electric current **flows** through a wire, a magnetic field appears around the wire.

    ⓐ travels   ⓑ vibrates

    ⓒ alternates   ⓓ fluctuates

05 San Francisco's Chinese community, comprising 67,000 **inhabitants**, is the largest concentration of Chinese outside of Asia.

    ⓐ adults   ⓑ workers

    ⓒ visitors   ⓓ residents

06 Concrete is a durable, watertight, and incombustible material that is, **moreover**, inexpensive to make.

ⓐ in addition   ⓑ more or less

ⓒ however   ⓓ consequently

07 Monkeys constantly groom one another, thus **reinforcing** the social bonds necessary to their survival.

ⓐ expressing   ⓑ stressing

ⓒ strengthening   ⓓ forming

08 Marcus Garvey, who **urged** the back to Africa movement, attempted to establish colonies of Black Americans in Africa.

ⓐ advocated   ⓑ envisioned

ⓒ lectured on   ⓓ planned for

09 Critics have never been able to find adequate praise for Marian Anderson's **matchless** contralto voice.

ⓐ memorable   ⓑ peerless

ⓒ faultless   ⓓ impressive

10 Steel is an alloy composed **primarily** of iron and carbon.

ⓐ traditionally   ⓑ ironically

ⓒ carefully   ⓓ principally

11 The common characteristic of fish, amphibians, reptiles, birds, and mammals is that all have **backbones**.

ⓐ lungs   ⓑ spines

ⓒ claws   ⓓ fur

12 Underground storage **reservoirs** are important in the conservation of natural gas.

    ⓐ laboratories   ⓑ receptacles

    ⓒ reactors   ⓓ showcases

13 Strict sanitary procedures help to **forestall** outbreaks of disease.

    ⓐ prevent   ⓑ control

    ⓒ minimize   ⓓ preview

14 **Deceptive** labeling of certain types of merchandise is not allowed under the Pure Food and Drug Act of 1906.

    ⓐ Alarming   ⓑ Misleading

    ⓒ Extravagant   ⓓ Tasteless

15 Alexander Woollcott's **flamboyant** personality combined sharpness of wit with sentimentality.

    ⓐ devious   ⓑ humorous

    ⓒ singular   ⓓ showy

01	c	ⓐwater=v. ~에 물을 대다 ⓑfertilize=v. 비옥하게 하다 ⓓtamper with=~을 간섭하다
02	c	ⓐwander=v. (떠)돌아다니다 ⓑbreed=v. 낳다, 기르다 ⓓexercise=v. 연습(운동)하다
03	a	ⓑsquare=n. 정사각형 ⓒnumerator=n. 분자 ⓓlist=n. 목록(명부)
04	a	ⓑvibrate=v. 진동하다 ⓒalternate=v. 교체하다 ⓓfluctuate=v. 동요하다
05	d	ⓐadult=n. 어른 ⓑworker=n. 일하는 사람 ⓒvisitor=n. 방문객
06	a	ⓑmore or less=다소 ⓒhowever=adv. 그러나 ⓓconsequently=adv. 따라서
07	c	ⓐexpress=v. 표현하다 ⓑstress=v. 강조하다 ⓓform=v. 형성하다
08	a	ⓑenvision=v. 마음에 그리다 ⓒlecture on=강의(훈계)하다 ⓓplan for=~을 계획하다
09	b	ⓐmemorable=adj. 기억할 만한 ⓒfaultless=adj. 결점이 없는 ⓓimpressive=adj. 인상적인
10	d	ⓐtraditionally=adv. 전통적으로 ⓑironically=adv. 반어적으로 ⓒcarefully=adv. 주의하여
11	b	ⓐlung=n. 폐 ⓒclaw=n. 갈고리 발톱 ⓓfur=n. 모피
12	b	ⓐlaboratory=n. 실험실 ⓒreactor=n. 반응을 나타내는 사람(동물) ⓓshowcase=n. 유리 진열장(상자)
13	a	ⓑcontrol=v. 통제하다 ⓒminimize=v. 최소화하다 ⓓpreview=v. 시사(시연)를 보다
14	b	ⓐAlarming=adj. 놀라운 ⓒExtravagant=adj. 사치스런 ⓓTasteless=adj. 맛없는
15	d	ⓐdevious=adj. 구불구불한 ⓑhumorous=adj. 익살스러운 ⓒsingular=adj. 단일의(남다른)

Lesson 23

particular

equivalent

handsome

endeavor

conscious(ly)

placid

restrict

pedestal

fluctuate

indispensable

bear[2]

depict

philanthropic

abiding

outburst

particular

adj. **1_특유의** specific, definite, certain, distinct

2_독특한 unusual, extraordinary

≠ordinary, common, general

n. **1_개개의 항목**

2_사항 detail, fact

3_특색

Most labor unions insist on being the sole representative of a **particular** group of employees. 대부분의 노동조합들은 특유의 고용인 그룹의 단독적인 대표단이 있어야 한다고 주장한다.

sole adj. 유일한, 독점적인, 단독의 n. 발바닥, 신바닥

representative n. 대표(자), 상속인, 국회의원, 전형 adj. 표현하는, 대리의, 전형적인

He'll be able to tell you about **particulars** of your program. 그가 당신 프로그램의 특색에 대해 말해줄 수 있을 것이다.

equivalent

adj. **동등한, 대등한** equal, same, alike, analogous, comparable

≠unequal, superior, unlike, incomparable

In terms of precipitation ten inches of snow is the **equivalent** of an inch of rain. 강설량에서, 10인치의 눈은 1인치의 비와 같다.

precipitation n. 강설(강수/강우)량, 낙하, 추락, 재촉, 조급

inch n. 인치, 신장, 근소한 거리, 소량

handsome

adj. **1_아름다운** attractive, good-looking, beautiful, elegant

2_균형 잡힌 well-proportioned

≠ugly, repulsive, plain

The large towers of the George Washington Bridge were not encased in masonry but were left exposed to reveal their **handsome** steel structure. 조지 워싱턴 다리의 큰 탑들은 벽돌 속에 싸여 있지 않고 그 아름다운 강철 구조물을 그대로 드러내고 있었다.

tower　n. 탑, 망루, 성채, 요새, 고층 건물, 안전한 장소

expose　v. 드러내다, 진열하다, 폭로하다　n. 폭로, 폭로 기사

reveal　v. 드러내다, 밝히다, 누설하다, 계시하다　n. 출현, 계시, 폭로

structure　n. 구조, 구성, 조직, 조립, 건조물, 건축물

endeavor

v. **1_노력하다** attempt, try, strive, venture,

2_열심히 해보다 undertake, tackle, struggle

n. **1_노력** effort

2_시도 attempt

After many years of unsuccessfully **endeavoring** to form his own orchestra, Glenn Miller finally achieved world fame in 1939 as a big band leader. 자신의 오케스트라를 구성하기 위해 헛된 노력을 하고서 몇 년 후, 글렌 밀러는 1939년 마침내 큰 밴드의 리더로서 세계적인 명성을 얻게 되었다.

fame　n. 명성, 고명, 평판, 세평　v. 유명하게 하다

conscious(ly)

adj.(adv.)

1_의식하고 있는 deliberately, knowingly

2_의도적인 intentional

≠unconscious, unwitting, inadvertent

Habits can be **consciously** strengthened, as when a student of the violin practices and memorizes different fingerings. 습관은 의도적으로 강화될 수 있다. 그것은 바이올린을 공부하는 학생이 다른 운지법을 연습하고 외울 수 있는 것과 같다.

habit n. 습관, 버릇, 관습, 풍습

practice v. 연습하다, 실행하다 n. 연습, 훈련, 공부, 숙련, 관행, 실행

memorize v. 외우다, 암기하다

finger v. 운지법에 따라 연주하다, 손가락으로 연주하다, 만지작거리다

placid

adj.

1_조용한, 차분한 quiet, calm, serene, composed, tranquil, undisturbed

≠agitated, aroused, stormy, turbulent

2_만족한 satisfied

From an airplane, the grasslands of the western prairie appear almost as uniform as a **placid** sea. 비행기에서 보면, 서부 대평원의 풀밭은 거의 조용한 바다와 같이 보인다.

uniform adj. 같은 형태의, 일정한, 언제나 변함없는 n. 유니폼

restrict

v. **제한하다, 한정하다** limit, confine, restrain, constrain, narrow
≠loose, loosen, free, open

By 1900, many municipalities had begun to **restrict** the
use of automobiles in order to ensure pedestrian safety.
1900년까지 많은 지방 자치체들이 보행자들의 안전을 보장하기 위해 자
동차 사용을 제한하기 시작했다.

municipality n. 지방 자치체, 시(읍)당국

ensure v. 확실하게 하다, 지키다

pedestrian n. 보행자, 도보 여행 adj. 도보인, 평범한, 시시한

pedestal

n. **대좌, 토대, 축받이** base, support, stand, foundation

Poet Emma Lazarus is perhaps best known for having
written the sonnet inscribed on the **pedestal** of the Statue
of Liberty. 시인 엠마 래저러스는 아마도 자유의 여신상 대좌에 새겨
진 소네트를 쓴 사람으로 가장 유명할 것이다.

perhaps adv. 아마, 필시, 어쩌면 ~일지도 n. 추측, 우연, 불확실함

write v. 쓰다, 편지를 쓰다, 작곡하다

inscribe v. 새기다, 쓰다, 적다, 등록하다

fluctuate

v. **1_ 동요하다** waver, vary, alternate, sway

2_ 물결처럼 움직이다 veer, alter

≠stabilize, settle, freeze, solidify

The manic-depressive usually **fluctuates** between great excitement and deep depression. 조울증 환자는 일반적으로 극단적인 흥분 상태와 심한 우울 상태 사이에서 동요한다.

manic-depressive n. 조울증 환자 adj. 조울증의

deep adj. 심한, 깊은, 깊숙한 데까지 이르는, 이해하기 어려운, 심오한

depression n. 우울, 의기소침, 강하, 저하, 저기압

indispensable

adj. **필수의, 무시할 수 없는** necessary, needed, critical, essential, vital

≠unnecessary, nonessential, superfluous, dispensable, disposable

n. **필요 불가결한 사람/것**

In the Navajo household, grandparents and other relatives play **indispensable** roles in raising children. 나바호 가정에서는, 조부모와 다른 친척들이 아이를 키우는 데 필수적인 역할을 한다.

relative n. 친척, 집안, 동족 adj. 비교상의, 상대적인, 관계가 있는, 상관적인

bear²

v. **1_낳다** produce, yield, generate

2_출산하다 give birth, reproduce, breed

3_떠맡다 sustain, brace

4_견디다 suffer, endure, stand, tolerate

n. **곰**

The walnut is a deciduous tree that **bears** valuable nuts.

호두나무는 금전적 가치가 있는 열매를 맺는 낙엽성 나무다.

nut   n. 나무 열매, 핵심, 도안

*bear는 다양한 뜻을 가지고 있어 Lesson 6에 이어 여기에서도 다시 한 번 소개한다.

depict

v. **1_표현하다** portray, express

2_그리다 paint, picture, sketch

3_나타내다 describe, tell, dramatize

Embroidery **depicting** scenic views became popular in the United States toward the end of the eighteenth century.

풍경을 표현하는 자수법은 18세기 말기 무렵에 미국에서 유행되었다.

embroidery   n. 자수(법), 자수품, 윤색

scenic   adj. 풍경의, 경치가 좋은, 무대의, 연극의, 극적인, 생생한

toward   prep. ~경, 무렵, ~의 부근에, ~을 위해, ~쪽을 향하여

end   n. 말기, 끝, 한계, 가장자리, 최후, 목적, 목표, 결과

depiction

n. 묘사 description, representation

philanthropic

adj. **1_인정 많은, 인자한** compassionate, altruistic, humane

≠miserly, egotistical, selfish

2_ 자선 사업의 charitable, humanitarian

The Ford Foundation is one of the world's wealthiest
philanthropic organizations. 포드 재단은 세계에서 가장 부유한
자선 단체 중의 하나다.

foundation n. 재단, 유지 기금, 건설, 토대, 기초, 기본

philanthropist

n. 자선가

philanthropy

n. 자선 활동, 자선 사업

abiding

adj. **지속적인, 불변의** enduring, lasting, continuing, durable,

perennial

≠transient, transitory, fleeting

The concept of upward social mobility has been an
abiding feature of American life. 수직적 신분 상승의 개념은 미
국인들의 생활에서 지속되고 있는 특성이다.

concept n. 개념, 관념, 구상

mobility n. 이동성, 가동성, 변동성

feature n. 특징, 두드러진 점, 용모, 얼굴, 이목구비, 대표작, 특종

v. 특징을 이루다, 특집 기사로 다루다

life n. 생활, 삶, 일생, 인생, 수명

outburst

n. **1_돌발, 폭발** explosion, eruption, surge, rush, burst

2_(감정 등의) 격발

The first major **outburst** of musical creativity in the United States occurred at the end of the nineteenth century. 미국에서 뮤지컬 창조의 가장 주요한 시작은 19세기 말에 발생했다.

creativity n. 창조성, 독창력

Lesson 23 Review Test

01 The walnut is a deciduous tree that **bears** valuable nuts.
  ⓐ replicates   ⓑ yields
  ⓒ replaces   ⓓ hides

02 In terms of precipitation ten inches of snow is **the equivalent** of an inch of rain.
  ⓐ the symbol of   ⓑ as same as
  ⓒ the product of   ⓓ as thick as

03 From an airplane, the grasslands of the western prairie appear almost as uniform as a **placid** sea.
  ⓐ fake   ⓑ seedy
  ⓒ hilly   ⓓ calm

04 Poet Emma Lazarus is perhaps best known for having written the sonnet inscribed on the **pedestal** of the Statue of Liberty.
  ⓐ inside   ⓑ base
  ⓒ torch   ⓓ replica

05 The first major **outburst** of musical creativity in the United States occurred at the end of the nineteenth century.
  ⓐ surge   ⓑ round
  ⓒ outcome   ⓓ performance

06 Most labor unions insist on being the sole representative of a **particular** group of employees.
  ⓐ fastidious   ⓑ biased
  ⓒ seasoned   ⓓ certain

07 By 1900, many municipalities had begun to **restrict** the use of automobiles in order to ensure pedestrian safety.

ⓐ test   ⓑ limit

ⓒ standardize   ⓓ prohibit

08 The manic-depressive usually **fluctuates** between great excitement and deep depression.

ⓐ recovers   ⓑ falls

ⓒ improves   ⓓ alternates

09 Habits can be **consciously** strengthened, as when a student of the violin practices and memorizes different fingerings.

ⓐ conveniently   ⓑ lasting

ⓒ intentionally   ⓓ robustly

10 The concept of upward social mobility has been an **abiding** feature of American life.

ⓐ enduring   ⓑ intriguing

ⓒ unaffected   ⓓ observing

11 In the Navajo household, grandparents and other relatives play **indispensable** roles in raising children.

ⓐ dominant   ⓑ exemplary

ⓒ essential   ⓓ demanding

12 Embroidery **depicting** scenic views became popular in the United States toward the end of the eighteenth century.

ⓐ distorting   ⓑ portraying

ⓒ commemorating   ⓓ emphasizing

13 The Ford Foundation is one of the world's wealthiest **philanthropic** organizations.

ⓐ profligate   ⓑ governmental

ⓒ humanitarian   ⓓ multinational

14 After many years of unsuccessfully **endeavoring** to form his own orchestra, Glenn Miller finally achieved world fame in 1939 as a big band leader.

ⓐ requesting   ⓑ trying

ⓒ offering   ⓓ deciding

15 The large towers of the George Washington Bridge were not encased in masonry but were left exposed to reveal their **handsome** steel structure.

ⓐ naked   ⓑ well-worn

ⓒ good-looking   ⓓ completed

01	b	ⓐreplicate=v. 모사(복제)하다 ⓒreplace=v. ~에 대신하다 ⓓhide=v. ~을 숨기다
02	b	ⓐthe symbol of=~의 상징 ⓒthe product of=~의 생산품 ⓓas thick as=~만큼 두꺼운
03	d	ⓐfake=adj. 가짜의 ⓑseedy=adj. 씨가 많은 ⓒhilly=adj. 구릉성의
04	b	ⓐinside=n. 내부 ⓒtorch=n. 횃불 ⓓreplica=n. 복사(복제)
05	a	ⓑround=n. 둥근 것 ⓒoutcome=n. 결과 ⓓperformance=n. 실행
06	d	ⓐfastidious=adj. 까다로운 ⓑbiased=adj. 치우친 ⓒseasoned=adj. 양념한
07	b	ⓐtest=v. 시험하다 ⓒstandardize=v. 표준화하다 ⓓprohibit=v. 금(지)하다
08	d	ⓐrecover=v. 되찾다, 회복하다 ⓑfall=v. 떨어지다 ⓒimprove=v. 향상되다
09	c	ⓐconveniently=adv. 편리하게 ⓑlasting=adj. 영구적인 ⓓrobustly=adv. 강건하게
10	a	ⓑintriguing=adj. 흥미를 자아내는 ⓒunaffected=adj. 영향을 받지 않는 ⓓobserving=adj. 관찰하는(주의 깊은)
11	c	ⓐdominant=adj. 지배적인 ⓑexemplary=adj. 모범적인 ⓓdemanding=adj. 요구가 지나친
12	b	ⓐdistort=v. 비틀다, 왜곡하다 ⓒcommemorate=v. 기념하다 ⓓemphasize=v. 강조하다
13	c	ⓐprofligate=adj. 방탕한 ⓑgovernmental=adj. 정부(정치)의 ⓓmultinational=adj. 다국적의
14	b	ⓐrequest=v. 요청하다 ⓒoffer=v. 제공하다 ⓓdecide=v. 결정하다
15	c	ⓐnaked=adj. 벌거숭이의 ⓑwell-worn=adj. 닳아빠진 ⓓcompleted=adj. 완성된

Lesson 24

complete

concentrate

field

counsel

injury

absolute(ly)

astound

extract

hypothesis

prominent

seal

beat

keen(ly)

range

advocate

complete

adj. **1_모든 것을 포함한** with all its parts

2_완성된 full-fledged

v. **1_~을 모두 갖추다**

2_마치다, 끝내다 accomplish, achieve, finish

Completing and patenting upward of fifty different inventions, Granville T. Woods appears to have surpassed nearly every other Black inventor of his time in the quantity and variety of his inventions. 50가지가 넘는 발명품을 완성하고, 특허를 낸 그랜빌 우드는 발명품의 양적인 면에서나 다양성에서나 동시대에 살았던 거의 모든 흑인 발명가를 능가했던 것처럼 보인다.

patent v. 특허권을 얻다 adj. 특허의, 명백한 n. 특허, 인가, 면허

surpass v. ~보다 낫다, 초월하다

completion

n. 1_완성, 완료

2_달성 fulfillment, realization

The urban renewal project is near **completion**. 도시 재개발 프로젝트는 거의 완성되고 있다.

renewal n. 재건, 재개, 복구, 부활, 갱신

concentrate

v. **1_~에 집결시키다** consolidate, collect, assemble

2_집중하다 focus

n. **농축물**

Modern dance teachers **concentrate** on helping students to express the concepts of space time, and energy through dance. 현대 무용 선생님들은 학생들이 춤을 통하여 우주 시간과 에너지에 대한 개념을 표현할 수 있도록 중점을 두고 있다.

modern adj. 현대의, 지금의, 근세의 n. 현대인, 새로운 사상의 소유자

concept n. 개념, 관념, 구상, 직관적 대상

concentration

n. 집중 focus

Concentration is what you need in passing this test. 네가 이 시험을 통과하는 데 필요한 것은 집중력이다.

field

n. **1_들, 벌판** grassland

2_현장 site

3_영역, 분야 area

Cornelius Vanderbilt's success in shipping prompted him
to extend his interests into the **field** of railroad
transportation in the early 1860's. 1860년대 초, 해운업에서
성공한 코넬리우스 밴더빌트는 그의 관심을 철도 운송 분야로 확대시켰다.

shipping n. 해운업, 선적, 선박, 상선

extend v. 확장하다, 넓히다, 전개시키다, 뻗치다, 연장하다

transportation n. 운송, 수송, 운수, 운임

counsel

n. **1_상담** guidance

2_조언 advice, suggestion

v. **조언하다** advise, recommend, suggest

Many large companies have begun to organize "wellness"
programs that **counsel** employees and offer them physical
fitness classes. 많은 큰 회사들이 고용인들에게 조언을 해주고
신체적인 건강 상태의 정도를 알려주는 "만족" 프로그램을 조직하기
시작했다.

wellness n. 좋음, 만족스러움, 소망스러움

physical adj. 신체의, 육체의, 물질의, 물질적인, 자연의, 물리학의

fitness n. 적당함, 적합함, 적절함, 건강(상태)

counselor

n. 1_조언자 advisor

2_카운슬러, 지도교사

3_법정 변론 변호사

injury

n. **부상**

injurious

adj. 해로운 harmful, hurtful

injure

v. 1_다치다, 해치다 wound, hurt

   2_손상하다 demage, impair

Since respiration is required for continual energy release, it is **injurious** to stop it for more than a short time. 호흡 작용은 지속적인 에너지 방출이 필요하므로, 짧은 시간 이상 호흡을 멈추는 것은 해롭다.

respiration n. 호흡(작용), 한 호흡

require v. 필요로 하다, 요구하다, 바라다

release n. 방출, 해방, 구출 v. 해방하다, 석방하다, 늦추다, 개봉하다, 양도하다

short adj. 짧은, 오래 가지 않는, 낮은, 부족한, 간결한

---

absolute(ly) adj.(adv.)

1_완전한 total, thorough

2_절대적인 supreme

3_명백한 clear

n. **절대적인 것** ≠relative

Many view him as the **absolute** authority on the subject. 많은 사람들이 그를 그 문제에 대한 완전한 권위자로 여긴다.

subject n. 문제, 주제, 과제, 화제, 교과, 동기, 원인, 신하

In many hunting and gathering societies, individuals are not **absolutely** restricted by kin-group membership in their choice of living groups. 많은 수렵 사회와 채집 사회에서, 개인은 자신들이 선택해 함께 살고 있는 집단의 구성원들에 의해 완전히 제한받는 것은 아니다.

kin adj. 친척인, 동류인 n. 친척, 일가, 혈족, 일가 사람, 동류의 사람

astound

v. **크게 놀라다** surprise, amaze, shock

astounding

adj. 놀라운 amazing, surprising,
　　shocking

The brief Alaska summer is accompanied by an **astounding** change in the flora and fauna of the tundra. 알래스카의 짧은 여름에는 툰드라의 식물상과 동물상에 놀라운 변화가 수반된다.

brief　adj. 단시간의, 잠시의, 간결한, 무뚝뚝한

flora　n. 식물상, 식물지, 식물

fauna　n. 동물상, 동물지

tundra　n. 툰드라, 동토대

extract

v. **1_뽑아내다** derive

2_추출하다 remove

n. **1_추출물**

2_발췌 excerpt

Extracted from flaxseed, linseed oil is the principal source of drying oil for paint and varnish. 아마인으로부터 뽑아낸 아마인유는 페인트와 니스에 사용되는 건조유의 주요한 원료다.

principal　adj. 주요한, 주된, 원금의　n. 우두머리, 주역, 본인, 기본 재산

paint　n. 그림 물감, 안료, 페이트, 착색, 입술 연지

　　　v. 그림 물감으로 그리다, 생생하게 표현하다

varnish　n. 니스, 니스를 칠한 표면, 겉치레, 외식, 속임수

hypothesis

n. **추측, 가정** supposition, theory, assumption

According to one **hypothesis**, cosmic rays originate from the destruction of atoms. 어떤 가설에 따르면, 우주의 빛은 원자의 파괴에 의해 생긴다고 한다.

originate v. 생기다, 일어나다, 비롯되다, 시작하다

destruction n. 파괴, 박멸, 파기, 멸망

atom n. 원자, 지극히 작은 것, 미량

prominent

adj. **1_유명한, 저명한** notable, eminent, distinguished

2_두드러진 conspicuous, noticeable

3_중요한 important

In the late 1800's Charlotte Gilman was a **prominent** lecturer and writer on such themes as feminism and labor. 1800년대 후기에 샬럿 길먼은 페미니즘이나 노동과 같은 주제를 다룬 유명한 강연자이며 작가였다.

lecturer n. 강연자, 강사

theme n. 주제, 제목, 테마, 소논문, 과제 작문, 주제곡

feminism n. 남녀 동등권주의(론), 여성적 특질

prominence

n. 유명 fame, eminence

seal

n. **1_도장** stamp

2_봉인

3_바다표범

v. **1_검인을 찍다** ratify

2_봉인하다 enclose

3_분명히 정하다 secure

4_밀폐하다 close

Salt added to the water used to boil eggs will **seal** a cracked egg by coagulating the leaking white. 달걀을 끓이는 물에 들어 있는 소금은 새고 있는 흰자를 응고시킴으로써 깨진 달걀을 밀폐한다.

boil v. 끓다, 분출하다, 익다, 뒤끓다

crack v. 날카로운 소리를 내며 깨지다(찢어지다, 부러지다), 녹초가 되다, 금이 가다

coagulate v. 응고(응결)시키다

leak v. 새다, 누설하다 n. 새는 곳, 새기, 누설, 배뇨

beat

v. **1_~을 치다, 두드리다** strike, throb

2_이기다 conquer, defeat

n. **1_구타**

2_박자 rhythm

A folk song will often vary its **beat** or alternate between major and minor keys. 포크 송은 박자가 다양하거나 혹은 메이저 키와 마이너 키 사이에서 번갈아 일어난다.

alternate v. 번갈아 일어나다, 엇갈리다, 교류하다 adj. 교대의, 상호간의, 대신의

keen(ly)

adj.(adv.) **1_예리한** sharp, edged

2_예민한 acute, clever, quick

Bloodhounds have a **keen** sense of smell. 블러드하운드는 예민한 후각을 갖고 있다.

Many young people are **keenly** aware of the advantages of a college education in today's competitive economy. 많은 젊은이들이 오늘날의 경쟁적인 경제에서 대학 교육의 장점을 빈틈없이 잘 알고 있다.

aware adj. 알아채고 있는, 정통한

advantage n. 유리한 점, 우위, 이익, 편의

range

n. **1_범위** scope, extend, limit, span

2_사정 거리

v. **1_변동하다** vary, fluctuate

2_뻗다, 퍼지다 extend

The polar bears of the Hudson Bay are a distinct population thriving at the southern end of their **range**. 허드슨 만에 있는 북극곰은 자신들 영역의 남쪽 끝에서 번성하고 있는 독특한 집단이다.

distinct adj. 독특한, 다른, 명료한, 선명한, 희한한, 눈부신

thrive v. 번성하다, 번영하다, 무럭무럭 자라다

Ranging from solitary to gregarious, beaked whales may travel in schools of several hundred during the breeding season. 혼자서 살기도 하고 무리로 살기도 하는 부리고래들은 번식기 동안에는 수백 마리가 떼를 지어 다니기도 한다.

advocate

v. **1_지지하다, 옹호하다** support

2_~을 추천하다 recommend

n. **1_옹호자** supporter, proponent

2_대변자

Shirley Chisholm has been one of the foremost **advocates** of welfare legislation since the 1960's. 셜리 치점은 1960년대 이후 가장 주목할 만한 복지법 제정 옹호자 중의 한 명이다.

welfare n. 복지, 행복, 번영

Lesson 24 Review Test

01 **Completing** and patenting upward of fifty different inventions, Granville T. Woods appears to have surpassed nearly every other Black inventor of his time in the quantity and variety of his inventions.

    ⓐ Inspecting   ⓑ Suggesting

    ⓒ Complementing   ⓓ Finishing

02 Modern dance teachers **concentrate on** helping students to express the concepts of space time, and energy through dance.

    ⓐ count of   ⓑ focus on

    ⓒ lecture about   ⓓ argue about

03 Cornelius Vanderbilt's success in shipping prompted him to extend his interests into the **field** of railroad transportation in the early 1860's.

    ⓐ area   ⓑ cargo

    ⓒ stations   ⓓ tracks

04 Many large companies have begun to organize "wellness" programs that **counsel** employees and offer them physical fitness classes.

    ⓐ exercise   ⓑ charge

    ⓒ advise   ⓓ hire

05 Since respiration is required for continual energy release, it is **injurious** to stop it for more than a short time.

    ⓐ harmful   ⓑ troublesome

    ⓒ contrary   ⓓ offensive

06 In many hunting and gathering societies, individuals are not **absolutely** restricted by kin-group membership in their choice of living groups.

    ⓐ totally   ⓑ often

    ⓒ intrinsically   ⓓ irresistibly

07 The brief Alaska summer is accompanied by an **astounding** change in the flora and fauna of the tundra.

    ⓐ alarming   ⓑ annoying

    ⓒ amazing   ⓓ alluring

08 **Extracted** from flaxseed, linseed oil is the principal source of drying oil for paint and varnish.

    ⓐ Derived   ⓑ Differentiated

    ⓒ Detached   ⓓ Descended

09 According to one **hypothesis**, cosmic rays originate from the destruction of atoms.

    ⓐ philosopher   ⓑ astronomer

    ⓒ theory   ⓓ experiment

10 In the late 1800's Charlotte Gilman was **a prominent** lecturer and writer on such themes as feminism and labor.

    ⓐ an insightful   ⓑ an interesting

    ⓒ a determined   ⓓ a notable

11 Salt added to the water used to boil eggs will **seal** a cracked egg by coagulating the leaking white.

    ⓐ deepen   ⓑ smooth

    ⓒ force   ⓓ close

12 A folk song will often vary its **beat** or alternate between major and minor keys.

    ⓐ lyrics   ⓑ notes

    ⓒ rhythm   ⓓ message

13 Many young people are **keenly** aware of the advantages of a college education in today's competitive economy.

    ⓐ sadly   ⓑ currently

    ⓒ anxiously   ⓓ acutely

14 **Ranging** from solitary to gregarious, beaked whales may travel in schools of several hundred during the breeding season.

    ⓐ Varying   ⓑ Roving

    ⓒ Grazing   ⓓ Turning

15 Shirley Chisholm has been one of the foremost **advocates** of welfare legislation since the 1960's.

    ⓐ predecessors   ⓑ judges

    ⓒ proponents   ⓓ historians

01	**d**	ⓐ Inspect=v. 면밀히 살피다 ⓑ Suggest=v. 제안하다 ⓒ Complement=v. 보충(보완)하다
02	**b**	ⓐ count of=세다(계산하다) ⓒ lecture about=강의(설교)하다 ⓓ argue about=논(쟁)하다
03	**a**	ⓑ cargo=n. 화물 ⓒ station=n. 역(정거장) ⓓ track=n. 철도 선로(궤도)
04	**c**	ⓐ exercise=v. 연습(운동)하다 ⓑ charge=v. 과하다(지우다) ⓓ hire=v. 고용하다
05	**a**	ⓑ troublesome=adj. 성가신 ⓒ contrary=adj. 반대의 ⓓ offensive=adj. 불쾌한(무례한)
06	**a**	ⓑ often=adv. 자주 ⓒ intrinsically=adv. 본질적으로 ⓓ irresistibly=adv. 저항할 수 없이
07	**c**	ⓐ alarming=adj. 놀라운 ⓑ annoying=adj. 성가신 ⓓ alluring=adj. 유혹하는
08	**a**	ⓑ Differentiate=v. 구별짓다 ⓒ Detach=v. 떼다 ⓓ Descend=v. 내려가다
09	**c**	ⓐ philosopher=n. 철학자 ⓑ astronomer=n. 천문학자 ⓓ experiment=n. 실험
10	**d**	ⓐ insightful=adj. 통찰력 있는 ⓑ interesting=adj. 흥미 있는 ⓒ determined=adj. 단호한
11	**d**	ⓐ deepen=v. 깊게 하다 ⓑ smooth=v. 부드럽게 하다 ⓒ force=v. 강요(강제)하다
12	**c**	ⓐ lyric=n. 서정시 ⓑ note=n. 악보(음표) ⓓ message=n. 전갈
13	**d**	ⓐ sadly=adv. 슬프게 ⓑ currently=adv. 일반적으로 ⓒ anxiously=adv. 근심하여
14	**a**	ⓑ Rove=v. 헤매다 ⓒ Graze=v. 방목하다 ⓓ Turn=v. 돌리다(회전하다)
15	**c**	ⓐ predecessor=n. 전임자 ⓑ judge=n. 재판관(판사) ⓓ historian=n. 역사가

revere

sort

foremost

extend

command

mushroom

ingenious(ly)

excel

treasure

obscure

build

detect

collide

acclaim

seclude

revere

v. **우러러 공경하다** venerate, respect, admire, honor

≠disrespect, dishonor, insult

reverence

n. 1_우러러 공경하는 마음

    veneration

    2_절 bow

    3_존경받고 있는 상태 respect

The Liberty Bell is an object of great **reverence** because it was rung in 1776 to proclaim the signing of the Declaration of Independence. 자유의 종은 1776년 독립선언의 서명을 선포하기 위해 울렸기 때문에 대단한 존경의 대상이다.

ring v. 울리다, 전화를 걸다, 둘러싸다, 둥글게 만들다

proclaim v. 선언하다, 칭찬하다, 금지하다

sort

n. **1_종류** kind, class, type, category

    2_성격, 성질 character, nature

    3_방법

v. **1_분류하다** segregate, separate, isolate, classify

    2_~을 가려내다 screen

There are two **sorts** of books required for basic bookkeeping. 기초적인 부기에 요구되는 2종류의 책이 있다.

bookkeeping n. 부기

foremost

adj. **1_ 맨 먼저의**

2_ 가장 중요한, 주목할 만한

3_ 주요한 chief, leading, principal

adv. **맨 먼저, 첫째로** chiefly, principally

In 1965 California replaced New York as the **foremost** state in the export of manufactured goods. 1965년 캘리포니아는 뉴욕을 대신해 주요한 공산품 수출 주가 되었다.

replace v. 대신하다, ~의 뒤를 잇다, 바꾸다

extend

v. **1_ ~을 잡아늘이다** elongate, stretch

≠shrink

2_ 연장하다 lengthen, prolong

≠shorten

3_ 뻗(치)다 stretch

4_ 확장하다 widen, enlarge

5_ (거리, 기간에) 이르다 reach

Biomedical research may soon discover a way to **extend** human life. 생물의학 연구는 인간의 생명을 연장하는 길을 곧 발견하게 될 것이다.

command

v. 1_~을 명하다 order

2_지배하다, 지휘하다 lead

3_~을 내려다보다

n. 지휘

commanding

adj. 명령조인, 위엄있는 forceful

As a performer, Martha Graham had a **commanding** personality and an intensity that captivated audiences. 연주자로서 마사 그레이엄은 청중을 사로잡는 강렬함과 위엄 있는 성격을 갖추고 있었다.

performer n. 연주자, 가수, 배우, 명인, 실행자

intensity n. 강렬함, 격렬함, 열심임

captivate v. 마음을 사로잡다, 매혹하다

mushroom

n. 1_버섯

2_버섯 비슷한 것

adj. 버섯 모양의

v. 1_버섯을 따다

2_빨리 성장(발전)하다 grow quickly, boom, snowball, swell

In the 1820's cities in the United States **mushroomed** as a result of the Industrial Revolution. 1820년대, 미국의 도시는 산업 혁명의 결과로 급성장하게 되었다.

ingenious(ly)

adj.(adv.)

1_ 교묘한, 정교한 skilled

2_ 독창적인 clever

3_ 착안이 좋은

4_ 발명의 재간이 있는 inventive

Duke Ellington's **ingenious** orchestration techniques made him perhaps the most remarkable artist that jazz has produced. 듀크 엘링턴의 독창적인 악기 편성 기술은 그를, 재즈가 낳은 아마도 가장 뛰어난 예술가로 만들었을 것이다.

orchestration n. 악기 편성법, 관현악법

remarkable adj. 주목할 만한, 현저한, 범상치 않은, 진기한

excel

v. 1_ ~을 능가하다 exceed, surpass, eclipse

2_ 뛰어나다, 탁월하다 be outstanding

Babe Didrikson Zaharias **excelled** in basketball, baseball, and track in her youth and later became a champion golfer. 베이브 디드릭슨 제어라이어스는 젊은 시절에 농구, 야구, 육상 경기에서 뛰어났으며 뒤에 골프 우승자가 되기도 했다.

track n. 육상경기, 철도, 궤도, 자국, 오솔길, 통로, 방식, 연속

excellence

n. 우월, 우수

excellent

adj. 뛰어난, 우수한 exceptional,
    outstanding

treasure

n. **1_보물** gem, jewel

2_귀중품

v. **소중히 하다** prize, value

Treasure *Island* by Robert Louis Stevenson is one of the most read books in the world. 로버트 루이스 스티븐슨의 『보물섬』은 세계에서 가장 많이 읽히는 책 중 하나다.

In the legends of the American West, Paul Bunyan's most **treasured** possession was Babe the Blue Ox, whose horns were said to span a distance of 42 ax handles. 미국 서부의 전설 속에서 폴 버니언이 가장 아끼던 소장품은 Babe the Blue Ox였는데 그것의 뿔은 도끼 손잡이 42개분의 길이였다고 한다.

horn n. 뿔, 뿔 제품

span v. 뼘으로 재다, 손으로 쥐고 재다, 걸치다, 미치다

obscure

adj. **1_애매한** uncertain

2_눈에 띄지 않은 inconspicuous, unnoticeable

3_컴컴한 dim

v. **1_～을 덮어 감추다** hide, conceal

≠reveal, expose, discover

2_～을 약화시키다 weaken

The old man cactus is so-called because of the long, silvery hairs that totally **obscure** its leafless, columnar stem. 노인선인장은 잎이 없고, 원형의 줄기를 거의 덮어 감추고 있는 길고 은빛 나는 털 때문에 그렇게 불렸다.

columnar adj. 원주의, 원형의

stem n. 줄기, 대, 자루, 저지, 장애

v. 줄기를 떼어내다, 생기다, 방지하다, 자제하다, 거슬러 나아가다, 저항하다

build

v. **1_짓다, 세우다** construct, establish

≠ destroy, ruin

2_쌓아올리다, 이룩하다 accomplish, achieve

3_건설하다, 건립하다 found

n. **1_구조** structure

2_체격 shape

The first studio was **built** by Thomas Edison in 1893. 최초의 스튜디오는 1893년에 토머스 에디슨에 의해 지어졌다.

detect

v. **1_~을 찾아내다** uncover, find, discover

2_정체를 간파하다

3_~을 측정하다 register, feel

Security officials say that computer crime is easy to accomplish and hard to **detect**. 보안 검색원의 말에 의하면 컴퓨터를 이용한 범죄는 저지르기 쉽고, 찾아내기는 어렵다고 한다.

crime n. 범죄, 죄, 못된 짓, 몰상식한 짓

accomplish v. 이룩하다, 수행하다, 완성하다, 경과하다

detection

n. 1_발견, 탐지

2_발각

detective

n. 탐정, 형사

Early **detection** is the key to overcome cancer. 초기 발견이 암을 극복하는 비결이다.

collide

v. **1_부딪치다, 충돌하다** bump, crash, clash

≠avoid

2_일치하지 않다 clash, conflict

≠agree, consent

collision

n. 충돌 impact

Whale sharks are not aggressive, but they have been known to **collide** with boats. 고래상어는 공격적이지는 않지만 배를 들이받는 것으로 알려져 있다.

acclaim

v. **1_~을 찬양하다** praise, hail, applaud, salute

≠criticize, blame, reprove

2_~을 환호하여 맞이하다

3_환호성을 올리며 선언하다

Margaret Atwood has been **acclaimed** as one of Canada's most talented writers. 마거릿 앳우드는 캐나다의 가장 재능있는 작가 중의 한 명으로 찬사를 받고 있다.

talented adj. 재능이 있는, 유능한

acclamation

n. 1_환호하여 맞이함

 2_박수 갈채

seclude

v. **1_ ~을 은둔시키다** sequester

2_ 고립시키다 isolate, remote

3_ 몰아내다

For centuries little was known about Antarctica, the most **secluded** continent in the world. 여러 세기 동안에 세계에서 가장 고립된 대륙인 남극 대륙에 대해서 알려진 것이 거의 없었다.

continent n. 대륙, 본토, 유럽대륙 adj. 자제의, 극기의

seclusion

n. 1_격리 separation, isolation

2_은둔 reclusion

3_벽지

Lesson 25 Review Test

01 The Liberty Bell is an object of great **reverence** because it was rung in 1776 to proclaim the signing of the Declaration of Independence.

    ⓐ sadness   ⓑ respect

    ⓒ fame   ⓓ worth

02 There are two **sorts** of books required for basic bookkeeping.

    ⓐ parts   ⓑ types

    ⓒ bindings   ⓓ covers

03 In 1965 California replaced New York as the **foremost** state in the export of manufactured goods.

    ⓐ most accessible   ⓑ aforementioned

    ⓒ fourth   ⓓ leading

04 Biomedical research may soon discover a way to **extend** human life.

    ⓐ improve   ⓑ duplicate

    ⓒ change   ⓓ lengthen

05 As a performer, Martha Graham had **a commanding** personality and an intensity that captivated audiences.

    ⓐ an outgoing   ⓑ an extravagant

    ⓒ a forceful   ⓓ a sympathetic

06 In the 1820's cities in the United States **mushroomed** as a result of the Industrial Revolution.

    ⓐ gradually decayed   ⓑ were subdivided

    ⓒ grew quickly   ⓓ became prosperous

07 Duke Ellington's **ingenious** orchestration techniques made him perhaps the most remarkable artist that jazz has produced.

ⓐ intricate

ⓑ melodious

ⓒ lyrical

ⓓ clever

08 Babe Didrikson Zaharias **excelled** in basketball, baseball, and track in her youth and later became a champion golfer.

ⓐ practiced

ⓑ taught

ⓒ was interested in

ⓓ was outstanding in

09 In the legends of the American West, Paul Bunyan's most **treasured** possession was Babe the Blue Ox, whose horns were said to span a distance of 42 ax handles.

ⓐ comical

ⓑ valued

ⓒ expensive

ⓓ colorful

10 The old man cactus is so-called because of the long, silvery hairs that totally **obscure** its leafless, columnar stem.

ⓐ mar

ⓑ support

ⓒ whiten

ⓓ hide

11 The first studio was **built** by Thomas Edison in 1893.

ⓐ constructed

ⓑ proposed

ⓒ financed

ⓓ organized

12 Security officials say that computer crime is easy to accomplish and hard to **detect**.

ⓐ explain

ⓑ plan

ⓒ uncover

ⓓ ignore

13 Whale sharks are not aggressive, but they have been known to **collide with** boats.

ⓐ bump into   ⓑ overthrow

ⓒ disorder   ⓓ guard against

14 Margaret Atwood has been **acclaimed** as one of Canada's most talented writers.

ⓐ viewed   ⓑ studied

ⓒ praised   ⓓ remembered

15 For centuries little was known about Antarctica, the most **secluded** continent in the world.

ⓐ elongated   ⓑ frozen

ⓒ hostile   ⓓ remote

01	**b**	ⓐ sadness=n. 슬픔 ⓒ fame=n. 명성 ⓓ worth=n. 가치, 값어치
02	**b**	ⓐ part=n. 부분 ⓒ binding=n. 묶는 것(붕대) ⓓ cover=n. 덮개
03	**d**	ⓐ accessible=adj. 접근하기 쉬운 ⓑ aforementioned=adj. 앞서 말한
		ⓒ fourth=adj. 네 번째의
04	**d**	ⓐ improve=v. 향상되다 ⓑ duplicate=v. 복사하다 ⓒ change=v. 변하다
05	**c**	ⓐ outgoing=adj. 외향상의 ⓑ extravagant=adj. 사치스런
		ⓓ sympathetic=adj. 동정심 있는
06	**c**	ⓐ gradually=adj. 점차로 decay=v. 썩다 ⓑ subdivide=v. 세분하다
		ⓓ prosperous= adj. 번영하는
07	**d**	ⓐ intricate=adj. 얽힌(복잡한) ⓑ melodious=adj. 곡조가 아름다운 ⓒ lyrical=adj. 서정(시)의
08	**d**	ⓐ practice=v. 연습하다 ⓑ teach=v. 가르치다 ⓒ interest=v. 관심을 가지다
09	**b**	ⓐ comical=adj. 우스꽝스러운 ⓒ expensive=adj. 값비싼 ⓓ colorful=adj. 색채가 풍부한
10	**d**	ⓐ mar=v. 훼손하다 ⓑ support=v. 지탱하다 ⓒ whiten=v. 희게 하다
11	**a**	ⓑ propose=v. 제의하다 ⓒ finance=v. 자금을 조달하다 ⓓ organize=v. 조직하다
12	**c**	ⓐ explain=v. 설명하다 ⓑ plan=v. 계획하다 ⓓ ignore=v. 무시하다
13	**a**	ⓑ overthrow=v. 뒤엎다 ⓒ disorder=v. 어지럽히다 ⓓ guard against= ~에서 지키다
14	**c**	ⓐ view=v. 바라보다 ⓑ study=v. 공부하다 ⓓ remember=v. 기억하다
15	**d**	ⓐ elongate=v. 연장하다 ⓑ frozen=adj. 언(냉동한) ⓒ hostile=adj. 적대하는

Index ∗숫자는 그 단어나 숙어가 나온 Lesson을 나타낸다

A

abandon 13
abandoned 1
abhor 17
abiding 23
ability 13
abnormally 6
abrupt(ly) 10
absolute(ly) 24
abundance 2
abundant(ly) 2
abuse 16
academic 19
academy 19
accelerate 15
accelerated 15
accent 1, 11
accept 8
acceptable 21
accessible 25
accident 13
acclaim 25
acclamation 25
accompany 4
accomplish 25
according to 17
accrete 7
accretion 7

accurately 4
achieve 15
acid 9
acquire 6
acrid 15
across 7
act 2
activate 11, 14
active 17
actively 1
activity 18
actor 15
actually 9
acute(ly) 19
adapt 12, 13
add 15
adequate 10, 22
adjoining 20
administration 18
admiration 1
admire 1, 16
adult 16, 22
advantage 24
adventuress 7
advertising 11
advisable 22
advise 16, 19
advocate 24

affection 3, 9
affectionate(ly) 9
aforementioned 25
agency 10
aggressive 11
aggressively 6
agrarian 4
a great deal 17
agriculture 19
aid 13
ailment 20
aim 1
air 18
alarming 22, 24
alignment 9
alleviate 2
allocate 8
allot 13
allow 13, 21, 22
alloy 22
alluring 24
ally 10
alter 3
alternate 22, 24
alternative 5
although 3
amendment 15
amenity 18

among 9

amorphous 9

amount 15

amphibian 22

amplification 6

analogous 2

analogy 2

analyze 21

anchor 11

ancient 16, 18

angle 19

angrily 1, 6

announce 10, 15

annoying 2, 24

antagonistic 11

anticipate 17, 21

anxiety 20

anxiously 24

apparel 13

apparently 12

appealingly 18

appear 5

appearance 18

appease 7

appetizing 2

applaud 14

application 18

apply 3

apprentice 13

appropriate 18

appropriately 9

appropriation 18

approximately 17

apt 16

arbitrarily 12

archaic 2

area 18

argue about 24

argument 20

arise 12

aroma 9

aromatic 9

arouse 12

arrive 16

arrogant 6

art 5

article 2

as 23

aspect 16

aspiration 10

aspire 10

aspiring 10

assign 10

assignment 21

assistance 6

assistant 1, 7

assume 7

assumed 18

astonishing 21

astound 24

astounding 24

astronaut 21

astronomer 24

astrophysical 16

at all cost 10

at any cost 14

at length 4

atmospheric 19

atom 14, 24

attack 1

attempt 4, 20, 22

attend 14

attendance 14

attractive 19

audience 1

austere 17

authentic(al) 18

authentically 18

authoritative 20

authority 14

authorize 19

autocrat 16

automatic 14, 19

automaton 16

available 5

aviation 7

aviator 7

avoid 2, 12

aware 24

B

back 20

backbone 22

bacteria 20

bag 8

band 13

bar 14

barely 17, 18

barrack 20

barter 15

base 14

basic 8

basically 21

beach 14, 17

bean 8, 19

bear 6, 18, 23

beat 24

beautiful 16

become 25

begin 3

behave 10, 11

believe 10

belong 9

beneath 6

beneficial 20

beware 16

beyond 4, 17

biased 23

bid 2

binding 25

biological 7, 16

bite 13

bland 9

blatantly 18

bleach 14, 18

block 3

blunder 20

blurry 4

body 9

boil 24

bond 2, 22

bondage 2

book 4

bookkeeping 25

boost 1

boot 17

borrow 14

botanical 12

boulder 21

bound 16

box 8

boycott 10

brain 14

braise 5

branch 15

break 2

break down 9

breed 7, 22

brevity 1

brew 9

brick 21

bridge 3

brief 24

briefly 21

brilliance 1

bring on 9

brink 17

brittle 10

bud 2

build 2, 25

bulk 21

bull 12

buoy 14

burn 21

burning 3

bury 20

business 9, 16

buy 6

buzz 1

C

cage 4

call 18

call for 2, 7

camouflage 12

campaign 9

candidate 1

canyon 6

captivate 25

capture 5

carbon 22

career 17

careful 9, 14, 16

carefully 6, 22

cargo 1, 24

carry 1, 15

carve 14, 20

case 7

casting 20

catalogue 5

catastrophic 20

catch 4

cattle 22

cause 4, 19

caustic 17

cavalry 14

cave 13, 14

cell 4

censure 2

ceramic 10

certain 13

certainly 8

challenge 19

change 25

character 5

characteristic 9

characterize 1

charge 6, 24

charm 3

chase 3, 7

chew 2

chief 10

childhood 6, 11

choice 18

circumstance 12

civil 7

civilization 15

classify 18

claw 16, 22

clay 10

clean 12

clever 17, 20

climate 8

climb 16

clinic 19

close 4

clump 11

clumsy 9

cluster 10

coach 16

coagulate 24

coarsely 18

coastline 14

coat 10

coercion 4

coherent 5

coil 11

cold-blooded 11

collaborate 18

collaborative 18

collaborator 18

collage 12

collection 5

collide 25

collision 19

colonial 4

colonist 6

color 9, 12

colorful 19, 25

columnar 25

combination 8

combine 22

comic 20

comical 25

comics 20

command 1, 6, 25

commandeer 8

commanding 25

commandment 4

commemorate 23

commentary 16

commerce 1

commodity 19

common 22

community 4, 19

community college 11

compact 9, 10

company 4, 19

comparatively 12

compensate 4

compete 18

compile 9

complain 1, 12

complement 24

complete 13, 24

completed 23

completely 3, 16

completion 24

complex 2, 18

complicated 14

comply 4

composer 4

compound 12

comprehensible 21

compress 7

compromise 20

compulsory 14

conceal 10

concentrate 7, 24

concentration 16, 24

concept 23, 24

concert 6, 14

conclude 3

conclusion 14

condition 10

conductor 6, 7

cone 10, 20

confident 17

conflict 21

confuse 6, 12

confusing 5

conglomerate 4

congress 18

conscious(ly) 23

consequence 16

consequently 22

conservation 6

consider 4

considerable 14

consistency 6

consistent 6, 11

consistently 6

constant 3

constellation 13

constitution 12

constitutional 4

constraint 20

construct 18

construction 8

consult 5, 19

contagious 13

contain 2, 9

contemporary 15

content 7

contiguous 17

continent 25

continental 8

continuation 19

continuously 20

contraction 14

contrary 24

contribute 8

control 3, 5, 22

controversial 18

conveniently 23

conventionally 15

conversation 1

convert 6

convertible 6

convince 5

cook 5, 19

cooperate 9, 12

cooperative 16

coordinate 14

coordination 21

copper 1

core 11

corner 14

corrupt 3

cosmetic 18

cosmic 7

cost 6

costly 1, 9

cough 19

counsel 24

counselor 24

courageous 6

course 4

court 10

courtroom 16

cousin 21

cover 8, 25

coverage 12

cover up 2, 3

crack 18, 24

crash 14

creation 10

creative 4, 20

creativity 23

creature 12

credential 13

creek 6, 19

crime 25

criminal 7

crisis 2

criticism 3, 21

criticize 3, 10, 17

crop 12

cross 14

crowd 1

crucial 18

crush 20

cultivate 15, 19

cultural 4

culture 4

curiously 13

current 5

currently 24

D

danger 3

dangerous 13

dark 8

darken 4

darkness 16

dauntless 17

dawn 19

daytime 4

dazzlingly 12

deadly 6

deal 9

dealer 16

decay 25

deceptive 22

decide 23

deciduous 15

decision 10

decisiveness 8

decline 8

decorate 20

decrease 2, 5

dedicate 3

dedication 3

deep 4, 23

deepen 24

defeat 5

defend 6

defender 12

define 15

deflect 10

degrading 2

degree 8

delay 1, 10

deliberate 14

delight 16

demand 6, 8, 21

demanding 23

demonstrate 19

denounce 3

dense 10

deny 6

dependably 4

depend on 4

depict 23

depression 2, 23

descend 21, 24

describe 14

deserve 21

design 7

desolate 17, 21

desperately 4

destruction 24

destructive 13

detach 24

detached 4

detach to 3

detail 4

detect 25

detection 25

detective 25

deteriorate 2

determined 24

determinism 16

detrimental(ly) 20

devastate 5

develop 8

device 19

devious 22

devise 21

devote 3

devoted 3

devotion 3

diagnose 21

diagnosis 6

diagram 15

differ 17

difference 11

differentiate 14, 24

difficult 16

diffuse 12, 17

dig 17

diligent 16

dinner 12

diplomatic 20

direct 11, 15

directly 3

dirt 22

disabled 21

disagree 18

discharge 18

disciplinary 11

discord 20

discover 2, 11

discreet 20

discreetly 18

discuss 15

discussion 7

disease 12, 13

disgust 16

disillusion 20

disintegrate 11

disintegrated 13

disorder 25

disparage 20

disparaging 20

dispensary 13

dispense 9

dispute 2

dissatisfied 4

dissolve 20

distill 9

distinct 24

distinguish 3

distinguished 3

distort 5, 6, 23

distracting 11

disturbing 2

diverse 1, 2, 20

diversely 18

diversified 2, 14

diversify 2

diversion 16

diversity 2

divert 12, 15

division 11

dock 20

domesticate 11

domesticated 11

dominant 12, 23

dormant 11

draft 15

drama 21

drastic 16

draw 10, 15

drawback 5

drink 13

drive to 17

drug 10

dry 18, 19, 22

due to 21

duly 7

duplicate 25

during 12

duty 1, 2

dwell 21

dweller 1

dwindle 9

E

earliest 12

early 7

earning 16

earth 17

earthquake 10

easy 15

eccentric 4

economic 4

economist 8

edge 17

editorial 1

educate 1, 13

effect 18

effective 16

effectively 8

elect 2, 7, 19

election 6

elementary 12

elongate 25

elude 13

embark 18

embed 9

emblem 15

embrace 20

embroidery 23

emerge 7

emergency 13

emigrate 20

eminence 15

eminent 15

emit 3, 17

emotion 9

emotional 9

emphasize 2, 20, 23

employee 15

enable 18

encase 10

encouragingly 3

end 12, 17, 23

endangered 3

endeavor 23

endorse 1

endure 2

enemy 12

energy 9, 16

engage 16

enigmatic 11

enormous(ly) 18

ensure 4, 23

enter 8

enterprise 16

entire 2

environment 3

envision 22

envy 17

epigram 1

equation 8

equivalent 18, 23

equivocal(ly) 6

era 6

eradicate 2

erosion 19

erupt 13

escape 5

especially 5

establish 13

establishment 19

ethnic 4

evangelical 13

event 12

evidence 5

exaggerate 13

excel 25

excellence 25

excellent 25

exceptionally 3

excess 15

excessive 11, 14

excited 5

excitement 15

exclusive 14

excuse 8

execute 14

executive 9

exemplary 23

exercise 14, 22, 24

exertion 17

exhaust 12, 21

exhaustive(ly) 3

exhilarating 20

exotic 16

expand 10

expansion 19

expect 2, 13

expensive 25

experience 15

experiment 24

experimental 18

expert 20

explain 25

explanation 12

exploit 1

exploration 19

export 11

expose 6, 23

exposition 20

express 5, 16, 22

exquisite 17

extend 24, 25

extinction 17

extract 24

extravagant 22, 25

extremely 5, 12

exuberance 16

F

fabric 12

fact 1

factor 2, 8

fade 12

failure 16

fair 20

faith 10, 16

faithful 11, 16

faithfully 3

fake 23

fall 23

fame 23, 25

family 9

famous 8, 17

fanciful 17

fare 6

fashion 22

fashionable 15

fast 8

fastidious 23

faultless 22

fauna 24

fear 2

feature 23

federal 2, 8

feeble 14, 15

feminism 24

ferocious 14

fertilize 22

fever 3

fidelity 15

field 15, 24

fierce 6

fiery 17

fight 6

figure 9

file 2, 11

film 16

finally 5, 7, 12

finance 25

find 5, 6

finding 3

finger 5, 23

fire 5, 10

first 13

fitness 24

fix 1, 5

fixing 9

flagrantly 18

flake 11

flamboyant 22

flashy 17

flatter 5

flavor 15

flavorful 9

flavoring 19

flaw 4

flawless 17

flexibility 12

flight 7

flora 24

flourishing 16

flow 12, 22

flower 10

fluctuate 22, 23

fluctuation 4

focus 1

foe 13

fog 20

foolish 14

foot 17

force 2, 24

ford 19

forecast 15

foreign 4

foremost 4, 25

forestall 22

forever 4

form 7, 22

formation 1, 8

formidable 9

fort 12

fortune 21

forward 18

fossil 17

foster 20

found 2, 19

foundation 23

founder 2

Founding Fathers 2

fourth 25

fowl 8

fragrant 17

frank 17

free 13

freeze 11, 20

frenzy 11

frequency 13

freshly 9

fringe benefit 10

frontiersman 11

frozen 25

frugal 15

fruitless(ly) 4

fruity 9

frustrated 14

frustration 2

function 6

funny 13

fur 22

furor 21

fury 16

fusion 9

G

gain 12

game 11

garden 1

gas 7, 14

gather 6, 20

gem 14

generally 4, 20

generate 8

genetic 6

genius 3

gentleman 4

gently 13

germinate 11

gift 14

gifted 4

give 3

glacier 6, 18

glance 5

glistening 17

glow 11

go ahead 5

goal 20

god 15

goods 8

gorge 19

govern 8, 13

government 2

governmental 23

governor 1

grade 5

gradual(ly) 1

gradually 25

graduate 20

grain 18

grant 6

graph 9

grassland 12

gratifying 15

graze 22, 24

greet 15

gregarious 8

grief 16

groom 22

ground 21

group 1, 13

grow 11

growing 15

growth 9, 21

grueling 20

gruesome 20

grumpy 15

guarantee 6, 14

guard against 25

guidance 7, 18

guide 18

guilt 5

guiltily 1

guilty 14

gullible 16

gulp 16

gun 1

H

habit 23
habitat 7, 10
halfheartedly 1
handsome 23
handy 13
hanging 19
haphazard 5
happiness 11, 15
harbor 1
hard 12
harden 10
hardly 5
harsh 2, 14
haul 11
hawk 11
hay 8
headache 3
health 9
hear 11, 18
hear about 12
heart attack 8
heat up 11
heavily 5
heavy 8
height 9, 17
herb 9
herd 8
heredity 11
hero 11
heyday 12

hide 2, 5, 11, 23
higher education 11
highest 14
highly 8, 21
high-powered 17
hilly 23
hire 24
historian 24
historic 19
hold 15
holding 5
hold out against 3
hole 16
hollow 17
home 8
hometown 9
homogeneous 12
honesty 8
hope for 6
hopefully 17
horizon 4
horn 25
hostile 25
house 5
household 15
however 22
huge 3
humble 17
humorous 22
hunter 12
hunting 11

hurriedly 1
husk 10
hypothesis 24

I

idea 10, 11, 14
ideal 14
identify 11, 16, 19
idol 4
idolatry 4
idolize 4
ignite 11
ignore 3, 5, 11, 25
illness 9
illustrate 9
illustration 9
illustrative 9
imagination 10
immature 21
immediate 16
immense 16
immigrant 15
imminent 4
impair 5
impede 15
imperfection 17
implant 4
implication 16
important 3
impressive 22

improve 10, 15, 16, 23, 25
improvisation 21
imprudent 12
impulse 6
inaccessible 21
inactivity 20
inadequate 19
inadvertent 7
inappropriate(ly) 1
inborn 7
incessant(ly) 12
inch 23
incombustible 22
income 1
incorporate 10
incorrectly 20
indemnify 13
independent 8
indicate 5, 10, 19
indication 4
indicator 16, 18
indiscreetly 1
indispensable 23
individual 18
indivisible 17
industrial 4
industry 7
inedible 8
inevitable 7
inevitably 15
inexpensive 22

infancy 12
infect 6
infection 6
infectious 6
inflated 2
influence 2, 7
influenza 13
informal(ly) 20
infuriate 21
ingenious(ly) 25
ingredient 18
ingrown 4
inhabitant 22
inherit 3, 6, 21
initiate 3
injure 21, 24
injurious 24
injury 24
in many cases 10
innovation 13
in order to 2
inscribe 23
insect 18
insecure 8
inside 7, 23
insightful 24
insinuation 16
insistence 4
inspect 10, 24
inspire 13
instead of 13

instinct 10
institution 5
instrument 10
insult 20
insurance 13
intact 7
integrity 8
intelligent 8
intensity 25
intention 2
intentionally 18
interact 9
interest 25
interestedly 17
interesting 21, 24
interference 13
interminable 7
interpretation 21
interpreter 10
in time of 17
intimidate 3
intricate 25
intrigue 21
intriguing 23
intrinsically 24
introduce 20
intrusive 20
invalid 21
invention 9
invest 16
investigate 16

invisible 4

invite 19

iron 3, 22

ironically 9, 22

irrefutable 19

irresistibly 24

irritating 5

island 22

isolate 15

isolated 4, 15, 19

isolation 15

issue 1, 7, 10

itinerant 13

ivory 10

J

jerk 17

join 11

judge 16, 24

junior 5

jurisdiction 7

just as 7

justice 7

K

keen(ly) 24

key 5

kin 24

kindergarten 15

knee 17

know 6

L

label 22

labor 11

laboratory 22

lack 2

language 10

last 2, 11

lasting 23

late 13

laud 4

laudable 4

laundry 18

law 1

lay 6

layout 7

lead 10

leader 10

leadership 15

leading 2

lead to 1

leak 24

leap 18

lease 6

least 2

leave behind 18

lecture 10

lecture about 24

lecture on 22

lecturer 24

legal 4

legend 7

legislative 9

legislature 15

legitimate 4

length 18

lengthy 20

library 13

life 23

lifetime 2

lighten 10

line 5

liquid 7, 12, 14

list 9, 22

literature 6

live 17, 18

load 1

locate 4, 13

located 4

location 4

lodge 4

log 20

logical 8

long 7

long for 21

long-lived 8

long-term 10

long-winded 5

look at 6

lot 1

lottery 18

loudly 21

lovely 19

lower 10

lowering 3

ludicrous 9

lump 12

lung 22

luster 10

luxuriant 17

lyric 24

lyrical 25

M

machinery 8

magnetic 22

magnificent(ly) 16

maintain 15

maintenance 4

major 2, 7

make up 8

making 18

mall 8

mammal 21

mammoth 8, 13

manic-depressive 23

manifestation 15

mankind 4

manual 5, 13

manufacture 6

manufacturing 7

map 6, 13

mar 25

marine 16

mark 16

marvel 2

masculine 12

mask 5

mass 8, 12

massive 5

mastery 20

match 11, 15

matching 4

matchless 22

mate 6

material 9, 12

mathematical 22

matter 21

maturity 9

meal 5

mean 22

means 20

measure 11

meat 5

mechanical 19

medicinal 9

medicine 5

medieval 7

meet 10

melodious 17, 25

melody 17

melt 10

memorable 22

memorize 23

menu 5

merchandise 22

message 19, 21, 24

migrate 1, 11

migration 1

migratory 1

mild 8

military 11

mimic 11

minimize 19, 22

miniscule 13

minute 1, 11

mirror 6

miserably 17

misguide 4

mislead 11

miss 20

missing 14

misunderstanding 20

mixed 3

mobility 23

model 2

moderate 3

modern 3, 8, 15, 24

modification 3

modify 3

modulate 13

moist 2

moisture 2

molecule 7

moment 16

mongoose 13

monster 9

monumental 2

mordant 20

more or less 22

moreover 22

more than 7

motion 7, 14

mount 13, 19

mountain 8

mountainous 9

mouse 13

mouth 7

movement 7, 9

movie 12

mud 21

multinational 23

municipality 23

muscular 3

mushroom 25

mysteriously 10

N

naked 23

name 1

national 8

nationalize 8

natural 2, 5, 10, 12

nature 12

near 6

necessary 14, 16

necessity 5

need 2, 10, 16

negative 10

neighboring 8

nerve 6, 11

nest 6

nice 13

nocturnal 10

noise 13

noisy 12

nomadic 16

note 24

noted 3

notice 22

noticeable 9

notion 16, 19

nuclear reactor 5

numerator 22

numerous 1, 3, 5, 8

nurture 21

nut 10, 23

nutritious 2

O

obedience 7

object 4, 14, 16

obligation 2

obscure 25

observe 5

observing 23

obtain 18

obvious 18

obviously 15

occasion 6

occasionally 6, 20

occupation 11

occur 11

occurrence 2

odious 17

off guard 5

offense 7

offensive 24

offer 19, 23

officer 19

official 2

often 21, 24

oily 9

old-fashioned 4

once 5

open 15, 16

operation 8, 20

opinion 4

opportunity 10

opposition 9

oral 18

orbit 14

orchestration 25

order 5, 15

ordinarily 9

ordinary 11

ore 10

organization 15

organizational 15

organize 15, 16, 25

organizer 15

origin 3

originally 12

originate 24

ornamentation 17

ostentatious 11

otherwise 6

ouch 20

out of 6

outbreak 22

outburst 23

outcome 19, 23

outdo 5

outgoing 25

outmoded 3

output 11

outrage 5

outside 14

outstretched 14

oven 10

overcome 16, 19

overly 12

overthrow 25

overturn 10

P

paddle 20

pain 3, 9

painstaking(ly) 17

paint 24

painter 19

palatable 10

paralyze 11

parched 21

parliamentary 9

part 6, 19, 25

partial 3

participate in 12

particular 23

particularly 15

partisan 11

partly 18

pass 14, 20

passage 13

passenger 15

passive 12

patent 21, 24

path 20

patient 20

patronage 10

pay 14, 19

peace 1

peak 6

peasant 21

peculiarly 1

pedestal 23

pedestrian 23

peer 3

penalize 13

penetrate 20

perceive 20

perfectly 8

perform 17

performance 15, 23

performer 25

perhaps 23

period 13

permission 6

permit 6

perplexingly 16

persecution 1

persist 1

persistent(ly) 1, 19

personal 14

personality 5

persuade 7, 19

peruse 5

petrified 10

pharmaceutical 21

philanthropic 23

philanthropist 23

philanthropy 23

philosopher 24

philosophy 6, 19

photograph 5

physical 24

physician 19

pious 16

place 11

placid 23

plan 5, 25

plan for 21, 22

planet 7

plant 9

play 13, 14

playful 15

plaything 8

pleasing 21

poisonous 19

polar 8

policy 16

polish 14

politician 21

popular 12

population 4

position 7

possess 8

possession 9

possible 19

pothole 17

pound 14

poverty 2

power 9, 15, 16, 18

powerful 4

practice 23, 25

praise 22

pray 17

preacher 13

precipitation 23

precise 8

predecessor 24

predict 10, 20

predictably 13

prefer 5, 14

prepare for 20

present 3, 4

preservative 19

pressing 18

prestige 10

presumably 10

prevalent 13

prevent 13

preview 22

previous 15

previously 20

primarily 2, 22

primary 7

primate 10

principal 24

private 6, 12, 17

prize 14

problem 9, 11

procedure 9

process 18

proclaim 3, 25

prodigious 20

produce 4, 7

product 8

productive 7

professional 17

profit 11

profitable 7

profligate 23

profoundness 1

program 7, 21

prohibit 4, 23

project 7

prolong 17

prolonged 17

prominence 24

prominent 10, 24

promise 1

prompt 9

propagate 17

propel 14, 20

proper 4

properly 1

property 18

proportion 13

proposal 1, 5

propose 6, 15, 25

proscribe 6

prosecute 13

prosperous 4, 12, 25

protect 7

protection 6

protestant 13

prove 6

provide 4, 10, 20

provided (that) 4

provocation 6

psychologist 7

public 11

purchase 5, 14

pure 3, 7

purpose 18

purposely 6

pursue 11

push 11

puzzling 18

Q

quaintly 1

quality 8

quantity 8

question 1, 7

quickly 16

quietly 21

quite 5, 17

R

radicalize 9

raise 8

ramification 5

range 14, 24

rapidly 5, 11

raspy 17

rate 9, 18

ratify 15

rattle 11

ravine 19

ray 15

reach 13

reaction 7

reactor 22

readily 8

real 14

realism 21

realize 16

really 5, 8

reasonable(ly) 8

rebound 10

rebuke 2

receive 15

recipient 15

recognition 21

recognizable 15

recognize 1

recommend 8

record 10, 15

recorded time 19

recover 23

recovery 1, 3

recreate 3

recurrent 7

reduce 18, 20

reflex 17

reform 3, 10

refuge 14

region 8

regional 7, 8, 18

regret 16

regular 21

rehabilitate 20

rehabilitation 20

reindeer 8

reinforce 22

relate 11

relation 11

relative(ly) 5, 23

relaxation 20

release 1, 24

relevantly 5

relieve 5

religion 2

religious 13

remain 21

remarkable 25

remedy 16

remember 25

remembrance 15

remnant 2

remodel 3

remote 18

remove 5

renewable 4

renewal 24

renovate 3, 13

repair 10, 15

repeatedly 10, 12

replace 23, 25

replica 23

replicate 23

represent 6, 14

representative 23

repudiate 16

reputation 7

repute 16

request 18, 23

require 24

requirement 4

reroute 1

rescue 2

research 7

resemble 9

reservoir 22

resist 10, 12

resolute 9

resonance 18

resort 17

resource 1

resources 5

respect 19

respiration 24

respiratory 13

respond 14

response 19

responsibility 7

rest 14, 21

restoration 21

restrain 2

restrained 9

restrict 6, 23

result 6

retain 8

return 1, 20

reveal 23

revere 25

reverence 25

reverend 3

review 4, 20

revise 9, 15

revival 10, 12

revolutionize 9

reward 14

rhythm 1

rhythmic 14

richness 1

ride 5, 20

rider 12

ridge 6

rigorous 21

ring 25

rise 14, 21

rising 15

rivalry 4

river 19

roar 13

robustly 23

rock 8

rodent 13

role 10

roll 16

root 10, 11

rot 11

rotate 11, 18

rough(ly) 8, 18

round 23

route 6

rove 24

rowdy 20

rugged 16

ruin 1

rule 5, 18

rumor 16

run 4

rye 9

s

sadly 21, 24

sadness 25

safety 5

sanction 4

sanitary 22

satisfactorily 13

saying 1

scare 12

scatter 5

scenery 21

scenic 23

scheme 20

scholar 3

school 13

scope 18

scorn 1

scrub 18

sea 9

seal 24

seaport 7

season 5, 6

seasonally 10

seasoned 23

seclude 25

seclusion 25

secondary 13

secret 18

secrete 6

section 14

sector 6

secure 4

security 2

see 18, 19

seed 11

seedless 8

seedy 23

seek 6, 21

seek after 8

seek out 18

segment 11

seldom 21

sell 15, 17

semester 20

send 6, 11

sensation 12

sensational 11

sense 1, 3

sentimentality 22

separate 5, 8

separation 7

serene 17

serious 9

seriously 12

servant 21

serve 13

service 16

settle 6, 11

shady 1

shape 13, 18

share 15

sharp 8

sharpen 7

sharpness 22

sharpshooter 8

shell 14

shellfish 8

shift 3

shifting 3

shipping 24

short 24

show 4

showboat 12

showcase 22

shrink 11, 12

shrub 5

shuttle 14

shy 12, 17

sick leave 6

sight 2

sign 18

signal 19

significant 12

significantly 3

silence 13

similar to 7

simple 7, 18

simply 8

simultaneous(ly) 1

single 18

singular 22

site 19

size 17

skeptically 12

skill 7

slant 10

slave 5

slimy 13

slope 11, 15

slowly 2

sluggish 9

slyly 1

small 1

smell 3, 12

smooth 14, 24

smoothly 4	speech 9, 13	step into 10
snobbish 19	speedily 8	stern 11
social 2	spend 10	steward 19
soft 10	sphere 16	stewardess 7
soil 4, 12	spin 18	still 7
solar 4	spirit 15	stockade 17
sole 23	split 13	stockpile 17
solution 5	sponge 16	stone 6
some time 5	spray 13	storage 22
somewhat 13	spread 6	store 4, 8
song 13	spur 2	storm 15
sophisticate 18	square 22	strangely 12, 16
sophisticated 4, 20	squirt 6	stream 10
sort 25	stabilize 1	strength 5, 9
sound 19	stable 2	strengthen 19, 22
sound wave 6	stand 14	stress 11
sour 9	standard 11	strict 22
source 3, 5, 7	standardize 23	strike 5, 9
souvenir 14	star 13	striking(ly) 8, 16
sovereign 4	starve 11	structural(ly) 7
space 3	starved 5	structure 4, 23
span 25	state 1	struggle 4
sparkling 10	statement 1, 6	stubborn 12
speak 15	station 13, 24	study 11, 25
speaker 1	statistics 22	stuff 9
spear 16	statue 13	stumble 17
specialize 8	steal 2, 10	stun 11, 21
specialized 7	steam 1	stylistic 14
species 3	steel 22	subdivide 25
spectacular 12	steer 5	subject 13, 24
speculate 9	stem 11, 25	subject to 21

submerge 12

subsequent(ly) 7

subsequently 13

substitute 20

subterranean 13

subtle 17

successful 20

succumb 3

suggest 5, 24

suit 7, 10

suitable 10

sum 22

summer 12, 14

summit 5

sunlight 18

sunset 2

supervisor 6

supplant 16

supply 5

support 2, 4, 25

suppress 19

supremacy 7

supreme 10

surgery 1

surmise 19

surpass 15, 24

surprised attack 5

surprisingly 6

surround 20

surrounding 14

survival 10

sustain 2

swamp 6

sway 13

sweet 8

swell 16

symbol 14

sympathetic 25

symptom 1, 3

T

table 13

tail 10

take down 21

take place 5

tale 7, 13, 21

talent 21

talented 25

talk 1

tame 7

tamp 22

tamper with 22

taste 2

tasteless 22

tax 1, 2, 8

teach 6, 25

tear 12, 14

tear down 16

technique 18

teeth 19

temperature 18

tend 6, 10

tendency 6

tenderize 5

tenderness 15

tentative 19

term 3

terminate 18

terrain 16

terrifying 9, 18

territory 16

terrorize 2, 3

test 21, 23

thaw 5

theme 7, 24

therefore 7, 13

thick 20

thin 18

think little of 21

thoroughly 18

thoughtfulness 15

thread 18

threat 3, 10

threaten 3

threatened 3

threatening(ly) 3

thrill 20

thrive 1, 24

throat 12

through 6, 13

thrust 19

thunder 15

thus 20
tier 11
time 10
timely 14
tiresome 12
tissue 11
toe 17
tolerable 20
tolerate 1, 17
tongue 19
tool 8, 13
tooth 11
torch 23
total 5, 17
touch 15
touchdown 14
tough 8
toward 23
tower 23
toxic 13
trace 3
trace to 3
track 3, 24, 25
tract 13
trade 17
trademark 4
tradition 16
traditional 16
traditionally 22
train 11
training 13

trait 7
tranquil 19
translation 20
transport 15
transportation 24
trap 7, 14
travel 8
treasure 25
treatment 16
treaty 4
trench 19
trial 7
tributary 7
trigger 2
triumph 16
trivial 3
tropical 7, 16
trouble 9
troublesome 24
tube 10
tundra 24
turn 6, 18, 24
turn into 1
turn out 8
twice 17
type 10

U

ultimate 20
unaffected 23

unavoidable 9
uncertain 20
unconcerned 3
underestimate 21
underground 22
underplay 21
underscore 5
understand 8, 11, 16
undertake 18, 21
undoubted(ly) 10
undulate 18
uneven 11
unexpected 9, 16, 19
unhappy 5
unharness 13
unification 10
uniform 23
unintelligible 21
uninteresting 20
union 10, 19
unique 3
universal 1
university 13
unleash 18
unlike 7
unnecessary 9
unofficial 13
unpleasantness 12
unpolished 12
unpolluted 10
unquestionably 8

unravel 12, 18

unrestrained 9

unscientific 12

unsettled 16

unsuitable 21

unusual 19

unusually 21

unwittingly 9

unyielding 11

upland 22

upward 19

urge 22

usage 12

use 9

use up 5

useful 9

usually 4

utilize 8, 16

utter(ly) 5

V

vacancy 1

vacant 1

vacation 17

vacuum 10

vague 12

validate 17

valuable 9, 18

valued 9

valve 19

variable 1

variety 2

various 11

varnish 24

vassal 16

venom 11

venture 11

verify 9

vessel 1

vibrate 22

victim 13, 21

victory 14

view 16, 25

vigilant 17

vigorous 17

vigorously 14

vindictive 11

vine 5

vinegar 9

violently 4

virtual 16

visitor 22

visual 21

vitally 3

voice 11, 15

volcanic 6

volcano 14

voluminous 17

voluntary 14

voter 21

vowel 12

voyage 12

vulnerable 7

W

wage 10, 13, 14

wait for 20

wander 22

warm 20

warning 3, 6, 11

warrior 12

water 14

waterfall 17

watertight 22

way 13

weaken 21

wealth 15

wear 14

weather 15

weave 9

weaver 9

weaving 9

wed 20

wedding 20

welfare 24

wellness 24

well-regulated 2

well-worn 23

western 7

wheat 9

whiten 25

whole 18

widely 16

widespread 2

wild 8, 11

wildlife 2, 7

wildlife preserve 7

willingly 13

win 21

wind 13

wind chill 8

wing 14

wire 22

wish for 3

wit 1

withhold 14, 18

within 16

withstand 18

witness 2, 12

wonder 7

woo 21

wood(s) 6

wool 12

word 12

worker 22

world 17

worm 18

worsen 19

worth 17, 25

wound 6

wounded 5

wrath 15

write 23

writing 18

Y

yell 10

yet 20

young 5

youth 21

A **accelerate** v. 1. 촉진하다 increase 2. 빨라지다 speed up

acclaim n.(v.) 1. 칭찬(하다) praise 2. 인정 recognition

achieve v. 이루다 accomplish

achievement n. 위업 attainment

actually adv. 사실상, 실제로는 really, in fact

acute adj. 1. 중대한, 심각한 critical 2. 격렬한, 심한 intense

adjacent adj. ~에 인접한, 근접한 near, nearby

adopt v. 1. 채택하다 enact 2. 받아들이다 take on

advent n. 출현, 도래 arrival, appearance, coming

adverse adj. 1. 반대하는 opposed 2. 불리한 negative

afford v. 제공하다 offer, provide

aggressive adj. 1. 공격적인 combative 2. 적극적인 forceful

alert v. 주의를 환기하다 notify, look out

allocate v. 1. 배치하다 designate 2. 배분하다 distribute

apparent adj. 명백한 evident, obvious

appoint v. 임명하다, 지명하다 designate, name

approximately adv. 대략 about, roughly

arduous adj. 1. 어려운 difficult 2. 힘든 strenuous

arid adj. 1. 물이 없는 anhydrous 2. 메마른 dry

aromatic adj. 향긋한, 향기로운 flavorful, fragrant

arouse v. 1. 흥분시키다 excite 2. 자극하다 stimulate

arrange v. 1. 계획하다 plan 2. 배열시키다, 정렬(정돈)시키다 put together

article n. 1. 항목, 물품 item 2. 물건, 물체 object

assemble v. 모으다, 집합시키다 gather

        n. 집회, 모임 gathering

assert v. 1. 주장하다 maintain, claim 2. 단언하다 declare

astonishing adj. 깜짝 놀라게 하는 startling

astonishingly adv. 놀랍게도 astoundingly

astounding adj. 놀라운 amazing, surprising

attempt n.(v.) 1. 노력 effort 2. 시도(하다) try

attract v. (주의, 흥미 등을) 끌다 appeal

attractive adj. 매력적인 pretty

attribute n. 특성, 특징 characteristic, trait

autonomous adj. 자치의 independent

autonomy n. 자치(권) independence

available adj. 1. 사용할 수 있는 accessible 2. 얻을 수 있는 obtainable

B **barren** adj. 1. 불모의 infertile, sterile 2. 생물이 없는 lifeless

base n. 1. 밑부분 bottom 2. 작전 기지 center of operation

bind v. 1. 묶다 tie 2. 붙이다 join

bizarre adj. 1. 색다른 exotic 2. 이상한, 기괴한 odd, strange

blend v. 혼합하다, 섞다 combine, mix

boom v. 번영하다 flower

        n. 급속한 성장 rapid expansion

border n. 가장자리, 경계 opposite to center, edge

bound n. 1. 억제 constraint 2. 한계 limit

boundary n. 경계선 dividing line

bountiful adj. 풍부한 plentiful, abundant, fertile

breach n. 1. 갈라진 틈 rift 2. 위반, 침해 violation

breathtaking adj. 굉장한 exciting, stunning

breed v. 1. 부화하다 hatch 2. 기르다 raise

burrow n. (동물의) 굴 den, hole

C **capture** v. 잡다 catch, seize

certain adj. 1. 피할 수 없는 inevitable 2. 명확한 specific

chaotic adj. 1. 혼란한 confused 2. 무질서한 tumultuous

chiefly adv. 주로, 대부분 mainly, mostly, principally

cite v. 1. 언급하다 mention 2. 인용하다 refer to

classify v. 분류하다 categorize, group

coin v. 1. (어구를) 새로 만들다 invent 2. (화폐를) 주조하다 mint

collide with phr-v. ~와 부딪치다, 충돌하다 bump into, hit each other

commodity n. 상품, 제품 goods, product, article of trade

community n. 1. 촌락, 부락 settlement 2. (지역) 사회 society

complex adj. 1. 정교한 elaborate 2. 뒤얽힌 involved

component n. 요소, 부분, 성분 element, part

composed adj. 작곡된 created, written

comprise v. ~으로 구성되다, 이루어지다 consist of, be made up of

concept n. 개념, 생각 idea, notion

conflicting adj. 상반되는 contrary, opposing

confound v. 1. 당황하게 하다 bewilder 2. 혼동하다 confuse

congested adj. 혼잡한 crowded, overcrowded

consciously adv. 의도적으로, 고의로 intentionally, purposely

consequence n. 결과 result

consequently adv. 1. 그 결과로서 as a result 2. 따라서 thus

consider v. 간주하다, 생각하다, 고려하다 deem, regard, take in account

considerable adj. 1. 상당한 substantial, great 2. 중요한 significant

considerably adv. 상당히, 꽤 very much

conspicuous adj. 1. 뚜렷한 noticeable 2. 분명한 obvious

constant adj. 연속된 continuous, unbroken

constantly adv. 끊임없이 continually, continuously

constrain v. 1. 구속하다 bind 2. 억제하다 inhibit

constrict v. 1. 수축시키다 contract 2. 제한하다 restrict

consumption n. 1. 소비 use 2. 먹기 eating

contemporary adj. 1. 현대의 current 2. 동시대에 존재하는 existing at the same time

create v. 1. 야기하다 bring about 2. 만들어내다 devise

crucial adj. 1. 중대한 critical, important 2. 불가결한 essential

crude adj. 1. 조야한 roughly made 2. 가공하지 않은 unprocessed

cultivate v. 1. 재배하다 grow, raise 2. 경작하다 farm

customarily adv. 습관적으로, 통상적으로 usually, habitually

customary adj. 습관적인, 통례의 typical

D **deal with** phr-v. 1. 대처하다 cope with 2. 대하다 concern with

debate v. 논쟁하다 argue

　　　n. 1. 논쟁 argument 2. 토론 discussion

definite adj. 일정한 fixed

definitely adv. 명확하게 clearly

deliberate adj. 1. 신중한 careful 2. 고의의 intentional

deliberately adv. 일부러 purposely

depend v. 1. ~에 달려 있다 be determined by 2. 의지하다, 믿다 rely

depict v. 표현하다 define, describe, picture, represent

deposit v. 1. 두다, 놓다 lay, place 2. (알을) 낳다 lay

derive v. 1. 찾다 obtain 2. 유래하다 originate

descent n. 출신, 가계, 혈통 ancestry, origin

despite prep. ~에도 불구하고 regardless of, even though

detect v. 1. 발견하다 discover 2. 탐지하다 measure, register

detective n. 탐정, 형사 investigator

device n. (기계적) 장치 instrument, mechanism

devote v. 1. 바치다 dedicate 2. 할당하다 reserve

dictate v. 정하다, 명하다 determine, prescribe, require

dim adj. 1. 애매한 ambiguous 2. 희미한, 약한 faint, weak

diminish v. 줄이다, 감소하다 reduce, decrease

dire adj. 무서운, 두려운 dreadful, fearful

discard v. 1. 제거하다 get rid of 2. 버리다 throw away

dispute n. 논쟁 argument, disagreement

v. ~에 의문을 제기하다, 문제삼다 question

disseminate v. 유포(배포)하다, 퍼뜨리다 disperse, spread

dissemination n. 씨뿌리기, 살포 spreading

distinct adj. 1. 별개의, 다른 different, separate 2. 명확한 definite

distinction n. 구별, 차이 difference

distinctive adj. 독특한, 특이한 characteristic

distinctly adv. 뚜렷하게 clearly

do away with phr-v. 폐지하다 abolish, eliminate

domain n. 범위, 영역 field, region

dominant adj. 지배적인 leading, prevailing, prevalent

dominate v. 지배하다 be prevalent, govern

dramatically adv. 1. 급격하게 radically 2. 극적으로 strikingly

duplicate v. 복사하다, 모방하다 copy, imitate

adj. 똑같은 identical

durable adj. 영속성이 있는 lasting, long-lasting

dwell v. 거주하다 live, habit

dwelling n. 거주지 house, living quarter, residence

E **effort** n. 노력 an earnest attempt, exertion

elaborate adj. 정교한, 복잡한 complex, complicated

elaborately adv. 정교하게 done in great detail

emanate v. 나오다 appear, emerge

embrace v. 1. 포함하다 include 2. 채택하다 take up

emerge v. 출현하다, 나타나다 appear, come into prominence

emergence n. 1. 출현 appearance 2. 발생 rise

enable v. 1. 가능하게 하다 help 2. 허용하다 allow

encompass v. 1. 포함하다 include 2. 둘러싸다 surround

enhance v. (질, 능력 등을) 높이다 heighten, improve

entirely adv. 1. 오로지 solely 2. 전적으로 totally

environment n. 환경 ecology, setting

era n. 시대 epoch, age, period

eradicate v. 근절하다 eliminate, completely destroy

erect v. 세우다 build

    adj. 수직의 straight

erection n. 건조물 construction

especially adv. 1. 두드러지게 notable 2. 특히 particularly

essential adj. 필수적인 vital

essentially adv. 기본적으로 basically, fundamentally

establish v. 설립하다 create, organize

estimate v. 1. 평가하다 assess 2. 추정하다 predict

eventually adv. 결국 finally, ultimately

evident adj. 분명한 apparent, noticeable

examine v. 1. 탐구하다 explore 2. 조사하다 inspect

exceed v. 1. ~을 초과하다 go beyond 2. ~보다 낫다 surpass

excel v. 1. 탁월하다 be outstanding in 2. 능가하다 be superior to

exceptionally adv. 1. 예외적으로 abnormally 2. 대단히 extremely

exercise v. 1. 연습하다, (권력, 권리 등을) 행사하다 practice 2. ~을 이용하다 use

exhibit v. ~을 전시하다, 내보이다 show, present

explicitly adv. 명백하게 accurately, specifically

express v. 표현하다 represent

expression n. 표현 term

expressly adv. 1. 명백히 definitely 2. 특별히 specially

extend v. 1. 확장하다 enlarge 2. 늘이다 increase, stretch 3. 늘이다, 연장하다 lengthen

extensive(ly) adj.(adv.) 넓은 wide

extra adj. 1. 추가된 additional 2. 여분의 surplus

extract v. 뽑아내다 derive, remove

extremely adv. 1. 예외적으로 exceptionally 2. 극도로 intensely

F **fade** v. 1. 퇴색하다, 바래다 lose color 2. 사라지다 disappear

  fairly adv. 1. 상대적으로 relatively 2. 다소 somewhat

  feature n. 1. 특징, 특색 characteristic 2. 구성 element

field n. 분야 area

figure n. 1. 모양, 형상 shape 2. 수치 amount

finely adv. 1. 미세하게 minutely 2. 훌륭하게 highly

fit v. 맞추다 adjust, conform to

fix v. 1. 고정하다 set 2. 결정하다 determine 3. 고치다 repair

flaw n. 결함 defect

flawed adj. 결함이 있는 imperfect

flawless adj. 1. 흠 없는 unblemished 2. 완벽한 perfect

flourish v. 번창하다 prosper, thrive

fool v. 속이다 deceive, trick

former(ly) adj.(adv.) 이전의 previous

forsake v. 버리다, 떠나다 abandon, leave

framework n. 1. 뼈대, 골격 skeleton 2. 구조 structure

frantic adj. 1. (흥분, 공포, 고통 등으로) 정신없는 frightened

　　　　　　 2. 광란적인 frenzied 3. 미친 insane

furnish v. 공급하다 provide, supply

further v. 1. 발전시키다, 촉진시키다 advance 2. 증진하다 increase

fuse v. 결합하다 combine, join

G　**gain** v. 얻다, 획득하다 acquire, earn, win

　　　 n. 이득, 이점 advantage

generate v. 발생하다 produce, create

gently adv. 1. 약하게 slightly 2. 부드럽게 softly

gigantic adj. 거대한 enormous, huge

gorgeous adj. 훌륭한, 멋있는 beautiful, magnificent

gradually adv. 차차, 서서히 slowly, by degrees, little by little

H　**haphazard(ly)** adj.(adv.) 무작정의 random

harm v. 손상하다 do damage

harmful adj. 해로운 detrimental

harsh adj. 1. 신랄한 acid 2. 엄한 severe

haul v. 1. 운반하다 carry, transport 2. 끌어당기다 pull

head v. ~을 이끌다, 지도하다 lead

    n. 지도자 leader

hearten v. 1. 용기를 북돋우다 encourage　2. 기운 나게 하다 cheer up

hide v. 숨기다, 감추다 conceal

    n. 짐승의 가죽 skin

highlight v. 강조하다 accentuate, emphasize

house n. 집, 거주지 dwelling

    v. 보관하다 contain, place

hue n. 빛깔 color, tint

I

illustrate v. 1. 설명하다 picture　2. 묘사하다 represent

immense adj. 거대한 enormous, large, huge

importance n. 중요성 significance

important adj. 중요한 significant

incessant adj. 끊임없는 constant, unceasing

incise v. 1. 조각하다 carve　2. 베다 cut

indispensable adj. 1. 없어서는 안 될 essential　2. 필요한 requisite

induce v. 야기하다 bring about, cause

infinite adj. 무한한 limitless, unlimited

informal(ly) adj.(adv.) 비공식의 casual, unofficial

inherently adv. 본래부터 fundamentally, intrinsically

inhibit v. 제지하다 limit, hinder

initial adj. 1. 초기의 early　2. 처음의 first　3. 최초의 oldest

initiate v. 시작하다 begin, originate

innate adj. 타고난, 선천적인 inborn, inherent, natural

innovative adj. 창조적인 creative, original

insolent adj. 건방진 impudent, impertinent

institute v. 1. 설립하다 establish　2. 시작하다 start

intricate adj. 복잡한, 정교한 complex, complicated

isolated adj. 외딴 remote, solitary

J

jeopardy n. 위험 danger, risk

K **keen(ly)** adj.(adv.) 1. 날카로운, 예민한 acute, sharp 2. 격렬한 intense

keep v. 1. 유지하다 maintain, retain 2. 보관하다 store

L **largely** adv. 주로, 대개 generally, mainly, mostly

last v. 1. 계속하다 continue 2. 견디다 endure

lasting adj. 영구적인 enduring

launch v. 시작하다 begin, establish

launching n. (미사일, 로켓의) 발사, 출발 send-off

leading adj. 1. 주요한 chief, principal 2. 뛰어난 starring

lethargic adj. 무기력한 sluggish, drowsy

link v. 1. 연결하다 connect, put together 2. 관련시키다 relate

lure v. 1. 유혹하다 attract 2. 불러들이다 draw

M **magnify** v. 1. 확대하다 amplify 2. 세게 하다 intensify

maintain v. 유지하다 sustain, preserve, keep up

major adj. 1. 주요한, 중대한 important, principal, significant 2. 큰 sizable

mark v. 표시하다 indicate

marked adj. 두드러진 pronounced

markedly adv. 두드러지게 noticeably, significantly, strikingly, substantially

massive adj. 거대한 colossal, enormous, huge

meager adj. 풍부하지 못한 limited, scanty

mechanism n. 1. 장치 device 2. 수법 means

method n. 1. 순서 procedure 2. 수단 means

methodically adv. 조직적으로 systematically

mimic v. 모방하다 imitate, copy

minute adj. 미세한, 작은 fine, tiny

mirror v. 1. 반영하다 reflect 2. 닮다 resemble

mixed adj. 혼합한 blended

mode n. 1. 양식 fashion, form 2. 수단 means

moderate adj. 1. 온화한 gentle, temperate 2. 중간의 medium

modification n. 변경, 개조 alteration, change

modify v. 1. 변경하다, 수정하다 alter, change 2. 한정하다 restrain

moreover adv. 게다가, 더욱이 additionally, in addition

mundane adj. 1. 속세의 earthly 2. 평범한 ordinary

myriad adj. 무수한 many, numerous, innumerable

N **narrow** adj. 1. 가는 thin 2. 한정된 limited

nature n. 특징 character, characteristic

O **obscure** v. 가리다 conceal, cover, hide

obsolete adj. 1. 구식의 outdated 2. 무용지물의 unused

obtain v. 1. 획득하다 achieve 2. 얻다 acquire, get

obvious adj. 명백한, 분명한 apparent, evident

ordinary adj. 일상의, 보통의 unexceptional, routine

outstanding adj. 뛰어난, 현저한 excellent, remarkable, prominent

owing to phr-prep. ~때문에 because of, due to

P **particular** adj. 특별한, 특정한 specific

particularly adv. 특히 especially

pass v. 1. 움직이다 move 2. 지내다 spend

passable adj. 무난한 adequate, acceptable

pastime n. 1. 오락 entertainment 2. 취미 hobby

patch v. 1. 수선하다 mend 2. 고치다 fix, repair

path n. 진로, 궤도 orbit

pathway n. 경로 course

peak n. 1. 절정 height 2. 최고점 maximum 3. 산꼭대기 mountaintop 4.정상 top

peculiar(ly) adj.(adv.) 독특한 distinctive, unique

penetrate v. 관통하다, 꿰뚫다 pierce, go through

perceive v. 지각하다 recognize

perceptible adj. 지각할 수 있는 visible

perceptive adj. 지각력이 있는 insightful

persist v. 지속하다 continue

persistently adj. 끊임없이 continuously

pioneer v. 개척하다 initiate

　　　　　　n. 1. 혁신자 innovator 2. 창시자 originator

pioneering adj. 선구적인 original

pledge n. 보증, 서약 guarantee, promise, warranty

potential(ly) adj.(adv.) 가능한 possible

powerful adj. 강력한 potent, strong

precise(ly) adj.(adv.) 정확한, 정밀한 accurate

precision n. 정확성, 정밀도 accuracy, exactness

preclude v. 막다, 방해하다 prevent, forbid, hinder

predicament n. 곤경, 궁지 dilemma, difficult situation

predominant(ly) adj.(adv.) 주된 principal, main, primary

prescribe v. 규정하다 dictate

prescribed adj. 규정된 certain

present(ly) adj.(adv.) 현재의 current

prestige n. 위신, 명성 honor, status

prestigious adj. 영광스러운, 영예로운 honored

presumably adv. 아마 maybe, probably

prevail v. 1. 우세하다 dominate 2. 이기다, 극복하다 triumph

prevailing adj. 1. 널리 행해지는 widespread, most frequent 2. 우세한 dominant

primal adj. 주요한 key, principal

principal adj. 주요한 central, chief, main, major

prior to phr-prep. ~이전에 before, preceding

profitable adj. 1. 유리한 advantageous 2. 유익한 gainful

profoundly adv. 1. 심오하게 deeply 2. 매우 strongly

prominent adj. 1. 눈에 띄는 conspicuous, outstanding 2. 저명한 distinguished
　　　　　　　　　　3. 유명한 famous, notable

promise n. 가망(성) potential

promising adj. 장래성 있는 likely

prompt v. 격려하다 encourage, motivate

proper adj. 적당한, 적절한 suitable, appropriate

prospect n. 1. 기대 expectation 2. 가망 possibility

protrude v. 내뻗다 extend

protruding adj. 돌출한 projecting

proven adj. 입증된, 증명된 established, shown

provide v. 1. 주다 give 2. 공급하다 supply

provided conj. 만일 ~이라면 if

provision n. 조항 clause, stipulation

proximity n. 근접 closeness, vicinity

pungent adj. 날카로운, 신랄한 sharp

pungently adv. 얼얼하게, 자극적으로 strongly

pure adj. 순수한 unadulterate

purely adv. 완전히 exclusively

purify v. 정화하다 clean, clear, refine

Q   **quest** n. 1. 추구 pursuit 2. 탐색 search

R   **radical** adj. 1. 근본적인 fundamental 2. 과격한 drastic, extreme

radically adv. 1. 근본적으로 basically 2. 과감하게 drastically

raise v. 1. 기르다 propagate 2. 증식(번식)시키다 rear

rare adj. 드문 infrequent, scarce, unusual

readily adv. 즉시, 쉽사리, 기꺼이 easily, quickly, willingly

realm n. 범위, 영역 area, field

reap v. 수확하다, 획득하다 gain, obtain

recognize v. 인정하다, 인지하다, 알아보다 acknowledge, appreciate

recruit v. 1. 신병(새 회원)을 들이다 enlist 2. 더하다 obtain

release v. 내뿜다, 방출하다 discharge, emit, give off

relinquish v. 그만두다, 포기하다 abandon, give up

reluctant(ly) adj.(adv.) 주저하는 hesitant, unwilling

remarkable adj. 1. 비범한 extraordinary 2. 주목할 만한 noticeable

remarkably adv. 매우 incredibly

remnant n. 유물, 자취 remains, trace

render v. 표현하다, 묘사하다 represent, portray

renowned adj. 유명한, 저명한 acclaimed, celebrated

repel v. 1. 쫓아내다 drive away 2. 격퇴하다 repulse

require v. 1. 명령하다 insist 2. 필요로 하다 need

required adj. 필수의 necessary

resolute(ly) adj.(adv.) 단호한 firm, determined

retrieve v. 되찾다, 회복하다 recover, bring back

right adv. 즉시, 곧바로 directly, immediately

rigorous adj. 1. 심한 severe, hard 2. 혹독한 harsh

rotate v. 1. 교체하다, 순환하다 alternate 2. 회전하다 turn, swirl

roughly adv. 대략, 거의, 약 about, approximately, around, more or less

rudimentary n.(adj.) 기본(의) basic

run v. 1. 지휘하다 direct 2. 작동하다, 경영하다 operate

S **scrupulous** adj. 1. 조심성 있는 careful, cautious 2. 양심적인 honest

scrupulously adv. 꼼꼼하게 diligently, meticulously

secluded adj. 고립된, 외딴 isolated, remote

secrete v. 1. 분비하다 produce 2. 방출하다 discharge

secure v. 획득하다 obtain

　　　　adj. 1. 안전한 safe 2. 확실한 firm

securely adv. 단단히, 확실히 firmly

seek v. 1. 시도하다 endeavor 2. 조사하다 search for

seem v. ~인 것 같다, ~처럼 보이다 appear

seemingly adv. 겉으로는 apparently

sequence n. 1. 진행 progression 2. 결과 result

serene adj. 평온한 calm, peaceful

settle v. 1. 해결하다, 결정하다 decide 2. ~에 살다 inhabit

sharp(ly) adj.(adv.) 1. 뚜렷한 clear 2. 급한 sudden 3. 가파른 steep

shed v. ~을 버리다 discard, lose, cast off

shelter n. 피난처 cover

sheltered adj. 보호된 protected

shift v. 바꾸다 change

shifting adj. 이동하는 moving

similar adj. 1. 비슷한 comparable 2. 닮은 resembling

simultaneously adv. 동시에 concurrently, at the same time

site n. 위치, 장소 location, place

sketch n. 1. 스케치 drawing 2. 개략 outline

sluggish adj. 1. 활발하지 못한 lethargic 2. 느린 slow

solemn(ly) adj.(adv.) 진지한, 엄숙한 serious, somber

somewhat adv. 다소 rather, to some degree

sophisticated adj. 1. 복잡한 complex 2. 정교한 highly developed

sparsely adv. 드문드문 lightly, thinly

spawn v. 알을 낳다 create, produce

spectacular adj. 눈부신 striking, impressive

speculate v. 1. 깊이 생각하다 reflect 2. 추측하다 hypothesize

speculation n. 추측 guess

speculative adj. 확실치 않은 unproven

sporadic adj. 1. 드문드문한 infrequent 2. 때때로 일어나는 occasional

spot v. 발견하다, 탐지해내다 detect, see, sight

　　　n. 장소, 지점 location, point

stable adj. 1. 안정적인 fixed 2. 동요되지 않는 unchangeable

staggering adj. 압도적인 overwhelming, astonishing

standard adj. 표준의 usual

standardized adj. 표준화된 uniform

standing n. 지위, 신분 status

　　　　adj. 멎어 있는, 흐르지 않는 not flowing

standpoint n. 관점, 입장 perspective, situation

stationary adj. 1. 고정된 fixed 2. 이동하지 않는 immobile, unmoving

status n. 명성 prestige, standing

staunch adj. 1. 견고한 strong 2. 확고한 unwavering

steadily adv. 꾸준히, 계속해서 consistently, constantly, continuously

stem from phr-v. ~에서 생기다 arise from, derive from, grow out of

stick v. 달라붙다 adhere, attach, cement

still adj. 1. 고요한 calm 2. 정지한 motionless

adv. 그럼에도 불구하고 nevertheless

stimulate v. 격려하다 encourage, motivate

stock v. 저장하다, 비축하다 store

　　　n. 축적 repertory

strenuous adj. 격렬한 arduous, hard

stress v. 강조하다 define, emphasize

　　　n. 압박, 스트레스 tension

strike v. 1. 마주치다 come in contact with 2. 치다 hit 3. 접촉하다 make contact with

　　　n. 파업 walkout, work stoppage

striking adj. 1. 인상적인 impressive 2. 두드러진 prominent

strikingly adv. 놀랍게 remarkably

stringently adv. 엄격하게 severely, rigorously

strongly adv. 1. 강력히 emphatically 2. 심하게 heavily

stunt v. 방해하다 hinder, inhibit

subside v. 1. 가라앉다 die down 2. 감소하다 diminish, reduce

substantial adj. 1. 상당한, 중요한 considerable, significant 2. 많은 large

substitute v. 대체하다 exchange, replace

　　　n. 대용품 replacement

suggest v. 1. 암시하다 hint, imply, indicate 2. 제안하다 propose

suit v. ~을 적용시키다 accommodate, adapt

supplant v. 대신하다, 대체하다 displace, replace

supplement v. 보충하다, 추가하다 complement, add to

support v. 1. 원조하다 assist 2. 지탱하다 hold 3. 입증하다 uphold

supreme adj. 1. 우위를 차지하고 있는 dominant 2. 두드러진 outstanding

surge v. 1. 갑자기 증대하다 increase 2. 가속하다 accelerate

susceptible adj. 1. 받아들일 수 있는 acceptable 2. 영향을 받기 쉬운 prone

　　　　　3. 민감한 sensitive

sustain v. 1. 유지하다 maintain 2. 경험하다 suffer 3. 떠받치다 support

swiftly adv. 신속히 quickly, rapidly

T **temperate** adj. 온화한 mild, moderate

textile n. 직물 fabric, cloth

thaw v. 녹다 defrost, melt

therefore adv. 그러므로 consequently, thus

thrive v. 번영하다 flourish, prosper

throughout prep. 1. ~의 도처에 all over 2. ~동안 during

timid adj. 1. 겁 많은 fearful 2. 소심한 shy

tiny adj. 1. 작은 little 2. 미세한 minuscule

trace v. 찾아내다 connect

      adj. 근소한 very small

tradition n. 전통, 관례 custom

traditional adj. 전통의, 전통적인 usual

transform v. 바꾸다 convert

transformation n. 변형 change

tremendous adj. 거대한 huge, great

tremendously adv. 굉장히 greatly

typical adj. 전형적인 average, usual

U **ultimately** adv. 결국 eventually, finally

under way phr. 진행중인 in progress, continuing

underneath prep. ~의 아래에 below, beneath

unequal adj. 같지 않은 asymmetric, uneven

uniformly adv. 1. 한결같이 consistently 2. 균일하게 evenly

unique adj. 1. 독특한 distinct, particular 2. 유일한 peerless

unparalleled adj. 견줄 나위 없는 unequaled, unique

unrestrained adj. 1. 제지되지 않은 unchecked 2 . 마음대로의 at will

usually adv. 대개 commonly, customarily

utilitarian adj. 실용(주의)의 practical, pragmatic

utterly adv. 완전히 absolutely, completely

V **vary** v. 1. 바꾸다 change 2. 다르다 differ

vast adj. 거대한 broad, enormous, immense, large

vessel n. 1. 그릇, 통 container 2. 배 ship

vigorous(ly) adj.(adv.) 1. 격렬한 strong 2. 활기 있는 energetical

virtually adv. 1. 거의 almost, nearly 2. 사실상 practically

vivid adj. 1. 생생한 graphic 2. 선명한 bright

vulnerable adj. 1. ~에 취약한 susceptible 2. 상처 입기 쉬운 easy to damage

W **wane** v. 쇠약해지다, 적어지다 decline, decrease

wary adj. 1. 조심성 있는 cautious 2. 방심하지 않는 distrustful

whereas conj. 1. ~이므로 since 2. ~에 반하여 while

while conj. 1. ~이지만 although 2. ~반면 whereas

wholly adv. 완전히, 전적으로 completely, entirely

widely adv. 1. 광범위하게 extensively 2. 일반적으로 generally

widespread adj. 1. 널리 퍼진 far-reaching 2. 일반적인 general

wild adj. 야생의 uncultivated, undomesticated

wildlife n. 야생동물 animal

withstand v. 1. 견디다 resist 2. 버티다 tolerate

worldwide adj. 세계적인 global, international

Y **yet** adv. 아직 hardly ever

conj. 그럼에도 불구하고 nevertheless